THE COMPLETE IDIOT'S GUIDE TO

Life After Death

by Diane Ahlquist

ALPHA

A member of Penguin Group (USA) Inc.

I would like to dedicate this book to all those who have had near-death experiences. Some have felt comfortable sharing their stories; others have been reluctant to discuss their experience with anyone. Whichever group you are in, know that you have experienced something extraordinary. You have been truly blessed to have been given a glimpse into the amazement that lies on the Other Side.

ALPHA BOOKS

Published by the Penguin Group

Penguin Group (USA) Inc., 375 Hudson Street, New York, New York 10014, USA

Penguin Group (Canada), 90 Eglinton Avenue East, Suite 700, Toronto, Ontario M4P 2Y3, Canada (a division of Pearson Penguin Canada Inc.)

Penguin Books Ltd., 80 Strand, London WC2R 0RL, England

Penguin Ireland, 25 St. Stephen's Green, Dublin 2, Ireland (a division of Penguin Books Ltd.)

Penguin Group (Australia), 250 Camberwell Road, Camberwell, Victoria 3124, Australia (a division of Pearson Australia Group Pty. Ltd.)

Penguin Books India Pvt. Ltd., 11 Community Centre, Panchsheel Park, New Delhi—110 017, India

Penguin Group (NZ), 67 Apollo Drive, Rosedale, North Shore, Auckland 1311, New Zealand (a division of Pearson New Zealand Ltd.)

Penguin Books (South Africa) (Pty.) Ltd., 24 Sturdee Avenue, Rosebank, Johannesburg 2196, South Africa

Penguin Books Ltd., Registered Offices: 80 Strand, London WC2R 0RL, England

International Standard Book Number: 978-1-59257-651-7
Library of Congress Catalog Card Number: 2006920582

13   12   11   20 19 18 17 16 15 14 13 12 11 10

Interpretation of the printing code: The rightmost number of the first series of numbers is the year of the book's printing; the rightmost number of the second series of numbers is the number of the book's printing. For example, a printing code of 07-1 shows that the first printing occurred in 2007.

Printed in the United States of America

Note: This publication contains the opinions and ideas of its author. It is intended to provide helpful and informative material on the subject matter covered. It is sold with the understanding that the author and publisher are not engaged in rendering professional services in the book. If the reader requires personal assistance or advice, a competent professional should be consulted.

The author and publisher specifically disclaim any responsibility for any liability, loss, or risk, personal or otherwise, which is incurred as a consequence, directly or indirectly, of the use and application of any of the contents of this book.

Most Alpha books are available at special quantity discounts for bulk purchases for sales promotions, premiums, fund-raising, or educational use. Special books, or book excerpts, can also be created to fit specific needs.

For details, write: Special Markets, Alpha Books, 375 Hudson Street, New York, NY 10014.

Publisher: *Marie Butler-Knight*
Editorial Director: *Mike Sanders*
Managing Editor: *Billy Fields*
Executive Editor: *Randy Ladenheim-Gil*
Development Editor: *Lynn Northrup*
Production Editor: *Kayla Dugger*
Copy Editor: *Amy Borrelli*

Cartoonist: *Shannon Wheeler*
Cover Designer: *Bill Thomas*
Book Designer: *Trina Wurst*
Indexer: *Tonya Heard*
Layout: *Brian Massey*
Proofreader: *John Etchison*

Contents at a Glance

Contents

Appendixes

Introduction

The idea of whether death is the end of our entire experience in this universe or just the beginning of another entire existence is something that humans have pondered for centuries.

Life after death is an expansive subject, and many books have been written about many of the individual concepts I present here. Due to space limitations, I include only general thoughts and theories. If you're interested in a particular subject, I highly encourage you to find out more. (The books listed in Appendix B are a good place to start.)

This book explores spiritual beliefs, near-death experiences, ghosts, psychic mediums, and many other topics you might be interested in when considering life after death or immortality. The belief in an afterlife brings comfort to those of us who may have a fear of dying. Additionally, it brings consolation to those who have suffered the loss of a loved one and wonder how and what his or her soul may be doing.

Some of these categories are considered by some to be evidence that life exists beyond the body. However, certain concepts, such as deathbed visions and soul travel, can be very controversial. Although this book is not meant to provide both sides of the argument for life after death, it still includes general information about skeptical beliefs.

Whether you believe in life after death, you're not sure, or you scoff at the entire concept, I think you'll find this book interesting and gain some knowledge on the subject—whether that knowledge convinces you or not.

With the invention of modern technology, the interest in the afterlife is suddenly drawing more attention. Paranormal researchers and investigators are more common than they were years ago. Is this renewed interest due to the fact that we've entered an age of growth where we're meant to finally uncover the mysterious key to life after death? Is something or someone trying to break through? You decide.

What You Will Find in This Book

This book is divided into four parts:

Part 1, "Religion and the Afterlife," discusses the basic religions of the world with which many people are familiar, as well as less common religions or spiritual groups. The controversies of heaven and hell, not to mention views from nonbelievers, are included.

Part 2, "Portals to the Light," talks about near-death experiences and deathbed visions. These are key to the evidence of the afterlife. Where you begin your journey to the other side and how you get there are discussed, along with what to do with souls that may choose to hang around.

Part 3, "What Do Dead People Do?" presents theories that suggest there may be cities on the other side or different dimensions in which the soul resides. Questions such as "Can I get my body back?" "What will I look like?" and "Will I see my dead friends and relatives?" are answered.

Part 4, "The Return to the Planet," gives you concepts about reincarnation and lessons to be learned before the soul can go to its final home. Even a lesson on how to conduct your own past-life regression is provided.

You'll also find four helpful appendixes: a glossary, a list of resources, a life after death journal, and a ten-day method for making contact with the deceased.

Extras

Within the pages of this book you'll discover four boxes that give you information to make your journey into the concepts of life after death easier.

def•i•ni•tion

Explore these boxes for the meanings of words or phrases that you may not be familiar with.

What Skeptics Say

Here you'll find ideas and opinions that nonbelievers have to offer.

Ethereal Potpourri

Check these boxes for miscellaneous information that is enlightening, interesting, and useful.

Eternal Thoughts

These boxes feature quotes regarding eternal life that will make you contemplate life after death, as well as quotes that may bring a smile to your face.

Acknowledgments

There are so many people to whom I wish to express my gratitude that if all were included these pages themselves would amount to a book.

First of all, I want to thank all the individuals who shared their stories of near-death experiences, deathbed visions, and other miscellaneous results of their research of the afterlife. Your interviews were invaluable to the writing of this work.

All my loving family members—you, too, Bob and Patty!

My agent, Jacky Sach, for her efforts and faith in me to pull this project together.

Editors Randy Ladenheim-Gil and Lynn Northrup for putting up with me for yet another book.

To everyone at Alpha Books who made this book shine.

Shelly, your talent, patience, and energy made all the difference.

Carolyn Drogan, for your insights and contributions to this book. What a beautiful mind!

Dr. Victor Zammit, you were absolutely precious to me in your knowledge and support and still are. Go, Victor!

Tom and Lisa Butler are to be thanked for their interview with me regarding EVP and the information they unselfishly shared.

My special thanks and blessings go to Garrett Husveth for furthering my knowledge about EVP and hauntings in a professional and sensible manner. Lots of phone calls and lots of e-mails, but you made a difference.

Al Rauber, a seasoned and fantastic paranormal investigator, who has been a wealth of information. Even with your busy schedule you still took the time to assist me in bringing clarity into my ghost chapters. You and Garrett Husveth both supplied valuable information.

Pat and Steve Samuels, for maintaining continual support. Additionally, your assistance toward the completion of this book was a godsend. You two are the best!

Jerry Mroczlowski, I thank you for participating in the chapter on NDE and your fascinating story of 9/11.

Linda Mroczlowski, for your insights about your husband's near-death experience.

Arthur R. Bresser, DDS, for keeping my teeth looking good, not to mention the surprising NDE story you shared. You keep everybody smiling with your care and good nature. You are my hero.

Sharyn Lonsdale, one of my favorite writers and supporters.

My dear friend, Roger Goff. Your NDE still astonishes me. Your recovery was amazing, and of course, you are too.

Joyce Miller, walking into my book signing was no mistake. Thank you for allowing me to interview you about your NDE.

To all of my other friends who have always shown love, understanding, and are not judgmental.

A special mention should go to Kathy Downes, Jeralyn and Jay Sheldon, Terri Bordner, Mike Seery, and Lou Davis for your good intentions.

Respectfully, I wish to thank Rabbi Arthur I. Baseman for the way you eloquently explained your thoughts about life after death. Took a while to connect but well worth the wait!

Pastor Lee A. Magneson, you answered many of my questions and even through the Christmas season found the time to share your thoughts. No wonder everyone loves you!

BNVP, you know who you are, or at least I hope you do. Thank you for your support behind the scenes.

All my dead relatives and friends. Just in case you're reading this, who looks good at the racetrack this year?

Trademarks

All terms mentioned in this book that are known to be or are suspected of being trademarks or service marks have been appropriately capitalized. Alpha Books and Penguin Group (USA) Inc. cannot attest to the accuracy of this information. Use of a term in this book should not be regarded as affecting the validity of any trademark or service mark.

Part 1

Religion and the Afterlife

Whatever you believe about life after death may be firmly rooted in your religious beliefs. Many people are taught to think one way about the afterlife at an early age, and they never think to question whether these beliefs suit them later in life. In these chapters, you'll learn about many religious traditions and their various beliefs in the afterlife; I'll also talk about New Age thought. It's my hope that you'll use this information to expand your own point of view and ask yourself, "What *do* I believe happens after death?"

What the Major Religions Say About Life After Death

In This Chapter

- ♦ Afterlife beliefs of Buddhism
- ♦ Christian doctrines and the departed
- ♦ Hinduism and the other side
- ♦ Islam (Muslims) and life after death
- ♦ Shinto (Japanese) thoughts of death
- ♦ Taoist dogma on the dead
- ♦ Judaism and the here-and-now

Beliefs in life after death often have their roots in religion—even if the beliefs have taken on a life of their own, so to speak, which have very little to do with religion at this point! For this reason, I want to start with an overview of the major religions and what they tell us about the next life.

An extensive exploration of each religion is far beyond the scope of this book. Therefore, I'll introduce the basics, simplistically and briefly.

This, in turn, will give you a general idea of what a specific religion observes, before I present their ideas about life after death. If any particular faith intrigues you, I encourage further research.

Buddhism: Cycle of Life

Buddhism is an ancient religion founded in India more than 2,500 years ago. Followers believe the soul is recycled over and over until it reaches the highest level of enlightenment.

Many people are beginning to consider Buddhism as more of a tradition or philosophy than a religion, but technically, it still falls into the category of religion. Buddhism has made great strides in general acceptance; it was seldom talked about in the Western world 30 years ago, but nowadays, people all over the world are embracing its basic principles.

The focus of Buddhists is personal spiritual development. They aim for a keen insight into the nature of our existence, as they believe that all life is interconnected. Compassion is a significant part of the Buddhists' teachings. Gods and deities are *not* part of the Buddhist practice. Buddhists strive for enlightenment through developing wisdom, morality, and meditation practices.

Eternal Thoughts

When Buddha was on his deathbed he noticed his young disciple Anan was weeping.
"Why are you weeping, Anan?" he asked.
"Because the light of the world is about to be extinguished and we will be in darkness."
The Buddha summoned up all his remaining energy and spoke what were to be his final words on earth:
"Anan, Anan, be a light unto yourself."
—Buddhist scripture

Buddha wanted to demonstrate the path of honor to the entire planet and, in doing so, eliminate anguish. Even though Buddha didn't accept a god or deities, he wasn't atheist or agnostic. He said, "Do not bother about questions like 'Is there God?' 'Do I exist?' 'Is the world real or not?' Do not waste your time and energy in useless discussions. Purify your heart. Control the mind. Lead a virtuous life. You will attain Nirvana or emancipation of eternal bliss."

The path to *Nirvana* is accomplished on an individual level; it's *self-realization*. This spiritual state frees us from the cycle of *reincarnation*.

def•i•ni•tion

Nirvana is a form of liberation from attachment. It frees us from fear of death. It is eternal bliss, the highest form of transcendence. When you have reached Nirvana, you've conquered desire, hatred, and delusion. **Self-realization** is understanding or having the knowledge of one's true self, the act of achieving the highest spiritual level, a level where the soul doesn't have to incarnate again. **Reincarnation** is the belief that the soul returns to another life form after death; it goes through the cycle of life over and over until it's free from desire and self. At that point, the soul reaches Nirvana.

Karma: Been There, Done That

According to Buddhist tradition, a person's destiny after death is determined by how that individual lives his life in the present. The person's karma, meanwhile, has determined the type of life he's living right now. Karma is the Buddhist belief that the conditions in a person's lifetime represent his deeds from a previous lifetime. Likewise, a person's actions in *this* lifetime determine the shape of his next life. Good actions and deeds lead to a higher rank, such as someone who is successful and financially secure. Bad or evil deeds lead to a lower form or state. This thinking obviously encourages one to walk respectable paths in life and explains why some people suffer from "bad luck" or what appear to be unjust circumstances.

Other Buddhist Sects

In Tibetan Buddhism, the soul or spirit of the dead begins a 49-day process of adjustment, which is divided into three stages called "bardo." At the conclusion of the bardo, the person either enters Nirvana or returns to Earth for rebirth.

The most well-known Tibetan Buddhist is His Holiness the Fourteenth Dalai Lama. The Dalai Lama, in the role of teacher to his fellow Tibetan Buddhists, provides many explanations concerning life after death. In *Advice on Dying and Living a Better Life*, for example, the Dalai Lama talks about how in the nature of cyclic existence, everything that was gathered will eventually disperse or disconnect from relationships with parents, teachers, friends, and so on—all things separate with time, and all things die without exception. Therefore, since no one knows when this will occur, it is important to be prepared. The following list contains a summary of the Dalai Lama's views on how to prepare oneself for death and the afterlife:

Ethereal Potpourri

Tibetan astrology plays a meaningful role in the death of a Tibetan Buddhist. The astrologer is brought in to check the death calculations (Shin Tsi) of the deceased, to see if he or she has any lives remaining.

1. If you cultivate a sense of the uncertainty of the time of death, you will make better use of your time.

2. To prevent procrastination with regard to spiritual practice, take care not to come under the influence of the illusion of permanence.

3. Realize that no matter how wonderful a situation may be, its nature is such that it must end.

4. Do not think that there will be time later.

5. Be frank about facing your own death. Skillfully encourage others to be frank about their deaths. Do not deceive each other with compliments when the time of death is near. Honesty will foster courage and joy.

Zen Buddhism is a sect practiced mainly in Japan, China, Korea, and Vietnam. It's based on the practice of meditation and has different beliefs from the other Buddhist concepts. It maintains that enlightenment can be accomplished through self-contemplation, meditation, and intuition. Faith and devotion to a superior being is not the way to enlightenment. I once heard a Zen follower say, "To practice Zen is not to practice Zen."

Zen Buddhists don't believe in an afterlife, but do believe there is a constant continuation of energy, as we are all universally part of each other and one. Therefore, nothing really dies. And although they don't believe in the "soul" per se, they feel the connection to a higher source continues on.

Christianity and the Departed

Christianity is considered the largest religion in the world, a religion centered on the belief that Jesus Christ is the son of God and his death saved us from eternal damnation. His teachings and life are presented in the New Testament of the Bible.

A monotheistic religion, Christianity is centered on the belief that there is only one God.

Ethereal Potpourri

The word *Christ* means "anointed one." It's *not* Jesus' last name!

I have heard a few different theories as per these modern times. Not all followers now believe the same things, and many are forming their own opinions as in so many other religions. Because

Christianity is so diverse with many denominations, thoughts and beliefs seem to be changing. Some followers believe that the soul is judged at the moment of death and is sent to heaven or hell. Other very Orthodox faiths believe the body and soul lay still after death and do not go to heaven or hell but wait for the day of judgment when they will then rise and be judged.

Basic Christian Beliefs

There are different sects or denominations of Christianity, but the basic foundation is a belief in the teachings of Jesus Christ, which include the following:

◆ Jesus physically rose from the dead.

◆ The dead will rise to be judged by Jesus when he returns, according to scriptural fulfillment. This will be the final judgment.

◆ Sins can be forgiven by repentance. Therefore, everyone who has asked for forgiveness will have an opportunity to enter into heaven.

Christianity is perhaps best generally described by saying that salvation is achieved through a relationship with the one and only God. Jesus exonerates sins and releases us from God's judgment.

Christian Beliefs About Life After Death

Some Christians believe that when a person dies, the soul leaves the body and is judged immediately. The soul goes to one of two places, depending on the outcome of the judgment (there's also a third destination reserved exclusively for Catholics):

◆ *Heaven:* The highest state a soul can travel to. Eternal life and bliss. Those qualified to enter heaven must have lived a near-perfect life that included a serious devotion to God.

◆ *Hell:* Fire, torture, eternal damnation. Reserved for the worst sinners who haven't asked for forgiveness; also, those who reject God can expect to end up in hell. Christians believe there is no way out. We condemn ourselves by not asking for forgiveness and not using free will.

◆ *Purgatory:* This is like a waiting room where you're cleansed of the sins you committed. After a time, you'll be released and you can enter heaven. Only Catholics subscribe to this idea.

Chapter 3 deals with the ideas of heaven and hell in more detail. However, it should be noted that some Christians feel that a place of flames and torture was an extreme example of punishment that came to be in the Dark Ages in order to keep people in line. So while the theory of fire and brimstone is losing favor, many still believe there is a place called hell that is a place of darkness.

Hinduism: Belief in the Supreme Spirit

Hinduism originated in India and is the third-largest religion in the world, with approximately one billion supporters. Many consider Hinduism the oldest living religion in the world. It's taken many centuries to develop Hinduism, and it's based on many religious texts, the *Vedas*, which include spiritual insights and offer down-to-earth guidance for religious living. Hinduism encompasses numerous religious denominations, beliefs, and practices, and has no single founder.

Brahman is the supreme spirit Hindus believe in. This is worshipped in numerous forms, symbolized by individual deities such as Shakti (Mother Goddess), Shiva (Auspicious One), and Vishnu (All Pervading). Hinduism encompasses various practices so a person can experience the divinity that is everywhere. "The Self" is genuine, meaning the all-knowing individualized spirit of God or the "Divine Self." This puts the focus on self-improvement for the ultimate purpose of attaining divinity. Like Buddhists, Hindus believe in karma and reincarnation.

def•i•ni•tion

The **Vedas** are the main scriptural texts of the Hindu religion, and could be compared to cosmic forces such as light, heat, gravity, and motion, in that they have no worldly origin. They are everywhere. They do not begin, they do not end. These teachings and learnings have been passed by word of mouth through the generations.

Islam and the Word of Allah

The word *Islam* means "surrender," or commit to God, or Allah. A Muslim is a follower of the teachings of Islam. *Muslim* means "one who makes or does Islam."

Islam is a monotheistic religion based on the *Qur'an* or *Koran*, the main religious text of Islam. Islam is considered the second-largest religion in the world. Though there are different denominations of the Islamic religion, they all maintain the same fundamental beliefs. Muslims believe the literal word of Allah was disclosed to Muhammad, a prophet and a political leader. Over time, he wrote Allah's word in the Qur'an. Muslims contend the Qur'an is exact, and that it contains the final teachings of God.

Muslims believe that there is a place or state called the Barzakh, or "Partition," which the soul enters before judgment. In this intermediate state, the soul is conscious and if the individual hasn't lived a good life, he'll experience what's referred to as the "Chastisement of the Tomb," also referred to as "Horror of the Grave." The soul is tormented here until the Judgment Day.

If the person had been of good faith, he or she will be happy and contented. But since no one's perfect and most people have some type of sin to be forgiven for, even the faithful usually have to experience some type of suffering.

On the final Judgment Day, the individual soul is judged and leaves this middle area, headed for its eternal destination.

Shinto and Sacred Spirits

There is no single founder or sacred scripture in Shinto, but it's a very deep part of Japanese culture and traditions. In fact, from 1871 to 1945, Shinto was the official state religion. It's believed Shinto creates a bond between the individual, his community, and his native land.

Shinto means "the way of *kami*," which means mystical, superior, or divine. Shinto gods are called *kami*. These are sacred spirits that take the form of things and concepts important to life such as rain, wind, moon, stars, mountains, trees, rivers, waterfalls, seas, fire, some animals, and fertility.

Shintos believe that when humans die, they become *kami*, or divine beings. The dead are revered by their families as ancestral *kami*, which are honored in Shinto rituals.

Ethereal Potpourri

Shinto sometimes associates death with corruption and decay. If people die happy and at peace, they become revered ancestors. If people die violently or unhappily, family members try to soothe the spirit, such as leaving flowers or other offerings on an altar, which acts as a shrine to that person.

Taoism: The Way

Taoism (pronounced *Dow*-ism) is a fundamental Chinese concept that implies or translates as a method, principle, or doctrine—the "way" or "path"—which one should follow.

Lao Tzu, founder of Taoism, laid down no rigid code of behavior for his followers. He believed a person's conduct should be governed by instinct and conscience and that "simplicity" is the key to truth and freedom. Lao Tzu encouraged his followers to observe and understand the laws of nature; to develop intuition and build up personal power; and to wield power with love, not force.

def•i•ni•tion

Tao is the final resting place for the Taoist's soul; it's perfection and immortality. It's akin to the Buddhist's interpretation of Nirvana.

In the writings of *The Tao Te Ching* (a time-honored text that translates more or less into *The Book of The Way and its Virtue*, written by Lao Tzu), Tao is described as having existed before heaven and Earth. It's formless; it stands alone without change and reaches everywhere without harm.

Taoists' view of the world is a philosophy and a religion. They believe that there is no purpose in anyone interfering with what nature has set into motion. No matter how unbearable a situation is, it will soon become better. Taoists believe that the way to find peace and harmony is to live the tranquil, rural life in union with nature or live in harmony with Tao. As they strive to be one with nature, Taoists seek to embrace the secrets of nature or principle fundamentals of nature's way and become immune to physical harm, disease, and death.

It's said that Taoism and Confucianism are two different expressions of the same concept. Confucianism deals solely with life here on Earth rather than the afterlife. It takes a pragmatic approach and teaches that order will be maintained if everyone follows the natural order of life.

Taoism teaches the survival of the spirit after death. To have attained the human form must always be a source of joy for the Taoist. Death is truly a reason to rejoice because despite whatever is lost, life always endures. The Taoist soul doesn't die at death; it migrates to another life. This process, the Taoist version of reincarnation, is repeated until *Tao*, a transcendence of life, is achieved.

The Taoist is told to use the light that is inside to revert to the natural clearness of sight. By divesting oneself of all external distractions and desires, one can achieve immortality. In ancient days, a Taoist who had transcended birth and death and achieved Tao was said to have cut the Thread of Life, which binds a soul to this earth.

The goal in Taoism, as in Buddhism, is to reach the ultimate level, to transcend life on Earth as a physical being, to achieve harmony with nature and the universe, to achieve immortality. Whatever the name of this ultimate goal—Tao or Nirvana—the followers of these religions believe there is an existence beyond life that can be achieved if they follow the right path or behaviors. The cycle of life continues indefinitely until the Thread of Life is broken. Only through proper living, by following the correct path guided by the inner light, can one achieve the ultimate goal of Tao or Nirvana.

> ## Eternal Thoughts
>
> Confucius made some comments on the supernatural that give insight into how he viewed life after death. In *Sayings of Confucius* (1917) by Lionel Giles, he once said, "Absorption in the study of the supernatural is most harmful." When asked about the subject of death, he had this to say in *Confucius, The Analects* (1979) by D. C. Lau: "Chi-lu asked how the spirits of the dead and the gods should be served. The master said, 'You are not able to serve man. How can you serve the spirits?' 'May I ask about death?' 'You do not understand even life. How can you understand death?'"

Life After Death in Judaism

An ancient religion that goes back 4,000 years, Judaism has its roots in Hebrew scripture and is based on the teaching of the Old Testament and the Torah, or "law." The Torah refers to a total pattern of behavior, applicable to all aspects of communal and individual life. These teachings are found in the Old Testament Scriptures and in a wide variety of oral traditions, ritual, ceremonies, stories, and commentaries.

There are different sects of Judaism, including ...

- ◆ Orthodox Jews, who adhere strictly to traditional customs.
- ◆ Reform or liberal Jews, who are interested in adapting Judaic teachings to modern life.

- ◆ Conservative Jews, who try to find a middle ground between Orthodox and Reform doctrines.

- ◆ *Hasidic* Jews, who ascribe to mystical teachings. (Some Hasids are better described as even *more* conservative Orthodox Jews.)

> **Eternal Thoughts**
>
> We must live this day. We don't live to die, we live to live. We live to make the world a better place. And in the course of that action, when we die, our spirits, our soul muscle, that which made us the kind of person we are, becomes a part of God. That's our immortality of soul.
>
> —Rabbi Arthur I. Baseman

In Judaism, the end of life is not the end of the existence of the soul. However, there is no hardened dogma as to what exactly happens in a step-by-step process to the transition of death according to Jewish tradition.

The focus of this belief is living in the here-and-now, and not what happens when we die. Therefore, it allows the individual to form many personal opinions.

There seems to be no one set of rules or concepts that the Jewish are taught they "must" believe about life after death. God is the higher power, and we eventually go back to the God-source or the essence of God when we die.

Jews believe "Dust we are and unto dust we return, but the spirit born of God's spirit, returns to God who gave it," meaning God is a spiritual entity which becomes enhanced by the positive and loving contribution that a person brings with him or her upon death. Judaism is about making the world better, and if we do a good job the afterlife will take care of itself.

In order for the Rabbis or the religious teachers of this faith to make the people understand better, they might say that when we die, God will not ask, "Have you believed in me?" but rather, "Have you been fair in your dealings with others?" It's an attempt to give a quality to life that may not have been apparent otherwise. When I asked Rabbi Baseman, "But if we stand before God, so to speak, after our death, and he asks, 'Have you been fair in your dealings?' and we say 'no,' what happens?" The Rabbi commented that his motto is "Leave a little to God." I thought that was a beautiful statement.

The Least You Need to Know

◆ Buddhists believe the soul is reincarnated until it reaches Nirvana, or a state of perfection.

◆ Christians believe that upon dying, the soul is judged and sent to heaven or hell.

◆ Hindus are also believers in reincarnation.

◆ Muslims believe that when the soul crosses over, it goes to a place called the Barzakh, where it awaits judgment.

◆ Shinto is a religion practiced almost exclusively in Japan. It involves the worship of many gods, called *kami*.

◆ Taoists teach reincarnation; their state of immortality or perfection is called Tao.

◆ Jews believe that the soul lives on and joins back with God from which it came.

2

Theories of Life After Death, Past and Present

In This Chapter

♦ The aborigines' Dreamtime

♦ Preparing for the journey to the next world, Egyptian-style

♦ Modern religions and their afterlife teachings

♦ Diverse Native American beliefs

♦ Voodoo and the soul

♦ The Wiccan Summerland

In Chapter 1, I discussed the more familiar religions and their views of life after death. It's also worthwhile to take a look at beliefs that may be less familiar to you. Some of these tenets offer different twists on life after death, and the concepts alone are fascinating.

Some of these ideas originated in ancient times, but I don't believe that makes them invalid. After all, the stories have been passed from generation to generation, so at least some of what we believe about the afterlife today most likely originated with ideas and practices that were in vogue hundreds or thousands of years ago.

While I've tried to include as much information as possible, there are many other groups that aren't included here; therefore, if some concept strikes your fancy, explore it on your own by visiting your local library or by doing an Internet search of the topic. You may just come up with some original ideas of your own about life after death!

Aborigines and the Afterlife

The Australian aborigines are the native people of Australia. It's thought they came from Asia over 40,000 years ago. These mystical people are very spiritual and often rely on their intuitive gifts to help them make decisions, sense danger, and feel the needs of others whether they're near or far.

Different clans have somewhat different beliefs about life after death. They've handed down stories, myths, and songs throughout the generations as their way of learning and keeping tribal traditions intact. They believe that the world of the spirits is inter-related to the physical world. Therefore the transition from life to death isn't that significant a journey.

The Dreamtime

The *Dreamtime*, or "dreaming," is the aborigines' mythological belief or adaptation of how the universe began. Dreaming explains how nature works and the cycle of life and death. They feel the past, present, and future coexist and are not limited by time and space.

The majority of the aborigines believe that humans, animals, and plant growth are a part of a single system or are associations that can be traced back to the Great Spirit ancestors of the Dreamtime.

def•i•ni•tion

> Aborigines believe that the **Dreamtime** (or dreaming) is the entire cycle of time—past, present, and future—existing all at once. There is no beginning and no end to life according to this theory.

Different Tribes, Different Thoughts

Some aboriginal clans feel that when a person dies, his or her spirit remains in the location where the person literally ceased to exist. Hence, they also believe in ghosts and won't utter the dead person's name again to avoid disturbing them.

Certain circles of the aborigines believe in reincarnation—that is, the soul being reborn into another human form. Like other religions who believe in reincarnation, the aborigines believe that the better a person you were in this life, the better life form you'll return in. Reincarnation is discussed in more detail in Chapter 22.

The Eora aborigines, who lived in the coastal area around Sydney, theorized about the *transmigration* of the soul, which means that when a person dies, his or her soul moves into another life form, but not necessarily a human one.

def•i•ni•tion

Transmigration is similar to reincarnation, but includes the belief that a soul can return in animal or even plant form.

James Backhouse, a missionary and botanist, reported that a group of aborigines stood shocked and disheartened when they saw Europeans shooting dolphins. The local aborigines believed that when their warriors died, they were reincarnated as dolphins. This idea was supported by the fact that dolphins herded fish toward the fishermen and also protected people from shark attacks.

Many Australian aborigines have now converted to Christianity and believe in heaven and hell, but there are also those who continue to hold firm to the beliefs of reincarnation and transmigration of the soul.

Egyptian Beliefs of Immortality

When we think of ancient Egypt, we almost instantaneously associate it with life after death and the belief in many gods or deities. In fact, some scholars would say that the ancient Egyptians were *obsessed* with the afterlife. Pyramids, mummies, and grave goods were an important part of the ancient Egyptians' mourning rituals. I'll talk about each of these practices in this section.

Pyramids

Pyramids were constructed as burial monuments for royalty. Most of these mysterious structures sport stairs ascending toward the apex, or peak, of the structure. The stairs were built to guide the dead souls to the heavens. The apex had to be aligned in correlation to stars and planet positions, serving as a type of launch pad. The soul would quickly project up and out, eventually finding comfort in the home of the gods and achieving immortality.

The tombs of the pyramids were filled with grave goods, items thought to help the departed in the afterlife. These consisted of everyday items such as bowls and tools, as well as more elaborate things like jewelry, amulets, gold, and silver. (Hey, you just never know what you might need on a long trip!)

The tombs also contained painted images depicting the deceased enjoying life on Earth with family and friends. Sometimes images of servants were included, suggesting that often servants were sacrificed so they could accompany their masters to the afterlife and serve them there.

A Little Light Reading for the Journey

The *Book of the Dead* is a name that was given to the collection of Egyptian funeral texts known as *The Chapters of Coming Forth by Day*. The chapters were typically illustrated and written on papyrus and placed in the tomb of the dead person for easy access. Some of the chapters were also written and illustrated on the walls of the tombs.

Now, you may be asking yourself, "*Why* would a dead person need reading material?" Well, these texts weren't designed to simply help pass the time. The chapters consisted of spells and formulas that would help the dead person pass through the perils of the Underworld, or the land of the dead. In this place, the recently departed would find a labyrinth. He would be asked many questions from the door keepers; if he answered correctly, he would advance through the maze. If the dead person passed *all* the tests, he would then be allowed entry into paradise.

However, if the dead person didn't make the transition to the land of the dead or pass the tests, it was believed that he was then *really* dead, with no chance at achieving a spot in the afterlife.

> **? What Skeptics Say**
>
> I don't believe in an afterlife, so I don't have to spend my whole life fearing hell, or fearing heaven even more. For whatever the tortures of hell, I think the boredom of heaven would be even worse.
>
> —Isaac Asimov, author and biochemist

Field of Reeds

There are a few different names for what the ancient Egyptians believed to be paradise. Some translate it as Field of Offerings, Elysian Fields, and Fields of Peace. The most common term is the Field of Reeds. The Field of Reeds was believed to be a utopia similar to life along the Nile, only better and more peaceful.

Those who made it to this magical place would find the perfect agricultural community. The fields were fertile, the livestock were plentiful, and hunting was simple. One could fish, listen to music, dance, and do all the things one associated with pleasantness and happiness.

Interestingly enough, unlike burial in the pyramids, the Field of Reeds was not just for the wealthy and royal—it was for all Egyptians.

Mummification

The ancient Egyptians used to bury their dead, but at some point they came to believe that a dead person's body needed to be mummified to guarantee safe passage to the afterlife, where the physical body would be resurrected. For this reason, they used mummification, a means of preserving the body, as part of their ritual in preparing the body after death. They felt that the physical body was as important for eternal well-being as the soul or spirit.

In the mummification process, the body was dried and the internal organs were removed—except for the heart. The Egyptians believed that after death, the heart would be weighed against a feather on a scale. If one had led a good life, the feather and the heart would balance each other and the deceased would pass into the afterlife. If the heart weighed more than the feather, the deceased would be denied entry to the afterlife and the heart would be eaten by an evil monster.

Ethereal Potpourri

Sometimes mazes are found at the entryway of ancient tombs. It has been concluded that the mazes were assembled to stop the dead from coming back to Earth as ghosts, as ghosts were thought only to be able to travel in a straight line.

After removal of the organs, the body was sewn up and soaked in Natron (a hydrated sodium carbonate) to prevent decomposition and promote dehydration. Then the body was carefully wrapped in linen cloths and placed in its tomb.

Eckankar

Eckankar is the religion of the Light and Sound of God, or the Ancient Science of Soul Travel. It's considered a new religion, established in 1965 by Paul Twitchell. The word *Eckankar* means "co-worker with God."

Followers believe when you recognize, through practice, that your soul can travel beyond the limitations of the body, you're released from your fear of death as it is apparent the soul continues.

Their goal is spiritual freedom within this lifetime. Thereafter, you become a co-worker with God, both here and in the next world. They also believe that when the body dies, the soul goes to exist on other planes or to different spiritual worlds of God.

The soul may stay on these planes for one day or thousands of years. What determines this is the mission of the soul, karmic responsibilities, and the level of spiritual development. Karma and reincarnation are fundamental beliefs for followers of Eckankar.

> **Eternal Thoughts** _____
>
> The best hotels and the most luxurious accommodations on earth seem like dark huts compared to the things you see on the inner planes. The worlds of God are light and spacious, and the joy that one experiences there is beyond human understanding. This is what the Soul is trying to get to, and it comes through the spiritual exercises.
> —Sir Harold Klemp, author and spiritual leader of Eckankar, in *The Cloak of Consciousness* Mahanta Transcripts, Book 5 (1991)

Kabbalah

Kabbalah is a system of Jewish mysticism and spiritual wisdom intended to be used to improve one's life. It teaches you how to remove pain, suffering, and chaos from your life. Followers believe that Kabbalah allows followers to find deeper meaning in the Hebrew bible and divinity.

The goal of Kabbalah is to bring understanding and freedom to the lives of those who practice it. To the Kabbalist, death is merely an illusion. They feel the soul is seeking to advance spiritually; therefore, as in the Eastern religions, Kabbalah teaches reincarnation, the idea that when we die we are reborn into another life and start over again. This cycle continues until the soul progresses to the level of spirituality where it can dwell near God.

Some Kabbalists adhere to the fact that the concept of the resurrection of the dead will take place on a final Judgment Day. Other Kabbalists believe a final judgment is a form of self-judgment, where the individual sees what he or she actually did compared to what he or she could have done.

Scientology

Scientology takes its meaning from the Greek and Latin words translating to "the study of truth." It's considered a new religion, founded by L. Ron Hubbard in 1954.

Scientologists give credence to the fact that man is a spiritual, everlasting being. A person's potential or capabilities are limitless once they are realized.

Belief in a Supreme Being

Scientologists believe in a Supreme Being, but the religion doesn't embrace its worship. This is a unique characteristic of this religion. Followers believe that only through spiritual enlightenment and freedom for the individual will you have an understanding of the Supreme Being. Therefore, following a doctrine and/or finding ecstasy in king-dom come isn't part of their belief system.

Past Lives

Scientology believes in past lives, but not necessarily in what we would call reincarna-tion. It's important to note that there are different interpretations of reincarnation. Sometimes the word implies being born again into any sort of life form. Scientolo-gists believe you're only born into human bodies.

Followers usually experience their own past life or lives while undergoing an auditing session, or a form of spiritual counseling that typically brings up past-life experiences. These sessions are meant to help the individ-ual move forward in a more productive way. Once the Scientologist gets everything right, he or she won't have to reincarnate anymore.

Ethereal Potpourri

Scientology aims to give its followers the tools to help them break away from upsets and "aberrations" due to circumstances from a past life. These circumstances prevent followers from progressing in *this* lifetime.

Native American Links to Life After Death

Native American beliefs about the afterlife are quite diverse. Some tribes believed that the soul moved to another world upon dying; some believed in reincarnation;

while others believed that we return as ghosts. And then there are those who felt that no one really knows. Here are a few examples of some of the specific beliefs of well-known tribes:

♦ Some ancient clans of the Cherokee believed that their people continued a life in a special place for the dead where dancing, relationships, and rituals were continued. However, others thought the souls stayed close to their remains.

♦ The Iroquois buried their dead but believed the soul was immortal and never died. Judgment took place by the Great Spirit when the body died. They believed that one would be punished in the afterlife if he or she didn't live a good life on Earth.

♦ The Navajo believed in ghosts and thought that ghosts resented the living. Therefore, when someone died, they burned the body quickly and destroyed the home of the deceased. They also took a roundabout way back to their village to prevent the ghost from following them. Later they would stand in smoke as a form of purifying themselves after being exposed to the dead.

Obviously, there are many more tribes than those listed here; the interesting thing is that each tribe has its own theory of what happens when the physical body dies. If you're interested in Native American culture, this topic alone is well worth looking into on your own.

The Faces of Voodoo

Voodoo, or Vodun, comes from the African word for "spirit" and is one of the oldest religions in the world. Although the essential beliefs were founded in different areas of Africa, the real structure of the religion began in Haiti. As in Christianity, there are different denominations of Voodoo. These various branches have different beliefs of gods, spirits, ceremonies, and so on. However, the two common beliefs they have are that there is only one Superior Being or God, and that there is an afterlife.

The Voodoo God, Bondyè, is a distant being. Therefore, followers look to spirits, lesser gods, and dead ancestors for help in all areas. They summon these entities by the use of ceremonies, which may involve music, dancing, drumming, and animal sacrifice.

Voodoo Tradition

I spoke with a Voodoo priest and asked about the animal sacrifices and frenzied dancing that are often part of the religious ceremonies. He told me the dance is of a spiritual nature; it allows followers to connect to the spirit world and sometimes involves the dancer becoming possessed by a spirit. (More on this in the following section.)

As for the sacrificing of animals, the priest explained that the animal's throat is slit, guaranteeing an instant death. Afterward, the blood is poured into a vessel for the ceremony and then the animal is usually cooked and eaten. The purpose of this is to make a blood sacrifice to the spirits of the ancients to keep them happy.

Bringing Back the Dead

Voodoo worshippers have great respect for the spirits of their ancestors. During a spiritual dance, a priest dressed in elaborate clothing spins through the village as he's possessed by a spirit. If anyone touches him, they could be killed, as the energy of the dead who are brought back to life is all-powerful.

Followers of Voodoo also believe that after death, the soul of the individual remains close to the deceased for nine days. During this time, the *ti bon ange* ("little angel"), the personality part of the soul, becomes vulnerable to sorcery. If a ritual (called "nine night") is not performed to ensure that the *ti bon ange* stays in the grave, it can be captured by a sorcerer and transformed into a *zombie*.

def•i•ni•tion

A **zombie** is a dead person who has been brought back to life by sorcery or black magic. He or she has no free will or soul and can only wander amongst us.

If the soul has escaped sorcery, a priest separates it from the body in ritual so it can live in "dark waters"—a restful state—for a year and a day. Eventually the soul is set free and lives amongst nature until it is reborn. After the soul is reborn 16 times, it merges into the cosmic energy.

Wicca

Wicca is a nature-based religion with a root belief that the soul is reborn into different bodies. Wiccans believe in gods, goddesses, or deities. Wiccans are pagans—simply meaning they aren't Christians and they have a high regard for nature. They are *not* a religious cult or satanic group. Wiccans don't believe in Satan, hell, or black magic; they don't believe in harming others, including animals.

Wicca is often judged harshly by people who haven't fully examined this belief system. Those who believe that Wiccans are worshippers of Satan, for example, might be surprised to learn that their idea of the afterlife doesn't include happily hanging out in the flames of hell.

Wheel of Life, Death, and Rebirth

So what do Wiccans believe? They pay homage to the cycle of nature: summer leads to fall, fall to winter, winter to spring, and the cycle starts over. This is also how they view life, death, and rebirth—as a cycle traveled by the soul. Wiccans believe that this life is the result of our deeds from a past lifetime and that the process of rebirth continues until the soul has learned all the lessons it needs and reaches enlightenment.

Some Wiccan groups believe that if your existence in this lifetime is negative, you can pay off your karma, the cycle of cause and effect (meaning if you do something wrong it will come back to you in the same way you sent it out), in the here and now and enjoy the rest of this life in a more positive mode.

The Summerland

The "Summerland" is the Wiccan form of heaven. Wiccans believe that when the soul doesn't have to come back to the planet for more lessons, the cycle of life, death, and rebirth comes to a stop. The spirit can finally get off the soul train and retire to this place of peaceful bliss.

Some Wiccans believe that the Summerland is the place the soul goes to renew itself after death but before coming back to Earth and reincarnating. It's the place where the soul takes a cosmic break.

Once the soul has learned all its lessons, it finally stays in the Summerland. It's kind of like when people run to Florida for the winter or take a vacation in the same place each year. They may not stay for good at the present time, but some day, they may settle there for the rest of their eternity.

The Least You Need to Know

- Some Australian aborigines believe people can reincarnate into human and animal forms.

- The ancient Egyptians built pyramids for royals with instructions in their tombs to act as a road map into the afterlife.

- Most modern religions believe in some form of afterlife.

- Different Native American tribes have different beliefs, including ghosts, the immortality of the soul, and reincarnation.

- Followers of Voodoo believe that after death, the soul remains close to the deceased for nine days.

- Wiccans believe after death, one goes on to the Summerland, their form of heaven.

The Concepts of Heaven and Hell

In This Chapter

- Is heaven on my atlas?
- Heavenly realms
- Dante's fiery poem
- Hell for eternity?
- Hope in the lower planes

Throughout time, people have fantasized about getting to heaven. Songs have been sung about it, poems have been written, and sacrifices have been made for the promise of paradise.

But the big question still remains: Is heaven an actual place, or is it something we made up to keep people in line and give meaning to our sometimes less-than-wonderful existence on Earth?

To say that the physical locations of heaven and hell are questionable is an understatement. People spend their lifetimes wondering where we go after we die—and why. We tend to think if we're "good," we go up to heaven; if we're "bad," it's a trip down to hell.

In Chapter 1, I talked about the existence of heaven and hell in regards to specific religious traditions. In this chapter, we'll go a step further and delve deeper into other concepts and theories.

Heaven Only Knows Where Heaven Is

There is an enduring fascination with the location of heaven, and since this is where many people think we'll spend the rest of eternity, it makes sense to want to know exactly where we're headed! If you were moving somewhere, wouldn't you want to know where your new home is going to be before you get there? What about the neighbors—and do they allow pets?!

Eternal Thoughts

To me Heaven would be a big bull ring with me holding two barrera seats and a trout stream outside that no one else was allowed to fish in and two lovely houses in the town; one where I would have my wife and children and be monogamous and love them truly and well and the other where I would have my nine beautiful mistresses on nine different floors.

—Ernest Hemingway, novelist and short-story writer

Can You Find It Using MapQuest?

When we think about the physical location of heaven, most of us think "up." It seems the most logical place, as most religious texts seem to tell us this; for example, the New Testament talks about Jesus rising up to heaven, and in ancient Egypt, heaven was thought to be beyond the earth and stars.

According to these theories, if you could reach the clouds and travel a smidgen more, you pretty much reached heaven.

With the invention of the airplane, however, the idea that heaven was just beyond the clouds was quashed. And with the advent of space travel and science enlightening us even more, the notion of the existence of heaven was further (and dramatically) challenged. Regardless, the concept of heaven being up above us prevailed—the location just became hazier. People began to think that heaven was still up there somewhere; we just haven't gone far enough to see it.

In Chapter 7, you'll read accounts from people who say they've visited heaven. These folks tell us that it does exist and it has a definite location. Still, no one can really offer simple directions, so that more or less takes us back to the beginning: *Where* are we headed after death?

Planet Heaven

Many people believe that heaven is actually a planet somewhere out there in the great expanse of the universe. People also sometimes refer to heaven as "going home." If we combine these theories, does it that mean "home" is another planet we came from and that we were sent to Earth to learn lessons and maybe even humble ourselves? Some people suggest that Earth is a type of school for the soul. We learn, we die, and we go back to our original planet and live a beautiful existence. Graduation isn't easy but well worth it.

If we accept the notion of heaven as a planet, the next logical question is, "Where is it?" There could be one planet or many planets that could serve as paradise. But since it's most likely located on an entirely different plane, we don't have a very good chance of finding this planet or cluster of planets, even if we sent our best space-exploring telescopes in search of it!

Ethereal Potpourri

To some, the concept of heaven as a planet is absurd, but think about it: the universe is a very big place. We have no idea what's out there. It would be very vain of us to think we are the only intelligent life form (and I use the word "intelligent" loosely) in comparison to what or who is out there!

So if heaven is a planet or if there are several heavens out there, does the departed soul just jet over to it at the speed of light? Chapter 16 addresses some of these issues; as for the others, we'll have to wait until we get to the other side to know for sure!

Seventh Heaven

In ancient astronomy, people talked about the "seven heavenly objects"—the sun, moon, and the five planets visible from Earth. Each celestial object was considered a layer of heaven.

At the time, it was believed that upon a person's death, the soul floated upward and out into the universe, stopping at each layer of heaven along his way. The outermost layer (which we call Saturn today) was where the person would meet God himself. Today, this theory has been disproved by space exploration, but there are still some cultures that believe in it. In some religious faiths such as Judaism and the Islam tradition, heaven has seven levels, the highest realm being the seventh. In fact, this is where the expression "seventh heaven" comes from. "Being in seventh heaven" is the ultimate happiness.

The Higher Realm

Maybe heaven isn't necessarily up ... maybe it's just out—way out!

Although it's been around for ages, the idea that heaven has different realms is just now becoming a very popular concept according to many spiritual philosophies, especially those that subscribe to Eastern practices, but also in some organized religions. This theory tells us that when you cross over, the location of *your* heaven depends on your actions during this lifetime. In other words, your spirit will be vibrating at a certain level after death, which determines which level you'll be sent to. The better a person you were on Earth, the higher the vibration you'll have and the higher the zone of heaven.

> **Ethereal Potpourri**
>
> An ABC News Poll done in 2005 said that nearly 9 out of 10 people in the United States believed in the existence of some concept of heaven.

For those who have communicated with the souls on the other side, it's said that the higher the realm, the more peaceful and exquisite the surroundings. The average person enters at level three, which is serene and beautiful, but you can still do better.

Some people wonder where the idea of the level three comes from. There are different theories about this; one is based on what is written in the Bible (2 Corinthians 12:2): "I know a man in Christ who fourteen years ago—whether in the body I do not know, or out of the body I do not know, God knows—such a man was caught up to the third heaven." If there is a third heaven, there must be a first and a second! Some people believe the Bible meant that Earth is one level, outer space is another, and the third level is heaven.

There are also nonbiblical teachings referring to levels or realms of heaven, and certain Buddhist teachings refer to six realms of rebirth.

Now, don't worry about being stuck in a lower level. You might be able to work your way up the heavenly ladder to reach the ultimate kingdom. This may take a while, but our spiritual communicators tell us it can be done, either via reincarnation, which involves coming back to Earth in another life to learn more lessons, or by learning lessons in the next life.

Spiritualism believes that there are these "realms of light"—higher levels in which the soul can enter as opposed to the lower, darker levels—and via reincarnation we can better our positions. In this theory, no one is damned to a place called hell—nor does anyone automatically enter into a domain called heaven. You more or less *earn* your place in eternity. The soul *wants* to graduate to the lighter realms.

def•i•ni•tion

Spiritualism is a type of religion or religious movement. Its unique characteristic is that followers believe we can speak to the dead by using a medium, a person who claims to be able to contact and receive messages from the departed.

The concept of heavenly or spiritual realms gives everyone a chance at the ultimate life after death existence, no matter what we've done in this life. This may not seem fair to everyone—if you've lived a good life, for example, but your neighbor has always been a creep, then why should he be given the same afterlife opportunities as you? Well, that's not up to you to decide! (And watch that judgmental attitude, or you'll have to unlearn it in your next life!)

66 99 Eternal Thoughts

Consciousness will always be present, though a particular consciousness may cease. For example, the particular tactile consciousness that is present within this human body will cease when the body comes to an end. Likewise, consciousnesses that are influenced by ignorance, by anger or by attachment, these too will cease. But the basic, ultimate, innermost subtle consciousness will always remain. It has no beginning, and it will have no end.

—His Holiness the Dalai Lama, spiritual leader of the Tibetan people

Is Hell a Scare Tactic?

We discussed different ideas about the location and existence of heaven. But what about its supposed counterpart, hell? Some people feel that hell is nothing more than a concept created by religious groups in order to convert people to their religion or to force people to adhere to some type of civilized behavior.

That may be so, but perhaps the concept of hell isn't such a bad idea if it forces people to really think about their actions and in turn makes the world a better place. Whether you believe that there's a place called hell located on the cosmic map is totally up to you. I'm not heaven-bent on changing anyone's mind. However, it does seem that as we evolve as human beings, the belief in hell is becoming less common.

Are You Trying to Scare the Hell out of Me?

Many people and religious groups believe it's unhealthy to have a group of followers living in fear and stressing over what may happen to them after death if they don't follow the rules of their religion. What's worse, since some actions are deemed especially evil by religious doctrine, these people may figure that since they're already going to hell, why try to change their ways?

Still, if people truly believed that they could get away with whatever they felt like doing, humans may never have evolved to this point. And no one should be faulted for attempting to have people live in a moral and loving atmosphere. In other words, it's hard to find fault with those who believe in hell.

However, those who use the threat of hell to intimidate and exploit others probably deserve to take a trip there.

What Skeptics Say _____

Religion has actually convinced people that there's an invisible man, living in the sky, who watches everything you do every minute of every day. And the invisible man has a special list of 10 things he does not want you to do. And if you do any of these 10 things, he has a special place full of fire and smoke and burning and torture and anguish where he will send *you* to live and suffer and burn and choke and scream and cry forever and ever until the end of time ... but he loves you.

—George Carlin, comedian

Eternal damnation is not really appealing to most, but it is said by many a comic it would be interesting to see who you would meet down there. I bet you'd find some smokin' characters.

What Does Hell Look Like?

We've all seen the depictions of hell that include flames, darkness, lots of fireproof red fabric draped everywhere, and screaming and other horrific sounds. Of course, with all that red fabric everywhere, who wouldn't scream?

We've also heard testimonials of those who have had near-death experiences (see Chapter 7). Many of these folks describe a heavenly place, but not too many describe hell. Therefore, we don't have much evidence on which to base the appearance of hell. And I'll beat you to the punch with the skeptical point of view. You're thinking there isn't evidence of heaven either. Well, in Chapter 4, we'll talk about some experts who feel that there is *indeed* empirical evidence of life after death ... so stay open-minded!

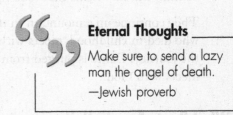

Eternal Thoughts

Make sure to send a lazy man the angel of death.

—Jewish proverb

Dante Alighieri's *Divine Comedy*

The concept of hell has been around since humans first learned to communicate, it seems. Obviously, the Bible is the best evidence of this, but other writers have tackled the concept, too.

In the fourteenth century, Dante Alighieri (1265–1321) wrote *The Divine Comedy*, a long narrative poem whose description of hell sparked a great deal of fear and controversy at the time. Dante's descriptions were so vivid that some thought the author actually visited hell and came back. (For some reason it didn't occur to these people that he may have just been a good writer with an inferno of an imagination!)

I'm going to give you a synopsis of this long poem, which was wildly popular in its day and remains a classic today (look for it in bookstores or online). Bear in mind that there are plenty of other stories focusing on a character's journey through hell (Goethe's *Faust* is considered the template for many of these stories). We have to ask ourselves: What is the author's point? Is it to scare, to inform, to entertain? Did these kinds of stories help to shape our views of the afterlife today?

The Story

This poem is a tale of Dante's trek through the three realms of the dead; Hell, Purgatory, and finally Paradise with an eventual meeting with God.

Thirty-five-year-old Dante finds himself lost in a dark and dreary forest where he's rescued by Virgil, who was commissioned by Beatrice (Dante's deceased love) to guide Dante through his journey.

After surviving the challenges of Hell, Dante and Virgil proceed to the terraces of Purgatory—one step closer to Paradise. The souls here have met challenges and can only leave when they have rebuilt the part of their personality that caused them to commit the sin or sins that took them there in the first place.

They continue up a mountain to the summit where Beatrice, whom Dante loved and who died in childhood, meets with Dante again. Virgil leaves and Beatrice takes over the journey. Dante is purged from his sins and eventually goes to heaven, where he meets with God.

What Dante Sees in Hell

Even though Dante has a happy ending to his story, his journey is far from smooth. In Dante's journey through the underworld, he sees many disturbing sights.

- ◆ The gates of Hell sport a sign that reads "Abandon Hope All Ye Who Enter Here."
- ◆ He takes a boat ride navigated by Charon, with other damned souls across a river Acheron to the Inferno or the center of hell. The trip is so horrendous he faints.
- ◆ Flaming deserts, a rain of fire, giant snakes, wasps, and violent winds are also a part of his vision.
- ◆ People are rolling boulders back and forth.
- ◆ Heretics are trapped in tombs of flames.

What do *you* think? Is this an accurate portrayal of hell? Are these the images you would expect to find there, or do you think we've moved past this interpretation of eternal damnation?

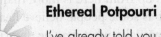

Ethereal Potpourri

I've already told you that *The Divine Comedy* scared the devil out of people when it was written. Here's an interesting thought to mull over: how would modern audiences have reacted to this tale? Would it scare anyone today, or are we so far past believing in the concept of eternal damnation that we would scoff at it?

I've Fallen and I Can't Get Up—or Can I?

If you've always believed that hell is just plain hell and there's no changing it, you may be surprised to learn that some sets of beliefs (such as those I talked about earlier involving Spiritualism and heaven's different realms) tell us that there is, in fact, a chance for improving your situation. You can improve your vibrational level. We talked about heaven as a multidimensional plane where you earn a better position over time. Following this theory, hell is better explained as the lower levels of the ladder or realms.

If you were cruel, selfish, and walked a dark path in this life, your vibrational level will be very low when you cross over and you'll have to exist for a time in the lower dimensions. For example, instead of starting at level three you might start at level one and have to work your way up.

The problem in the lower realms is that those who dwell there are so wrapped up in negativity even after death that they do not work too hard or even notice there is a glimmer of light shining from above! It may take a very long time for them to even look up or sense there is liberation. They can be somewhat stagnant. But eventually, these souls wake up and recognize that they must incarnate until they end up at a higher level—at which point, climbing the ladder is much easier!

It doesn't exactly sound like Dante's Paradise, but at least with this explanation there is still salvation and hope of heavenly bliss eventually. These souls will evolve toward the light, according to supporters of the viewpoint.

Hell on Earth

We've all heard people say, "I don't believe in hell because we're living in it right now." I think we all have those kinds of days, months, and even years.

The belief that this life is hell and we can only go up from here is more than a passing expression—many people do believe this. Just as some people believe heaven is an actual planet, some believe what we call Earth is actually what may be described as hell to inhabitants of other planets and dimensions.

Ethereal Potpourri _____

The idea that this life is actually hell is certainly an interesting way to look at it—especially for those of us who are reluctant to consider that heaven could be another planet. What if *this* planet is a cautionary tale on other planets, just as we use hell to warn each other about the perils of living a less-than-moral life?

Atheists and Agnostics in Heaven? No Fair!

Admit it—if you believe in God or a higher power, you want to believe that the skeptics, atheists, and agnostics are going to a lower dimension when they die. Hey, that's only fair, right?

Well, that's not how it works. Fortunately for these folks, personal beliefs don't determine where we end up after death—it's our deeds, how we treat people, our work ethic, and whether we have respect for human beings, animals, and nature. In fact, there are plenty of nonbelievers who will pass on at a higher vibrational level than those who rushed to a place of worship each week, but didn't walk their talk.

Of course, there's no reason that nonbelievers should be on a track straight to hell. Their beliefs don't make them bad people. They're simply looking for scientific proof of life after death or the existence of the soul. Of course, they may not find proof in this lifetime; the best evidence of what happens after death doesn't occur until … well, after death. Fortunately for the doubters, they'll be as welcome in the next life as anyone else!

The Least You Need to Know

- Heaven might be a different planet or a different dimension with different levels.
- The vibrational level that you encounter when you die is a result of your actions on Earth and will determine which plane of existence you will start out at in the next life.

◆ Dante's epic poem titled *The Divine Comedy* tells his story of passing through Hell, Purgatory, and Heaven.

◆ There are lower planes that can be described as hell. But the twist is there is always hope for the betterment of the soul even if you end up in the lower chambers.

◆ If we're judged by our good actions and not religious beliefs, then anyone who is kind, fair, and ethical can enter into a heavenly existence.

Chapter 4

Afterlife Skeptics

In This Chapter

♦ What's the difference between atheists, agnostics, and debunkers?

♦ The levels of skepticism

♦ What scientists believe about life after death

♦ Skeptics, séances, and Ouija boards

♦ Proving the existence of the afterlife

♦ Skeptic organizations

How can I present a book about life after death—a topic that is so speculative—and not include the opinions from atheists, agnostics, and debunkers? I figure that since there are groups out there who believe that the afterlife is nothing but hogwash, the least I can do is tell you *why* they think that.

Atheists, agnostics, and debunkers generally feel that because there's no physical proof of life after death, it can't exist. They wonder why other people would spend their time investigating and investing their energy exploring that which *they claim* can't be proved. They have strong points and theories about their disbelief in life after death, which to many are logical and make perfect sense.

To give you a complete view of this topic, it's important to include something in this book as a voice representing the opposite side. (I won't say the "other side," so as not to confuse you!) We believers are nothing if not open-minded, after all.

Defining Their Beliefs

These terms are sometimes used interchangeably, but they're not really the same things. To avoid confusion, let's break them down from the get-go:

◆ An *agnostic* is someone who claims no knowledge of the existence of gods, God, or any deities. He or she withholds judgment on the subject until solid evidence is brought forth.

◆ A *debunker* is someone who actively attempts to discredit claims of the paranormal and the afterlife that he or she claims can't be proven scientifically. Debunkers try to ridicule those who claim to have had paranormal experiences and those who investigate these experiences. They attempt to prove that things like near-death experiences (NDEs), psychic mediums, and ghosts are either fraudulent or caused by the biochemistry of the brain. They reject any "evidence" of the afterlife, saying it must be fraudulent because the afterlife does not and cannot exist.

◆ An *atheist*, generally speaking, is someone who has an absence of a belief in a single creator, God, or any deities. However, some atheists accept there is an afterlife.

Now, it should be noted that while atheists don't believe in a higher power, they also don't hold religion in very high esteem. They feel religion is a concept created by man to keep people on the straight and narrow. They don't see the logic or the compassion in a belief system that tells people, "If you don't follow the rules, you don't get into the afterlife."

The Finer Points of Skepticism

The word *skeptic* comes from ancient Greece and translates as "one who doubts," not "one who rejects." When we're talking about belief in the afterlife, there's a subtle but meaningful difference in the two translations.

Dr. Victor Zammit is a lawyer, a retired attorney of the Supreme Court and High Court of Australia, and one of the foremost defenders of life after death. He's also something of an expert in the area of skeptics, since he butts heads with them from time to time.

Dr. Zammit gives us the following breakdown on skeptics:

◆ We have open-minded skeptics. Many scientists and empiricists (who use scientific method to measure phenomena) both past and present have been open-minded skeptics. They doubt, so they investigate and experiment. Their acceptance of anything depends on their investigations and experiments.

◆ We also have closed-minded skeptics. They've already made up their minds and no amount of evidence is going to sway them to accept anything that's not consistent with their deeply entrenched beliefs.

◆ Lastly we have the debunkers, closed-minded skeptics who actively try to ridicule anything to do with the afterlife and the paranormal and try to discredit those who investigate or promote it. Their motivations often include gaining funding, establishing careers, and other areas of self-interest.

Dr. Zammit is quick to point out that the term "believer" doesn't necessarily apply to someone who isn't a debunker. Even if someone is open-minded enough to accept the *possibility* of life after death, it doesn't make that person a true believer—it just doesn't make him or her a nonbeliever. This person is looking for evidence to prove that there is an afterlife, unlike a debunker or closed-minded skeptic, who is looking for evidence to prove otherwise. So from this point forward, when I use the term "believer," I'm talking about people who are convinced that life after death is real—not someone who's still searching for proof.

(Later in this chapter, I'll tell you about an interesting challenge Dr. Zammit has posed to closed-minded skeptics!)

All religions believe that the soul continues and has some type of afterlife. Atheists generally believe that the continuation of the soul isn't real—it's something people tell each other

What Skeptics Say

Death is a part of life, and pretending that the dead are gathering in a television studio in New York to talk twaddle with a former ballroom-dance instructor is an insult to the intelligence and humanity of the living.

—Dr. Michael Shermer, founder of *Skeptic* magazine, executive director of the Skeptics Society, and author to make dying easier and to prevent themselves from being depressed and suffering from anxiety about the end of life.

It should also be noted that the majority of atheists, agnostics, and debunkers would prefer to be called skeptics. The above titles don't always define their complete personal opinions.

Do Scientists Believe in Life After Death?

Common sense has always told us that scientists are naturally skeptical of the afterlife—after all, these are people who deal with black-and-white, cold, hard facts every single day.

According to recent studies, however, somewhere around two thirds of scientists have a belief in some sort of Supreme Being, and nearly three quarters of doctors believe in life after death. This is surprising information, as conventional wisdom has always drawn a line between science and religion. In other words, the prevailing belief has been that if you study any type of science—biology, chemistry, medicine, whatever—you must almost automatically dismiss the idea of God, and therefore the afterlife. These are things that can't be proved, after all, and science is all about proof.

However, there is a differentiation to be made—many scientists think of themselves as spiritual, but not religious (which is where they differ from the atheists, of course). I think this differentiation is kind of beside the point here. The main issue is whether someone who works with facts on a daily basis can reach outside of themselves and embrace the idea of another dimension. According to the statistics, this is not only possible, it happens more often than not.

So the answer to the question, "Can a scientist believe in the afterlife?" is yes. Color me surprised!

Psychic Tools Under Attack

While this isn't a book about fortune telling or divination (for more on that topic, check out my book *The Complete Idiot's Guide to Fortune Telling*; see Appendix B), I do need to address how skeptics react to psychic tools. After all, we use things like séances and Ouija boards to connect with those who've already passed on to the afterlife. What might a skeptic say about these forms of ethereal chitchat?

Séances: Communicating with the Great Beyond?

Say the word *séance* in front of a skeptic and I can almost guarantee there will be a lot of eye rolling and eyebrow raising. A séance typically consists of meeting with a medium who attempts to communicate with someone who has passed on to the afterlife. The medium may go into a trance or altered state of consciousness so that the departed person can talk through him or her.

We sometimes see séances in movies, in scenes depicting mediums performing obviously fake sessions for profit (remember Whoopi Goldberg in *Ghost?*). Lights flicker, windows fly open, and sounds from the unknown are heard by participants, who are scared silly.

def•i•ni•tion

A **séance** (pronounced say-ahnce), which is sometimes also called a spirit-circle, is a gathering of three to twelve people, typically assembled in a circle, attempting to receive messages or communicate with the spirit of a person who has died.

Now, while the drama of windows opening and tables shaking has not been my experience, I don't discount these things. I've been to séances and have even tried to conduct a few myself. (I like it better when someone else is the medium, as I don't have a natural flair for it.)

I firmly believe that those on the other side are looking for a way to communicate with us and often need a go-between (a medium) to help them. Frequently people will ask, "If you can talk to the dead, why don't they just appear?" Well, just as we're trying to talk to them, those on the other side may be researching methods for opening the door of communication to us!

Ethereal Potpourri

One of the most noted skeptics of séances was Harry Houdini, the famous magician who later turned his interests to debunking psychics and mediums. Houdini would disguise himself and attend séances, hoping to reveal a piece of equipment the medium had planted in the room to create effects supposedly coming from the world of the dead. He took great joy in this process and newspapers eagerly published many of these exposures. (For more on Houdini, see Chapter 13.)

Ouija Boards: Messages from the Other Side?

To some (skeptics), the Ouija board is a game; to others (believers), it's a form of divination and communication with those who have passed over.

Using the Ouija ordinarily involves two people, using a pointer (called a planchette) and a board with the alphabet, numbers, and the words "Yes" and "No" printed on the surface. As one or two people put their fingers on the pointer and ask questions, it moves about the board, spelling out messages by landing on the letters or numbers. Believers say Ouija boards can help you receive messages from those who have crossed over and reside in the afterlife.

The participants are supposed to lightly place their fingers on the pointer; not push it around. The purpose of this is to help guide the pointer—the spirit who's been called upon is supposed to be doing the actual spelling.

Skeptics believe that there's no indication of paranormal activity when it comes to the use of a Ouija board. They claim the participants themselves are moving the pointer.

Ethereal Potpourri

I once did a Ouija board session by myself, and the letters I got spelled R-U-E-Z. I couldn't understand what "ruez" meant. Then I said each letter out loud and heard myself saying, "Are you easy?" Oh my! Who was I taking to, the Casanova of the other side?

They often suggest that the users should be blindfolded and that another person should write down the letters, numbers, or yes and no answers. Skeptics claim that if a third party were interpreting the answers, they would be gibberish.

What the doubters don't acknowledge is that most people who use Ouija boards often *do* get gibberish, with or without using blindfolds, and they honestly admit it. Those on the other side, you see, are sometimes "spelling challenged." (You would be, too, if you hadn't communicated by the written word for a long time—perhaps for centuries!)

Being Skeptical of the Skeptics

Skeptics and debunkers are always demanding evidence of life after death. Obviously, this is not an easy thing to prove. On the other hand, no one can *disprove* it. After all, the skeptics claim, no one has ever come back from the dead to tell us an afterlife does indeed exist. So on both sides of the issue—the believers and skeptics—people are always looking for facts. With more modern research, afterlife explorers are starting to come up with indications that might withstand the scrutiny of the debunkers.

Victor Zammit for the Defense!

As I mentioned earlier in this chapter, Dr. Victor Zammit is a retired attorney of the Supreme Court and High Court of Australia. He is also the author of *A Lawyer Presents the Case for the Afterlife—Irrefutable Objective Evidence*, which presents scientific evidence supporting the theory that the soul lives on after the physical body dies. (For more information on this book, see Appendix B.)

Dr. Zammit takes issue with debunkers who claim that there isn't any scientific evidence that proves the existence of an afterlife; he responds by noting that there isn't any scientific evidence *disproving* the afterlife. He has reviewed the work of several scientists who feel that they have proven through their research that the afterlife is, indeed, real. Dr. Zammit has taken this work and challenged skeptics to disprove it—in fact, his website offers a $1,000,000 sponsored prize to anyone who can prove that the afterlife is *not* real. The original compensation was offered in 2000 and to date, no one has collected on it.

Where would anyone come up with such an idea? To hear Dr. Zammit explain it, it seems perfectly natural. He says, "In assessing afterlife evidence, one needs to be a specialist in making the distinction between objective and subjective evidence. All personal beliefs (including skeptical beliefs) are subjective. Anything subjective is itself subject to error and to complete invalidation. This is the closed-minded skeptics'/debunkers' greatest vulnerability. A subjective belief or disbelief in something doesn't make it true.

"In come the empiricists. We use scientific method to measure afterlife phenomena. If we can duplicate the phenomena over time and space and obtain the same results while keeping variables constant, we have an empirical conclusion, which is a scientific conclusion."

Some skeptics argue that Dr. Zammit is challenging them to "prove the negative." He responds, "That's absolute nonsense designed to willfully mislead and fool those who are unaware. I've expressly presented some 22 areas of objective evidence of the afterlife. Now the onus shifts to the skeptic to show why the evidence ought not be admitted. That is not asking the skeptic to 'prove the negative'; that is asking the skeptic to formally rebut the objective evidence. And that has never been done."

One of the most important things about Dr. Zammit's work is that he's opened up a dialogue between believers and nonbelievers that's based on science—not religious beliefs. All too often, skeptics quickly dismiss life after death as religious doctrine; thanks to Dr. Zammit, skeptics are being given scientific evidence to mull over.

The Afterlife Experiments

Gary Schwartz, Ph.D., is the director of The VERITAS Research Program of the Human Energy Systems Laboratory in the Department of Psychology at the University of Arizona. He received his doctorate from Harvard University and is a professor of medicine, neurology, psychiatry, psychology, and surgery at the University of Arizona. (This man has some serious credentials!) He's also a *former* skeptic.

Schwartz conducted experiments in a laboratory setting to attempt to prove life after death using physic mediums such as John Edward and Allison Dubois. Some of the experiments were featured by HBO television airing in 1999.

In these experiments, the mediums were to attempt to contact friends or relatives of the "sitters," the people who were looking for communication. The sitters were hidden from view and never spoke a word, so as not to give the mediums any clues. The mediums were still able to bring forth information to the sitters that was, without a doubt, clear communication. With these extraordinary and surprising results, Schwartz abandoned his own skepticism. He published his findings in 2003 in *The Afterlife Experiments: Breakthrough Scientific Evidence of Life After Death*. (For more information on this work, see Appendix B.)

Regardless of the results, the skeptics still were not convinced. In an article from the January/February 2003 issue of the *Skeptical Inquirer*, titled "How Not to Test Mediums Critiquing the Afterlife Experiments," Dr. Ray Hyman, a former mentalist and magician who is now a noted scientific critic of parapsychology and one of the founding fathers of CSICOP (The Committee for the Scientific Investigation of Claims of the Paranormal), refutes these findings. He takes particular issue with the testing method, noting that the experiments were not *double-blind*.

def•i•ni•tion

Double-blind is a standard scientific method used to prevent the outcome of research from being influenced by prejudice or opinion. Both the investigator and the participant are unaware of certain aspects of the testing; it's only when the testing is complete that the investigator is made privy to all the pieces of the puzzle, so to speak, and he or she draws his or her conclusions at that point.

Those on Schwartz's team are basically responding to Hyman's criticism by saying, "Prove us wrong."

This is a great example of two sides being deadlocked on an issue. One side says, "Prove it!" and the other side says, "No, you *disprove* it!" In the absence of physical proof of life after death, the best we can hope for is to agree to disagree—peacefully.

Voices of the Skeptics, Unite!

Many skeptics organizations have been formed to discuss their beliefs. Just in case you're curious to learn more about them, I've listed a few here (see Appendix B for more information on these websites):

- The Committee for the Scientific Investigation of Claims of the Paranormal (CSICOP) is a nonprofit scientific and educational organization, started in 1976. The *Skeptical Inquirer* is its official journal. (Taken from their website: www. csicop.org. Recently they have changed their name to the Committee for Skeptical Inquiry, or CSI.)

- The Skeptics Society is a scientific and educational organization of scholars, scientists, historians, magicians, professors, teachers, and anyone curious about controversial ideas, extraordinary claims, revolutionary ideas, and the promotion of science. Their mission is to serve as an educational tool for those seeking clarification and viewpoints on those controversial ideas and claims. (Taken from their website: www.skeptic.com.)

- The James Randi Educational Foundation is a not-for-profit organization founded in 1996. Its aim is to promote critical thinking by reaching out to the public and media with reliable information about paranormal and supernatural ideas so widespread in our society today." (Taken from its website: www.randi.org.)

Ethereal Potpourri

James Randi, also known as "The Amazing Randi," is a skeptic and debunker of the paranormal. He was a stage magician and is now best known for his Million Dollar Challenge, which began in 1964 by offering a prize of $1,000 to anyone who could demonstrate evidence of the paranormal under test conditions. The prize money kept accumulating and is now set at the million-dollar mark. This is what prompted Dr. Victor Zammit to offer his challenge, which is to disprove the existence of the paranormal for the same amount of money! For more information about these challenges, go to James Randi's website (www.randi.org). Visit Dr. Zammit's website, too (www.victorzammit.com). Read the information and then *you* decide.

If you're curious to learn what skeptics have to say about life after death, these websites are a great place to start your research. At the very least, you'll have the opportunity to open your mind and examine your own beliefs more thoroughly—and that's always a good thing.

The Least You Need to Know

♦ Atheists don't believe in a higher power; agnostics claim not to know if a higher power exists; debunkers actively try to disprove theories of life after death.

♦ Open-minded skeptics are willing to investigate and experiment; closed-minded skeptics will not be swayed to accept anything that's not consistent with their deeply entrenched beliefs.

♦ Contrary to conventional wisdom, scientists are not always skeptics.

♦ Skeptics discount the use of Ouija boards and séances as means of communication with those who have passed on.

♦ There are groups of believers and skeptics who are trying to prove either the existence or the absence of the afterlife.

Send Me an Angel

In This Chapter

◆ Have you come for me?

◆ Guidance in crossing to the next dimension

◆ What do angels look like?

◆ The hierarchal order of angels

◆ Summoning an angel for help communicating with the dead

Many religions believe that angels are the guardians of our spirits, so it would make sense that they would be close at hand at the time of death. But do we all become angels as soon as we die? Is this what happens to all dead people, or is it a selective process?

There is much more to the subject of angels than what we usually hear in church or even in stories. For example, did you know that there are hierarchies of angels and that each group is held responsible for different tasks? I'll cover this information and talk about how to contact an angel in this chapter.

Angel of Death

Although most of us like to think of angels as messengers of peace, there have been many myths and stories throughout the ages telling us about the angel of death. Does an angel really appear when we are ready to pass? According to those who have had near-death experiences (see Chapter 7 for more details), angels of death sometimes make themselves known to those who are crossing over. Interestingly, though, different religions tell us different things about these heavenly operators that usher us across the etheric planes:

◆ Muslims believe that God created angels from light, which makes sense, as angels are usually depicted with glowing light encompassing them. Additionally, the Qur'an speaks of the charge of the angel of death in these verses: "The angel of death, who has been charged with you, will gather you; then to your Lord you will be returned." (As-Sajdah 32:11)

> **What Skeptics Say**
>
> The problem with the majority of alleged angelic encounters is that highly religious people are likely to interpret coincidence as divine intervention, or a mysterious "human" hero as an angel sent from God, when in fact, they were just benevolent human beings.
>
> —"Angels: An Objective View," Davy Russell (1998)

◆ Judaism teaches that God created the angel of death while he was creating the world. According to this theory, the angel of death has 12 wings and resides in heaven. The overall picture of this angel is rather scary: he supposedly waits at the head of the dying person with a sword that has one drop of gall at its end. When the dying person opens his mouth the angel drops the gall into it, and the person expires.

◆ Roman Catholics believe that St. Michael the Archangel is the angel of death. St. Michael is often depicted carrying a sword and a scale—the scale is viewed as a tool of judgment by which Michael allows the newly deceased one last chance to prove him- or herself worthy of entry into heaven.

Angels are referenced throughout scriptures in many other religions and belief systems, including the Greeks, Romans, and Babylonians. Different scriptures tell us that there are many different kinds of angels, and they all have different tasks. So although an angel of death might seem like a frightening specter, they should not frighten us. They have a job to do. It's probably better to have an angel escort or guide you than to try to make it across by yourself!

Angel of Peace

Just as there is an angel of death, we also hear about the angel of peace, especially in Judeo-Christianity.

This angel is considered nonjudgmental and balanced, existing in harmony of all things. She surrounds herself on equal ground in all things. The reason this particular angel has been classified as feminine may be because the qualities of this entity relate more to the feminine or gentler side of our psyche. And she has a very important role in bringing balance to our lives. For example, when something doesn't go the way you want it to in your life, you will see that this angel has taken what you thought of as a negative and made it into a positive.

It's also said the angel of peace can guide us to the next dimension after our death. Who would be a better angelic pilot to take us over to the other side than someone who has unconditional love for all? You may be thinking, "I thought that was the angel of death's job! So who *does* take us to the next life?" That may be determined by your religious and spiritual beliefs, and of course, we'll never know until the moment arrives.

Ethereal Potpourri

Do we become angels when we die? Most religious texts tell us no. Angels never had physical form—they were created by a Supreme Being. They never walked the earth like you and I, and they cannot become a guardian angel for the living.

What Do They Look Like?

Angel sightings are countless, and the stories concerning what they look like are equally so. From the beginning of time, we have seen primitive artwork depicting beings that would be nowadays labeled as angels. In ancient texts such as the Bible, there are numerous tales of the appearance of angels. We also hear accounts of angel sightings in modern-day life. We're seeing as many angels as ever!

People who claim to see angels report a variety of images. A friend once told me she saw an angel who looked like a lumberjack! I've heard accounts of angels who had hair, which doesn't sound so strange—except the hair was not attached to their heads! The hair somehow followed behind them and it didn't seem to catch up as they walked. Perhaps this is because the time frame from another dimension was not in sync?

Angels are spiritual beings and without any physical form that we can relate to. However, they can take on the appearance of humans when necessary, to give us an appearance we can relate to that will not frighten us. In near-death experiences some people see angels, but typically, they don't have wings. How can the dying tell if an angel is an angel without its wings? Call it intuition. You may wonder if angels come in a human form and how to differentiate between an angel and a ghost. Intuition helps you to know the difference. Somehow you just know. Perhaps it's a telepathic message you receive or a feeling that you are in the presence of a spiritual entity that is not of this realm.

I Only Go There for the Wings

If you look at artists' renditions of angels, many have wings and halos, but not all. The old masters' artwork and sculptures portray angels as winged creatures. So how did they know what angels really looked like? Did they all see angels, or were they simply relying on their own imaginations and the written or spoken word of those who had reported seeing angels?

> **Eternal Thoughts**
>
> As well-spent day brings happy sleep, so life well lived brings happy death.
>
> —Leonardo da Vinci, artist, scientist, sculptor

One of the reasons for this depiction is that these artists needed to differentiate between humans and these glorified entities on canvas—so they added the wings. Another reason for displaying wings in artwork or on sculptures was to represent the angel's flight between a heavenly dimension and Earth.

I've put together a list of "angelic" artists and their works that you may want to research on your own:

- Abbott Handerson Thayer, *Angel*
- Leonardo da Vinci, *Study of an Angel*
- Sandro Botticelli, *Annunciation*
- Joyce Birkenstock, *Angel of Peace*
- William Adolphe Bouguereau, *Angels Playing Violin*

Admittedly, not all artists depict angels with wings and halos, but many do feature some type of glow or mystical aura surrounding them. Again, this is usually done for the purpose of differentiating between humans and ethereal life forms, but what does that glow say to us? I don't know about you, but it sure makes me feel like I'm headed for a warm, safe place in the next life!

The next time you see angel art, take a closer look and determine what you think the artist is seeing (and saying) and whether you can relate to that image.

Are Angels Male or Female?

Sometimes we think of angels as being men and sometimes we think of them as being women. For example, the archangel Michael is always portrayed as being male. However, it's also been said that angels are androgynous, meaning they're neither male nor female. It seems it is all in the vision of the beholder.

The Bible and other religious texts don't uphold the fact that angels can be of either gender. They may refer to angels on occasion as male, but that's mostly for reading purposes more than anything, and typically even in present times we tend to use the masculine language to make our points. Regardless, it should be noted that that most of the angels' names we are familiar with end in the letters "el": Michael, Gabriel, Raphael, and so on. This is taken from the Hebrew root word meaning "of God." These names are all considered masculine; another reason people may assume all angels are male.

I subscribe to the notion that angels are without gender. If angels do not bear children, why would they be created with genders? It's just not necessary.

Ethereal Potpourri

Gallup Polls show that 85 percent of people in the United States believe in some form of angels.

Angelic Triads

If you believe in angels, then you have to wonder where they spend their time. Where do they live? What do they do all day long?

Thomas Aquinas (1225?–1274), an Italian philosopher and theologian, believed that there were angelic realms, or angelic choirs, made up of three orders, which were each further divided into groups of three. Each of these groups of three created what he referred to as a *Triad*. (Because of his philos-

def•i•ni•tion

According to Thomas Aquinas, **Triads** of angels refer to the hierarchical order of angels, which consists of three levels. Each level, in turn, contains three levels of angels. Each level is tasked with specific duties.

ophies regarding angels, Aquinas was known as the "Angelic Doctor," which elevated him to a high level of respect within the church. He was later made a saint.)

The First Triad

The first Triad is considered to be the closest to God. It consists of Seraphim, Cherubim, and Ophanim. These groups are the custodians of divine love and wisdom:

- The *Seraphim* are the first rank of the first Triad. They are the angels of love, light, and fire. They encompass the throne of God and sing the praises and glory of God. Because such intense light radiates from them, no other beings can look upon them.

- The *Cherubim* are the second rank of the first Triad, representing knowledge. They are the keepers of the divine records, a library of sorts that contains all the knowledge of the universe since the beginning of time, including dealings in the human experience, animals, minerals, and all things of matter, philosophy, and emotions. It's said the Cherubim will sound the four trumpets heralding the beginning of the apocalypse.

- The *Ophanim*, the third rank of the first Triad, are sometimes referred to as the many-eyed ones and often also called "Thrones." They guard the throne of God.

The Second Triad

The second Triad is the mid-level, for angels who rotate back and forth between the first level and the third level. These secondary groups are made up of Dominions, Virtues, and Powers:

- The *Dominions* are the first rank of the second Triad. They take their orders from the Seraphim and Cherubim, and on occasion, might receive orders from God himself. The main task of the Dominions is to keep the universe running smoothly. They hardly ever appear to humans.

- The *Virtues* are the second rank of the second Triad. They are believed to play a role in inspiring works of art and scientific discoveries. It's believed that the Virtues appear to humans as sparks of light.

- The *Powers* are the third rank of the second Triad. They oversee conscience and history, and are the angels of birth and death. Generally speaking, these angels are believed to be the "brains" of the ethereal operation, concerned with matters like philosophy, ideology, and religion.

The Third Triad

The third tier of angels is more connected to mankind. They consist of the Principalities, Archangels, and Angels:

♦ The *Principalities* are guardian angels of entire nations and deal in issues like politics and trade. Interestingly, one of their duties is to decide which humans are worthy of becoming rulers.

♦ There's some confusion and debate surrounding the *Archangels*. For the most part, they're regarded as guardians of heaven, in an almost militarylike way. St. Michael is probably the most famous archangel, and he's always shown with his sword at his side.

♦ What we call *Angels* are the lowest rank of all the angels. These beings are given tasks that relate to everyday care of human beings. Angels are given many tasks, most of them dealing with sending messages back and forth, from the living to the dead (or vice versa).

According to Aquinas's basic philosophy, this would sum up the angel groups. However, there may be other levels of angels that we are not aware of.

It is said that once angels have finished a mission on Earth they return to the afterlife until they are summoned by their supreme power (or by humans, as discussed in the next section) to make the excursion again. When they're back in their realm, they shed the appearance that makes us feel comfortable (the humanlike form) and go back to their cozy form of existence, which is free of any physical body.

Summoning Angels to Talk to the Dead

The word "angel," according to Greek, means *messenger*. They deliver messages back and forth from Earth to a supreme plane. It makes sense, then, that they may act as mediums between humans and the dead.

There are several methods of communing with angels for the purpose of contacting the departed. I have included just one here for you to try. I have used this method with many of my clients and it has been successful for some but not all. I would say the percentage was about 50/50. The worst thing that can happen is that you don't make contact; the good news is that there's no cost involved except for a candle.

Telepathic Communications with Angels

In order to communicate with an angel who will carry your message to a loved one who has passed over, you must be very specific about *why* you are trying to communicate and with whom. Now, specific doesn't mean overly involved. Your reason for wanting to make contact can be as simple as wanting to know that there is life after death or finding comfort in knowing the deceased have made the transition to a better place.

On the other hand, you might also want to know the location of the keys that will open that treasure chest your loved one has buried in the backyard. That's fair game, too. There are no laws. If your question isn't appropriate, you simply won't receive an answer. That said, remember: even if your request is appropriate, you may *still* not receive an answer. All of this is wrapped up in your intention and your ability to telepathically communicate.

The only item you need for this is a white candle, which stands for purity and will give you a boost to communication with a higher realm by its physical properties. (It may also help to focus on something like a candle to put yourself in an altered state of consciousness.) The candle can be any size, shape, or height. It should be set on a table or in a safe area.

The Steps of Communication to the Dead

Pick a time and date when you are alone and quiet. Face the direction west, as this is believed to be a portal to the other side. (I talk about the various directions and their associated energies in Chapter 9.) As you light your white candle, think about the person with whom you are trying to make contact. Then …

> **Ethereal Potpourri**
>
> You may want to envision a cloudlike, white light of protection around you before you begin this process. This will prevent a fallen angel from coming into your space.

1. Gaze into the flame of the candle and ask an angel (do not use any angel names) to help you communicate with your loved one. Focus on communicating with *one* departed person. Continue to gaze at the candle flame and ask your question, either out loud or silently. You might say something such as, "I put out my request to any angel who can hear my call for assistance in helping me communicate with [the name of the deceased]. I ask that you come in love and light with kindness."

2. Continue to gaze at the candle flame for a few minutes and see if telepathically you pick up any messages from the angel. You won't be hearing directly from the departed but from the angel.

3. If you feel you're making contact, you can continue to pick up messages or ask more questions.

4. When you grow weary or stop receiving messages, your time will be over. Thank the angel who helped you. Gently snuff out your candle and sit quietly for a while. When you feel you are no longer in your altered state, stand up and continue your daily routine.

It should be noted that you should not expect to actually *see* the angel—although that is not necessarily impossible, especially for those who have high levels of concentration and focus. Anything can happen.

As with all means of communicating with the dead, I recommend writing down your experiences so that you can reflect on them later and/or compare notes with other sessions. And if the first session doesn't work, I recommend trying again on another date. Obviously, we don't know much about the workings of the afterlife. If your angel is busy on one night, she or he may be free another time. It never hurts to give it another shot!

The Least You Need to Know

- Different belief systems recognize angels of death and of peace.

- Humans don't turn into angels when they die.

- Artists depict angels with wings to differentiate between humans and to represent the flight from the ethers to Earth.

- It is thought that there are three Triads or levels of angels, each with a different job or purpose.

- You can try to telepathically contact angels in order to get in touch with a dead loved one.

Chapter 6

Just Call Me Spiritual

In This Chapter

◆ Defining spirituality

◆ Combining traditional beliefs with new ideas

◆ Defining your own thoughts of life after death

◆ Are you a New-Ager?

Most of us have a religion imposed upon us at birth, but there are many people who investigate other religions and change faiths as a result of their search for God or a higher power. Other people throw their hands up and just don't adopt the "Almighty" at all, unless it can be proved.

And then there's an alternative group, people who don't believe in organized religions or structured belief systems at all. They're mostly of the opinion that there's something or someone out there who's our creator and with whom we are all universally connected; however, there's no one religion or faith group that accurately expresses their belief system. These people feel ill at ease embracing traditional religion. That sort of uneasiness propels them to form a very personal spiritual concept of their own—and with that personal view comes a unique view of life after death.

In this chapter, we'll explore what spirituality is (and what it *isn't*) and how spiritual philosophies help open up new doors to exploring life after death.

Spiritually Speaking ...

We've all heard people who describe themselves as spiritual but not religious. Their descriptions of themselves, and how they feel about their beliefs, may take form as one of these common views:

◆ "I believe in a higher power but I'm not really sure what or who it is."

◆ "I have my own thoughts about spirituality, but I feel it's very personal, so I don't talk about it."

◆ "Oh boy! That's a tough one. I simply do my own thing."

◆ "I almost think I could start my own religion because there isn't one out there that describes my thoughts."

Often, these individuals have examined numerous *orthodox* paths and have sincerely tried to find one that makes sense to them, but simply can't. Therefore, they often refer to themselves as "just" spiritual.

def•i•ni•tion

Orthodox, in this context, means conforming to an established conventional or conservative religious group or doctrine.

What Do Spiritual People Believe?

Let's define what I mean by the term *spiritual*, so we're all on the same plane. Even if you don't technically share the same definition, you'll understand what I'm referring to as you read this chapter.

A spiritual person is someone who ...

◆ May be of a religious nature, but isn't necessarily so.

◆ May not be connected to a specific faith but is connected or is striving to connect with a higher power, universal life force, or source, as well as their inner self.

◆ Generally wants to grow in awareness of themselves and others, has a will to gain wisdom, and has the desire to give and accept love, understanding, and patience.

◆ Typically believes that everything has a higher purpose or eventually happens for the best.

Do spiritual people believe in life after death? Usually, yes. In their analysis, it would be unreasonable to think that this life is all that exists. The concepts of reincarnation or past lives are respectfully considered in their contemplations, but not always necessarily their truth. Suffice it to say that spiritual people are open-minded.

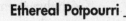

Ethereal Potpourri

Recognize that the "just spiritual" types are hardly "just" anything. I personally don't care for this terminology. It makes a person sound wishy-washy in his or her beliefs. If you're a spiritual person, say it loudly and proudly—and lose the "just"!

Spiritual Ideas About Dying

People who label themselves *spiritual* have numerous thoughts and ideas about life after death, the reason being they don't typically adhere to a fixed outlook—they can have literally millions of ideas during their life here on Earth. Ask 100 spiritual people what happens when you die and you'll most likely get at least 80 different answers.

So what are some of these beliefs? The following theories are based on interviews I've had with individuals as well as general research about "spiritual" but not "religious" people and what they're thinking about life after death:

◆ We proceed to another plane where we wait to return in another body. We reincarnate after choosing our own parents or guardians, who are already on Earth. In being raised by those specific individuals, we'll learn the lessons we need to learn to spiritually evolve and will continue to come back until we "get it right." (So if your teenager tells you, "I didn't ask to be born!" you can say, "Well, actually you did, and *you* picked *us*." That gets 'em every time.)

◆ We leave our body and our soul transcends to a place that is of total peace and fulfillment. We don't come back to Earth and we have no contact with those on this planet. We simply "live" in the awe of a different dimension.

◆ There's a whole city, so to speak, where we have a life like here on Earth, but in a different way. No death, hatred, or jealousy.

◆ When you pass on, an automatic review of life is unfolded, like watching your life on a DVD. From this review, a higher being decides what level of this new dimension you'll reside on—until you come back via reincarnation.

◆ We ascend to another planet or different planets, depending on our level of enlightenment. (This is *not* the mainstream New Age thinking, but I have heard several accounts of this philosophy.)

> **Eternal Thoughts**
>
> Religion is not identical with spirituality; rather religion is the form spirituality takes in civilization.
>
> —William Irwin Thompson, social philosopher and cultural critic

◆ You simply unite with your creator, and no one can possibly understand this state of being. People who believe this take great peace in knowing that the soul lives on, even though they're not sure in what manner. These thinkers feel that death is something to embrace, not fear. (But, of course, they also believe that we never should take our own life or anyone else's to try to get there faster!)

As you can see, spiritual theories about the afterlife can be as varied as the flowers growing in a sprawling garden. But what are these theories based on? We'll talk about how people form their spiritual theories later in this chapter.

Don't Forget the Question!

Hopefully, your spiritual voyage includes your thoughts about life after death—including the question of whether the afterlife exists at all.

Sometimes spirituality becomes so pronounced that we don't take the time to contemplate what happens when we die. Some people just don't want to think about it, while others think we do something or go somewhere upon the moment of our death but have no firm opinions or thoughts concerning the details. There are those who think Earth is a classroom and we have to keep attending "class" until we can finally graduate and make our final ascension. Then we have those who feel they are volunteers who didn't need to come back here but did anyway to help someone, or to be here for a special reason.

Feel free to use these ideas to intuit or "feel" the answers about life after death. Maybe you have your own beliefs. Ask yourself what they are and take the time to mull over your answers. As a spiritual person, you don't have a big organization behind you making it easy for you by telling you what you are expected to believe about crossing over to the other side. You'll have to do some work here!

The most important thing is that you believe *something* to be true about life after death. Even if you change your mind, form some type of theory for the present. Don't flip-flop for too long or you'll become spiritually lazy and find yourself perpetually looking for answers. Searching and questioning are excellent foods for the soul. But leaving your opinion of eternal life for another day, and then *another* day, won't bring you balance or peace. I can't tell you what to do, but I encourage you to formulate a view of life after death and see how it sits with you for a while. If it doesn't work, then try again. Eventually, you'll find your spiritual niche. With this idea, you conclude what happens after we die and hopefully you'll find serenity when contemplating this topic. Then you'll be able to approach the other aspects of your life.

Ethereal Potpourri

I call the process of daily living *life's midsection*. You know how you are born. And, when you know, or think you know, what happens when you die, all you need is the insights of what will happen in between. Holding firm to your beliefs of the afterlife helps you to answer philosophical questions in *this* life (like "Why am I here? What's the point of life?").

Mix Equal Parts Religion and Spirituality

You may be asking yourself, "Can I combine religious beliefs about life after death?" The answer is yes—and not only about the afterlife, but about any religious or spiritual notions. There are no rules here as to what you can or can't think.

In Chapters 1 and 2, I address diverse religious beliefs about life after death. If you thread two or more of them together and come up with your own afterlife theories, good for you! This reveals that you are contemplative, learning and concerned about the existence of the soul after death.

Believe It ... or Not

If you aren't of any particular religious persuasion but you *are* spiritual, you can believe whatever you want about the afterlife. Remember, you need not answer to any organization or feel guilty about not going along with the congregation. As a spiritual person, you are a solitary practitioner of your own thoughts, convictions, and theories.

But this isn't to say that you need to hold on to your spiritual beliefs with a death grip (no pun intended). Part of being spiritual is having a willingness to hear other ideas. To this end, interacting with others for the purpose of spiritual growth and enlightenment is something to consider. This exchange of ideas isn't intended to convert someone to your way of thinking; it's about sharing opinions and speculations—about life after death *and* other issues—that may prove to be interesting, enlightening, and intriguing.

Take One from Column A, Two from Column B ...

Combining religious and/or spiritual beliefs is becoming more common every day. For example, people often look at Buddhism as more of a philosophy than a religion. Those who view Buddhism in this way use it as a way to complement their base religion. I know many people who consider themselves Christian Buddhists or Jewish Buddhists.

But isn't this just picking and choosing the "best" parts of each religion and adapting them to your own beliefs? For the most part, it is. But isn't it beautiful that we're developing a frame of consciousness that will accept mainstream believers as well as those who establish a spiritual path of their own?

I believe that if you create your own belief system, your actions are within the law, it harms no one (including yourself), and it's rooted in a loving attitude, you have created your own spiritual reality. You've found your unique passageway. And the good news is you can make changes along the way if you feel they're necessary. Spirituality encourages your own unique process, not traveling the most "acceptable" route to life after death.

New Age Thought: Everything Old Is New Again

While standing in the checkout line at the grocery store as the cashier attempted to put a tape into the cash register, I had yet another opportunity to practice patience.

The lady in front of me made a comment that she liked a particular young actress who was on the cover of one of the magazines. I commented I liked her too, and added, "She's kind of new-agey." The woman said, "What do you mean, new-agey?" I answered I meant this actress subscribed to New Age thought. The woman looked at me like she hadn't a clue as to what I was talking about. I was just going to try to explain when she said, "Oh, yeah, all that psychic stuff."

My hair almost stood on end. Suffice it to say that *New Age* thought includes explorations that reach far beyond psychic readings.

def•i•ni•tion

New Age is a term that was popularized in the 1980s and is used to describe a set of beliefs that don't gel with traditional religion. New Age followers are spiritual, open-minded individuals searching for their own path. When it comes to life after death, they follow the beat of their own individual drummer. There is no common element, but believers believe the soul continues in some form into some type of an afterlife.

New Age interests may include psychic readings, as my friend in the grocery store pointed out, but typically also include alternative medicines, meditation, reincarnation, spiritual healing, and dream interpretations. Open-mindedness to UFOs and other mysteries also flash in the thoughts of this movement. Environmental issues are important, as are angels, prayers, holistic health, crystal healing, and meditative-type music for relaxation.

And even though the expression is "New Age," these thoughts and ideas are rooted in ancient traditions and philosophies. They're simply resurfacing to create a new spiritual era that's perhaps more open-minded and evolved than days of yore.

New Agers, or people who follow a New Age direction, are spiritual, discerning, and eager to learn and experiment to see what our mysterious planet and the universe have to offer.

The New Age Movement on the Move

Even if you never really knew what the New Age movement was all about, I'm very sure you've experienced some New Age concepts that are steadily flowing into mainstream areas of our everyday lives. Here are some examples of New Age thought that have become commonplace in our society.

◆ Some hospitals now boast meditation rooms.

◆ Yoga is now practiced by people of many faiths who used to find this form of relaxation and exercise unacceptable on a spiritual level. (It was originally practiced by Easterners and some of them included it in their religious practices. Therefore, here in the West there are those who would look at practicing yoga as incorporating another religion into theirs.)

◆ Aromatherapy, which is associated with alternative medicine, uses essential oils and other aromatic mixes to change someone's mood to a more positive and relaxed natural state. These products are found in most department stores, drugstores, and online.

New Age Beliefs About the Afterlife

New Age philosophies are working their way into the fabric of our everyday lives. Is it any surprise, then, that New Age beliefs about life after death are also becoming more commonplace and accepted in mainstream society?

So what *do* New Agers believe about death? Well, because this philosophy is a very individualized path, there are a lot of theories. I've put a few of them together here:

◆ Theories about past lives or reincarnation are very prevalent amongst New Agers. One theory is that we keep returning to the planet until our soul has learned its lessons. Once the soul "gets it right" by learning from the mistakes we've made, we become spiritually evolved or enlightened and don't have to return.

◆ Different planes or dimensions are another idea the New Age movement considers. This theory holds that when we depart from the earth, we go to a different dimension. Some dimensions or planes are better than others; where you end up depends on how you led your life on Earth. You can go up to a higher level once you've learned your lessons in this new dimension.

◆ Some New Agers believe that we journey to other planets when we die; others think that there are entire new cities out there waiting for us.

We'll discuss some of these ideas later in this book.

The interesting thing about New Age philosophy is that among those who follow this general direction, most don't judge others' opinions and ideas about life after death. It's all about having a "whatever you think is perfect for you *is* perfect" attitude.

The Least You Need to Know

- ◆ Spirituality is a highly individualized path that may or may not be based in traditional religious philosophy.

- ◆ It's okay to combine religions and their thoughts about life after death to come up with your own philosophy.

- ◆ New Age practices are actually not new at all; many have been passed on from ancient times.

- ◆ New Age notions are making their way into our everyday lives.

Part 2

Portals to the Light

When the soul passes, what happens? That is, how does it get from *here* to *there?* What does it see and experience along the way? You may be surprised to learn that while there are sometimes significant differences in reports of near-death experiences, there are also startling similarities. In these chapters, you'll read about passageways to the other side, including what happens in those final moments before the soul takes its leave of this life.

7

Near-Death Experiences

In This Chapter

- ◆ What happens during a near-death experience
- ◆ Real-life stories to die for
- ◆ What the skeptics say about NDEs
- ◆ How death changes life

A near-death experience, or NDE, as they're often referred to, happens to some people when they're close to death, when they've been deemed clinically dead, or are in a circumstance where they expect to die but are somehow saved.

People who've briefly crossed over to the other side often have a recollection of what took place while they were dead or close to dying—and many of these experiences are startlingly similar. And these are fairly common occurrences!

Believers in life after death feel this is first-rate evidence of life in other dimensions. Others refute these stories, saying they aren't scientific evidence and that they're probably the result of the brain shutting itself down.

No matter how you feel about these brushes with death, it's certainly interesting to hear the stories. In this chapter, I'll cover what happens in an NDE, along with the long-term changes for the people who've been there—and come back.

Phases of a Near-Death Experience

Each *near-death experience* (NDE) is unique, but there are often very similar happenings within the experiences. Typically, when a person reports what happened to them during an NDE, the order of events is the same, and what's seen, heard, and felt is also similar.

Death Has a Sequence

People often report following the same path, so to speak, to the other side. At the time of death, the person has a feeling of being removed from her physical body. This is usually described as a floating sensation, giving the person a sense of being unburdened by pain. She feels a sense of great peace; there is no fear.

def•i•ni•tion

A **near-death experience**, or **NDE**, occurs when a person is either declared dead or is close to death, briefly crosses over to the other side, and then returns to this life.

The person can often see herself looking down on her own body, which may lie in the wreckage of an accident or on an operating room table or wherever the person was when she died. The person is totally aware of what's going on around her. She can see loved ones crying or doctors trying to revive her. Some claim they can also see through walls and doors and can telepathically pick up the thoughts of those nearby.

The next phase varies from person to person, but it involves entry to another dimension. They may see deceased loved ones who seem to be waiting to receive them. Others see entities described as angels or religious figures. It's very common for people to say that they move through a tunnel or toward a bright light (as discussed in Chapter 10). Some say they walk along beautiful paths, hearing music that defies description. A feeling of all-encompassing love surrounds them at this point.

Some people who've had an NDE say they've seen cities in another dimension where they could live similarly to life on Earth but without pain or fear.

In the last phase of an NDE, the person returns to her physical body. Most spiritual travelers tell us they were given a choice to stay or return. Obviously, these people chose to come back. However, they say it wasn't an easy choice and usually came back because of an obligation to other loved ones here on Earth.

Some people report that they didn't want to come back but they weren't given a choice. They were made to return because it was not their time to pass.

> **Ethereal Potpourri** _____
>
> A life review is a commonly reported episode during an NDE. In a life review, the individual's past and actions unfold in front of them in a flash. They experience their wrongdoings and the good they may have done, as well. A Supreme Being ultimately judges the person's life and decides whether the person will have to incarnate back to Earth or proceed on to eternal life after death.

Why Don't We Hear About Scary NDEs?

Many religious traditions teach us that there are places like hell waiting for those of us who haven't led the noblest of lives. Do people who have NDEs *always* go to heaven? That's just not possible—is it?

It's true that the majority of reported NDEs include stories of pleasure, elation, and total love. However, there are some folks who've had negative experiences in the moments following their deaths. They saw evil beings, terrifying cities, or had an overall feeling of despair.

It should be noted, however, that many of these people were fearful or angry at the time of their death. When these people surrendered to the experience, their feelings of anger or fear of dying left them, and their negative experience turned into an NDE filled with love and great happiness.

It's also been reported that some people who've had scary NDEs asked a higher power for help. With this plea, their negative experience immediately turned positive.

Real-Life Stories About Coming Back from Death

Due to advances in modern medical technology, more people are being revived than ever before. Therefore, more people are experiencing NDEs and the subject is being discussed more and more. What's really interesting about NDEs is that all sorts of people have had them: children, adults, people of all races, all religions—even atheists have been "there" and back. A near-death experience is an equal opportunity for all.

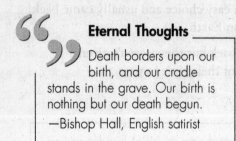

Eternal Thoughts

Death borders upon our birth, and our cradle stands in the grave. Our birth is nothing but our death begun.

—Bishop Hall, English satirist

There are many books written about NDEs and Internet sites containing stories from people who've had NDEs (see Appendix B for more on both), but I wanted to do my own research. Therefore, the stories presented here are straight from the (dead) horse's mouth, so to speak.

Some of my sources really surprised me! I guess you just never know who's going to have a close call with life after death ....

The Car Accident

My friend Roger told me years ago about his NDE. I never would have thought I would end up sharing it with so many others! In fact, I had forgotten all about it, but when I told him I was writing a book about life after death, he reminded me about his story.

Roger was driving down a four-lane highway in Michigan during a tremendous snowstorm at night. A friend of his was in the vehicle ahead of him; they were headed to go goose hunting, but Roger's car began to overheat. He flashed his headlights, signaling his friend to pull over. Roger parked on the side of the road and his friend pulled over in front of him.

Roger opened his hood, trying to find the problem. A passing driver didn't see Roger until it was too late, slid on the roadway and hit Roger's car from behind. The impact sent his body vaulting over the vehicle and he landed between the front of his own car and back of his friend's car. Roger slid down on the ground between the two vehicles. He was taken to the hospital in an ambulance.

The next thing Roger remembers were doctors sticking long needles in his stomach. At that moment he felt himself move away from his physical body. His second body, so to speak, floated only inches above his physical body, which was lying on the gurney below. He said he felt a "knowingness, serenity, and freedom of sorts."

Roger looked to his left, and suddenly, he was moving sideways. He saw a black void, which he didn't move toward, but which he sensed contained the presence of an energy, as he describes it, of some sort, which emanated love, understanding, and compassion. He didn't see the source of this energy or possibly a being; he just knew it was there. He also intuitively knew he was heading for a better place, where there was nothing to fear and everything to gain.

Unexpectedly, he heard a voice say, "Do you want to go back or stay here?" The voice was not that of a man or a woman, but it was peaceful, strong, and clear. Roger told me he didn't want to go back because he could feel that what was ahead was going to be something amazingly wonderful. However, Roger's love and conscience prevailed and he said, "I have a little baby son, and I would like to see him grow up." The voice casually said, "Okay."

In that moment, Roger was back in his body. He woke up to see a priest giving him his last rites, a religious sacrament performed on the dying. Roger was released from the hospital after 14 days, which included physical therapy, and after three months of rest he had a total recovery from his accident. He said his NDE changed his life. Roger used to be a hunter and had many guns for this purpose. When he finally went home, he got rid of all his guns and could never hunt again. He is filled with love for all things and has no fear of death.

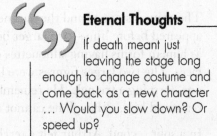

Eternal Thoughts

If death meant just leaving the stage long enough to change costume and come back as a new character ... Would you slow down? Or speed up?

—Chuck Palahniuk, American freelance journalist and satirist

The Drowning Child

I changed dentists this year, and after my second visit, I came home with a first-rate NDE story!

One day when Arthur (my new dentist) was about 7 years old, he went for his usual swim at an indoor recreational facility in the Bronx. However, on this particular day, the lifeguards were busy talking amongst themselves, paying little attention to the young swimming enthusiast.

While the lifeguards chattered away, a determined Arthur was teaching himself to swim. He courageously dove into the deep end of the pool. As he hit the water, he immediately inhaled water. He recalls, "I tried yelling, but I couldn't. I struggled up to the surface but I still couldn't yell."

Suddenly, a feeling came over him that made him want to simply let go of his panic. At that moment, he felt a comfort around him—warmth, quietness, and a sense of soothing calm. He remembers hearing what he describes as chimes and bells. He recollects that "they were wonderful sounds, but there was no melody." Arthur said that he never felt anything similar to this before, and probably never will again—at least not during this lifetime.

Arthur's experience wasn't restricted to a sense of peace and gentle sounds. He also saw darkness, which gave way to a light in the middle. Unlike many people who have an NDE, Arthur did not experience floating or walking through a tunnel or passageway. Instead, he was unexpectedly encompassed in this darkness, which had no border or shape, just the bright white light shining through. He felt no pain, only peace.

The chimes stopped and the darkness somehow seemed to get bigger. Three figures appeared before him—two larger beings and one smaller shape. Arthur describes them as human forms having silhouettes of arms, legs, a torso, and a head, but without visible faces. The two larger figures were behind and to the left and the right of the smaller one, forming a triangle. He remembers that these figures telepathically comforted and reassured him, although he cannot remember any details of the conversation.

In a split second, Arthur felt a terrible pain in the back of his head and the figures disappeared. He was being pulled out of the pool by one of the lifeguards! The peace he had just experienced was gone. Instead of comforting this frightened young boy who had drowned (or come pretty darn close), the lifeguards were annoyed, yelling at Arthur to "Get the hell out of here!"

Arthur went home and did not speak of his NDE for many years—until, as an adult, he heard of others who had come forward with their stories. At last, Arthur knew he was not alone in his experience.

In his adult life, Arthur has occasionally experienced depression. He has a simple explanation for this: "Living in this world hurts." This is not an unusual experience for those who've had a glimpse at the road to the afterlife. These people have experienced a place so peaceful and so beautiful that it's no wonder this life has lost its luster as far as they're concerned. But on the positive side, Arthur feels that because of his NDE, he became more mature and more understanding of people in general.

> **Ethereal Potpourri**
>
> Children who've had NDEs often report hearing or seeing children playing in a garden setting; they also report seeing angels without wings.

Like all those who have had an NDE, Arthur has no fear of death. He wanted to share his story with those who may have apprehension about the existence of life after death.

September 11, 2001

Through the chaos and confusion of the morning of 9/11, many life-changing experiences happened to many people. My friend Jerry was kind enough to share his experience with me, which of course was an NDE. I should mention that before this happened to him, Jerry had heard of NDEs but took no interest in them at all. He considered them mumbo jumbo and a bunch of baloney.

Jerry was in his mid-50s at the time, in New York to attend a business meeting that was to take place not far from the World Trade Center. He was in an excellent frame of mind, anticipating closing a big business deal as well as the wedding of one of his children. He was in a very positive mind-set.

In the cab on the way to the meeting Jerry and his colleagues heard a bulletin on the radio that one of the towers of the World Trade Center had been hit by a small plane. The cab driver told them not to worry; it was an accident. He kept driving toward their destination. As they neared the twin towers, it was then they saw a commercial jetliner roar overhead and hit the second tower of the World Trade Center.

The cab driver told them to get out of the cab, which they did. Unable to enter the building they had been heading to, they stood outside. The atmosphere was horrifying. Windows were shattered; the buildings were burning; people were crying, shouting, and screaming. It was at that point they were discussing what they thought they should do next. That's when the second building started to collapse. One of the men Jerry was with suddenly grabbed the corner of a nearby building and held on, in shock. Jerry said, "God help me!" Obviously, Jerry went from one extreme happy state of being into the opposite state of negativity, which must have thrown his psyche into shock.

During this turmoil, Jerry was neither injured nor hit. But perhaps due to emotional trauma, at that instant, Jerry remembers leaving his physical body. He says, "I was disconnected from my body, but I still existed." He wasn't sure if he was floating above his body, next to it, or soaring all around it. He just knew he was a separate entity at that point. He says, "I felt like nothing could hurt me. I was free."

He wasn't thinking about family, friends, or even the circumstances he was in. With a smile of recollection, he says, "I was glad to get rid of it, all the grief."

As I questioned Jerry as to what happened next, once the body detached from the soul, he said he had no further recollection. He does remember that he had no concept of time, as it didn't seem important. It could have been 10 minutes or an hour.

However, suddenly Jerry was back in his body, and where was he? Not in the place in where he detached from the physical, but in a four-lane intersection somewhere in New York. He was helping a man get his luggage over the median. He doesn't know how he got there or even where he was, exactly, as he wasn't familiar with New York. But he seemed to have a feeling that he knew this man well, although he had never met him.

As I asked Jerry about his thoughts about reincarnation, which I felt he was not sold on, he didn't really comment and just continued to say, "I just felt like I knew him."

Jerry certainly believes in NDEs now. I asked him if he had any parting comments and he said, "If anyone gets in trouble, ask for help from God or whoever you think your higher power is. Ask for help. That's the most important thing." I also asked how he felt about the experience now. He said, "It changed my life, made it better, made everything better."

> **Ethereal Potpourri**
>
> Reincarnation can come into play in an NDE. The man Jerry met in the intersection may have been someone he knew in another lifetime or past life. Jerry was led to help this man now. This is why he said, "I felt I knew him."

Heart Attack

When I was at a book signing several months ago for another book I wrote, a woman asked me what my next project was. When I replied, "It's a book about life after death," she told me she had had an NDE and was kind enough to share her story with me.

Joyce, 62, had been in poor health for some time. She was taken to the hospital after complaining of heart attack symptoms, and while she was there, she did indeed suffer cardiac arrest. Joyce says she thought she had just woken up, but found herself looking down on an operation from the corner of the room. She watched doctors trying to revive a gray-haired woman, and she thought that lady was a goner. She also felt a sense of freedom without knowing why.

Then one of the doctors said, "Come on, Joyce!" Joyce found it interesting that the lady on the operating table had the same name. She continued to watch and then realized it was *her* body down there!

She couldn't understand how she could be in two places at once. Then she understood that she was dead. She stopped watching and listening to what was going on in that operating room and saw a long tunnel with a bright light at the end of it. She began floating down the tunnel, which was drawing her in. Joyce somehow knew this was where she wanted to go.

When she came to the end of the tunnel, her dead mother was waiting, smiling and waving. Joyce also met up with her deceased grandmother, uncle, and childhood friend. All of them looked happy and healthy. They started to escort her down what appeared to be a beautiful garden path. As they walked, she and her loved ones chatted—telepathically.

As they continued to walk, Joyce could see a city ahead. She said she couldn't describe it well, but if she had to put an earthly twist on it, it looked like the Emerald City in the Wizard of Oz! She had her body but no pain; she felt good. Then she said she heard a message telling her not to worry about her body for the moment. She thought, "For the moment? Maybe I get a new one!"

Then, without warning, she was back in her body in the recovery room waking up. She was disappointed to be back.

Ethereal Potpourri _____

It's not unusual for people who've had NDEs to be depressed afterwards, even if they remember making the choice to return to this world. The depression comes from having seen paradise and leaving it behind. It's like returning to your cold, snowy home after a week in the Caribbean. Who *wouldn't* be depressed?

At first, Joyce believed she had had a dream and didn't mention her experience to anyone. But then a woman came into the room whom Joyce recognized. She was the surgical nurse who was assisting the surgeon in the operating room.

Joyce said, "Thank you for helping me. You're a good nurse."

The nurse looked at her and said, "But we never met till now. How did you know who I was?" Indeed, the woman wasn't even wearing her scrubs; she was in her street clothes, on her way home for the evening, but she had stopped to check in on Joyce before she left.

Joyce told the nurse her story and the nurse said, "This kind of thing happens more often then you think." The nurse guaranteed Joyce she had been dead on that table. She could not have seen the nurse at all, even when they got her heart beating again. Today Joyce says she has no fear of death and is looking forward to her new body and home!

The Skeptical View of NDEs

Believers consider NDEs evidence of life after death. However, some skeptics believe that an NDE can be explained away by neurochemistry and the state of the brain prior to dying.

British psychologist Susan Blackmore, author and skeptical investigator of near-death experiences, explains the feelings of peacefulness, tunnels of light, and the other experiences people have reported in their NDEs as hallucinations and the result of a "dying brain." And she isn't alone in her belief that NDEs are not real, at least as far as crossing over to another dimension is concerned.

Dr. Karl Jansen, psychiatrist and author of _Ketamine: Dreams and Realities_ (Multidisciplinary Association for Psychedelic Studies, 2001), claims that Ketamine—an anesthetic and hallucinogenic—can reproduce all the features common to those who've had NDEs, from the light at the end of the tunnel to talking to God. Out-of-body experiences are common while using this drug.

This point of view tells us that if a drug can reproduce these effects, that perhaps when the brain is dying it releases a chemical that may do the same. But those who believe in life after death argue that this _isn't_ conclusive evidence of the absence of an afterlife.

The controversy and the search for evidence and scientific proof regarding NDEs is extensive. If you're interested in finding out more, I suggest doing more research on your own (you'll find plenty of material on the Internet and in the library). I freely admit that *this* book is slanted toward believers!

Time Reveals Personality Changes

In addition to the previous real-life accounts, I heard several more reports of NDEs from credible sources. Although I couldn't include them all, I've made a compilation of some of their common features. These people have reported that their NDEs changed their personalities and their outlook on life and death in a positive and loving way. Aside from my own limited personal interviews about what happens to the personality of someone who's had an NDE, studies have shown that approximately 80 percent of adults and children undergo character changes after an NDE. Check out www.iands. org, the website for The International Association for Near-Death Studies, Inc., for further information about research and current information.

How Do Adults Change?

With the passing of time and the opportunity for reflection, many adults who've gone through an NDE confirm they are not exactly the same person they were before the event. The upside of their personality changes include …

> **Ethereal Potpourri**
>
> It appears that another characteristic of NDEers is that they become more interested in general spirituality as opposed to organized religion. Whether you consider this a plus or a minus is up to you.

- ◆ A deeper love of life.

- ◆ No fear of death.

- ◆ More charitable and sympathetic feelings toward others.

- ◆ Less attachment to people, places, and things.

- ◆ Becoming more accepting and forgiving of others' flaws.

- ◆ Living in the present becomes a primary concern.

Some of these adults report negative changes to their outlook on life, as well. These may include …

- Depression, as they've seen the other side as being the ultimate peace and happiness.

- Less attachment to their spouse.

- Less concern for the future.

- A complete lack of distrust; trusting others to a fault; they want to express nothing but love for their fellow human beings.

If you think about it, it certainly makes sense that an NDE could knock a person off balance. If you've seen the most beautiful sights, heard the most beautiful sounds, and felt an incredible and indescribable sense of peace and love, perhaps you'd hate to come back to your humdrum life. And if you were a nonbeliever to begin with, everything you ever thought to be true would be turned on its head!

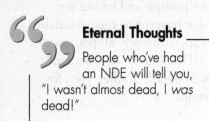

Eternal Thoughts

People who've had an NDE will tell you, "I wasn't almost dead, I *was* dead!"

The good news is that in time, most people are able to balance these positive and negative aspects and find peace in *this* life.

Children Who've Crossed and Come Back

Children who've had NDEs have the same upsides as the adults but with a few more to add to the list. Changes in children may not be as noticeable, because they're still forming their personalities. After their brushes with death, these kids typically ...

- Are more willing to learn.

- Are suddenly more mature than others their age.

- Take an interest in things that are unusual for their age.

- Are not as selfish.

- Are not overly attached to parents.

- Show increased intelligence.

- Are interested in future professions or careers that help and assist other people.

Just as happens with adults, there are some changes that the child who has had this astonishing experience may struggle with. Parents should be sensitive to these challenges and seek professional help if their child seems perplexed for a long period of time.

Which brings us to the downside of changes in kids' personalities, which may include ...

- Temporary withdrawal or depression.

- Difficulty relating to peers.

- Comparing the world they experienced to their present world, which seems to be filled with pain and hopelessness.

Once the children find their balance again, they usually grow up to be good-natured, loving, spiritual, and sensitive individuals.

The general consensus is that a person—whether an adult or child—is better off for having had this type of experience.

The Least You Need to Know

- There are reports of adults and children crossing over to the other side and returning in near-death experiences, or NDEs.

- NDE stories have common factors and sequences to them.

- Skeptics believe an NDE may be the result of a dying brain and its chemical releases.

- The personalities of those who've had NDEs usually change for the better, but there can be a downside to these changes as well.

8

Deathbed Visions

In This Chapter

◆ Researching the visions

◆ Children's visions

◆ Firsthand stories of those left behind

◆ Religious figures and glimpses of the afterlife

◆ Deathbed last words

This book covers a lot of territory, from religious beliefs to what may happen after the physical body dies. But what do we know about the person's last moments? In other words, before the person is dead, do they know what's happening? Do they have any idea where they're headed?

Right before dying (and sometimes in the days before death) people often have visions of deceased family members, beautiful places, and even mysterious beings. Living family members, doctors, nurses, and hospice volunteers are among those who can attest to the reality of deathbed visions.

Are these firsthand accounts of the existence of life after death? Read on and judge for yourself.

Studies on Deathbed Visions

Throughout the ages and different cultures, there have been reports of dying people having visions of the afterlife. The documentation on this topic is profuse—these visions were even recorded in ancient texts and drawings! As these visions are obviously still happening today, researchers have conducted studies on the subject.

Dr. Karlis Osis

Dr. Karlis Osis of the American Society for Psychical Research launched a study in the 1960s focusing on deathbed visions. In the 1970s, his studies, conducted in the United States, were compared to reports of deathbed visions in other areas of the world; his findings were found to be accurate across cultural lines. This indicates that his findings weren't tainted by his own religious or cultural views.

Thousands of case studies were investigated. Interviews with over a thousand doctors, nurses, and others who were somehow present at the time of death to those passing, also took place. Dr. Osis concluded:

> **What Skeptics Say**
>
> The debunkers of deathbed visions may argue that what the dying individual is actually seeing is either a hallucination caused by lack of oxygen to the brain or a wish fulfillment.

- Drugs that could cause any type of hallucinations were not administered to the patients involved in the study.

- The belief in life after death or any religious or spiritual belief had no bearing on the number of times an apparition was seen.

- Most bedside visions were of consistent length, lasting five minutes or less. (The length of the vision tended to vary from person to person.)

- The patients had the idea that whoever was visiting them from the other side had come to take them back with them.

- The most common vision the dying see are people they knew who were already deceased.

According to Osis's research, another common element is that the visions are always of a positive nature and the dying enjoy and embrace what they see. This is a great comfort to those observing these phenomena. Obviously, it would be disturbing to watch someone experiencing a terrifying deathbed vision.

A Second Study by Osis

In the late 1970s, Dr. Osis and his colleague, Dr. Erlenddur Harldsson, conducted further studies gathering information from medical personnel. The information that was gathered is as follows:

♦ Deathbed visions included not only seeing dead loved ones, but flashes of other worlds.

♦ In addition to these visions, Harldsson and Osis observed dying people experiencing feelings of exhilaration which couldn't be explained medically.

♦ Harldsson and Osis noted that as few as 10 percent of people were conscious right before their death. Osis felt that if more people were alert in their last moments, there would be more accounts of deathbed visions.

Many doctors and nurses note that even the angriest patients had facial expressions of serenity after they'd died. One would think that pain, fear, or anger at the end of a person's life wouldn't lead to an expression of contentment.

Dr. Osis died at the age of 80 on his birthday, December 26, 1997. It seems he may have cycled out on his exact day of birth.

For more about the studies done by Dr. Osis and Dr. Harldsson, you might be interested in reading *At the Hour of Death*, *Third Edition* (Hastings House/Daytrips Publishers, 2006), which provides detailed accounts from doctors and nurses in the United States and India who report on the deathbed visions of patients with whom they came in contact.

Sir William Barrett

In his book *Deathbed Visions*, published in the 1920s, Sir William Barrett, a professor of physics at the Royal College of Science, notes that the dying are often surprised to see a deceased friend or relative in their room. They believe this person is somehow alive and has come to visit them.

Barrett also notes that dying children have reported seeing wingless angels, and that these visions surprise them. He asks, "If deathbed visions are only wish fulfillments, then why don't children see angels *with* wings? After all, *that* would be what they expect."

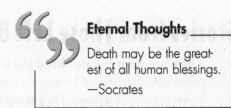

Eternal Thoughts

Death may be the greatest of all human blessings.
—Socrates

Children Led to the Great Beyond

Children most often report seeing deceased relatives as they near the end. The interesting thing is that some children have never met their dead relatives and may not have even seen pictures of them.

Other things that children have seen, as reported by those with them while they were dying, are ...

◆ Lots of beautiful colors.

◆ Other children playing and looking like they are having fun.

◆ Angels.

◆ Beautiful landscapes.

◆ What or who they perceive as God or a spiritual figure.

Parents of dying children often hope to be with a child when and if they see something before dying. This obviously is a comfort to all; the mourning process is less trying when a parent knows that their child's soul goes on and continues to a place with others who can help and guide them.

Ethereal Potpourri

In my research, I read an account of a mother at her dying child's bedside. The mother was holding her child's hand in the final moments. Unexpectedly, the child told her mother, "I can't hold your hand anymore." The mother asked her why. The daughter said, "Because Grandma wants me to take hers now." The child's grandmother had died many years prior to this event. The mother said she could not have asked for a better gift than knowing her daughter went from her hand to the hand of her grandmother. What a beautiful account of a deathbed vision.

Stories from Those Left Behind

There are countless deathbed stories from every continent in the world. If you haven't personally experienced someone having a deathbed vision, then you undoubtedly know people who have. They truly are *that* common.

I also did my own research and have come up with several accounts of those who had a friend or relative who had a deathbed vision. I will share some of them here.

Several books, such as *One Last Hug Before I Go: The Mystery and Meaning of Deathbed Visions* (see Appendix B) by Carla Wills-Brandon, Ph.D., offer interesting accounts of deathbed visions and should be considered for further exploration.

The Atheist

A personal friend of mine—we'll call her Kate—told me her account of a deathbed vision.

Kate was a realtor working for a real estate company in Florida. Her boss, Larry, was a kind, generous, loving, good father and husband—always lighthearted; nothing got him down. Larry was also an atheist. Regardless of Kate's strong religious beliefs, she never tried to convert him or even discuss the subject of the existence of a higher power with him.

One day Larry was in a car accident. He appeared to be uninjured until a week later, when he was rushed to the hospital with severe pain. He remained there while tests were performed to determine the cause of his pain.

Kate visited him at the hospital; they spoke about work and other everyday things. He told her he hadn't been given any pain pills that day; the pain was easing, and he wasn't a person who believed in taking unnecessary medication.

Kate reports that all at once, Larry got a big smile on his face and seemed to be stifling a giggle as he glanced around the room. She was sure he was going to tell her a joke or that he'd thought of a funny story. This would not be at all unusual of Larry's behavior.

Instead, Larry said, "There's so many of them!"

Still thinking it was some type of joke, Kate asked, "Okay, so many what?"

He replied, "Angels." Those were his last words … and he passed.

> **Eternal Thoughts**
>
> I see Hermes, unsuspected, dying, well-beloved, saying to the people, "Do not weep for me, This is not my true country, I have lived banished from my true country—I now go back there, I return to the celestial sphere where every one goes in his turn."
>
> —Walt Whitman, writer/poet

Where Is Aunt Joan?

Carol's grandmother was in a hospital recovering from a stroke. For several days, she had been telling Carol that she was seeing dead relatives coming and going from her room. Carol thought her grandmother's medication may have been causing hallucinations. Nevertheless, she asked her grandmother how the deceased relatives looked; her grandmother reported that they looked well and happy. Carol asked if they were talking to her and her grandmother said no, they just came in to check on her.

> ## 66 99 Eternal Thoughts
>
> In his book *Parting Visions* (see Appendix B), Dr. Melvin Morse says that spiritual visions not only take the fear away from the dying but help the grieving after their loved one has departed, as they know the soul will go on.

One day when Carol was visiting, her grandmother looked up toward the door and said "Oh look! It's Aunt Joan!" referring to a relative who lived in England and had phoned earlier in the week to check on Carol's grandmother.

Carol turned toward the door, not believing that Joan—an elderly woman herself—would travel to Texas to see her grandmother. She didn't see anyone, so she looked down the hall just to make sure Joan wasn't lurking around the corner. Her grandmother asked, "What are you looking for?" Carol answered, "Aunt Joan."

The grandmother said, "She's right here—don't you see her?"

Carol left for the day and her grandmother passed that evening. Later that same evening, she received a call informing her that Aunt Joan had also suddenly died—one day earlier.

Spiritual Guides

Tim and Lynn were with their dying mother in her Connecticut home. She wasn't suffering from any illness; old age had just finally worn out her body.

While the two of them were there one rainy October morning, their mother awoke and said, "Today is the day." They asked what she meant by this, but they feared they already knew. She told them that this would be the day she would be at peace.

Lynn asked her mother how she could be so sure of this.

"I had a dream last night and was told to get ready," her mother said.

Tim asked who had told her this; his mother said she wasn't sure. It hadn't been a person, she explained; just a peaceful voice in her dream. She said that in this dream she had seen a glow but no figure.

Lynn assured her mother that it was only a dream; there was no need to believe that this was the day she would die. Her mother said she knew that a message was sent to her in a dream so that she wouldn't be scared—and she assured her children that she *wasn't* frightened.

That day when both of her loyal children were at her side, the dying woman suddenly looked toward her bedroom closet at the other end of the room and started nodding her head up and down as if to say "yes" while smiling. They asked what she was smiling at. Their mother said, "I'll be leaving now. Can't you feel them?" Lynn admits she felt a shift in energy in the room. It was peaceful, like the slow energy of a Sunday afternoon.

Tim asked, "Feel who?" All his mother said was, "Them, right there. Them." Then she passed on with what her children described as an angelic smile.

An Opera Singer's Last Bow

Michael was a noted performer of the Lyric Opera in Chicago. He was talented and full of life. As the years rolled by, he retired from singing professionally and settled in a suburb of Chicago. My friend's mother, Vivian, was a very close friend of his and he shared many personal stories with her. One such story concerned a woman named Ella.

Michael would frequently see the same woman in the audience, very close to the stage, when he performed. This was not unusual; opera singers have followers just like any other performers. One day after a performance, he went out into the lobby and talked to this woman, whose name was Ella. She was about Michael's age at the time, approximately 45 years old. She also shared her last name, address, and phone number with him.

> **Eternal Thoughts**
>
> What we have done for ourselves alone dies with us; what we have done for others and the world remains and is immortal.
>
> —Albert Pike, attorney, soldier, writer, and Freemason

Through the years, they communicated and became friends. Suddenly, her telephone calls, letters, and in-person meetings stopped. Michael learned that Ella had moved away. Although he was disappointed, Michael didn't pursue finding her, not with the workload he had, and also because he had a wife.

When Michael was 82 years old, he gave a little performance at Vivian's home for about 50 people. Although his voice was shaky, he was still an obvious pro. After the performance, he quite unexpectedly addressed the crowd, saying, "You invited Ella. Where did they find you? You haven't changed a bit!" Everyone looked around, trying to figure out which lady was Ella. Vivian knew who he was talking about, but she said nothing.

As Michael sat down to catch his breath, he became ill and started to hold his chest. An ambulance was called, but Michael died on the way to the hospital. Shortly afterward, Vivian's son looked up Ella on the Internet and found that she had passed away many years earlier.

Spiritual Beings

The most common deathbed visions seem to be dead relatives who come to escort the dying to the other side, but people also often claim to see religious figures and even light beings they can't describe. In different cultures, dying people will see the higher power of their religious or spiritual tradition.

There have been claims of those who have seen *Ascended Masters* in their deathbed visions—spiritual beings who have lived on Earth, but left their physical form through death, when they became *Self-Realized*.

def•i•ni•tion

Deathbed visions often include visits from **Ascended Masters**, religious figures who have fully united with God. Ascended Masters are said to be **Self-Realized**; that is, they've freed themselves from ego and are one with God. The term "Ascended Master" was first introduced to the general public in 1934 with the publication of *Unveiled Mysteries* by Guy Ballard. The term caught on and was used to describe these cosmic spirits by many spiritual and religious organizations.

Ascended Masters have reached a vibrational level akin to the frequency of light, which allows them to come and go to the earth plane from other dimensions at will. They serve humanity and no longer *have* to be involved with the cycle of birth, death, and rebirth—they're above it all. However, this kind of pure goodness could never just walk away from humanity, so we see them from time to time.

What Do They Do and Who Are They?

The Ascended Masters guide and help those who are spiritual seekers looking for personal growth. They can hear us when our souls cry out for help. In addition to reaching us through deathbed visions, they can contact us through dreams, meditation, and soul travel.

There are many Ascended Masters from all cultures and areas of the world. I've listed a few here:

- **Jesus Christ:** Considered the Son of God and God made incarnate by most Christians. He was sent to Earth to provide deliverance by *atoning* for the *sins* of humanity.

- **Mother Mary:** The virgin mother of Jesus Christ.

- **Quan Yin:** The great goddess and Mother of Compassion. She is adored by many throughout Asia.

- **Gautama Buddha:** Known simply as Buddha. Buddhism was formed from his teachings.

- **El Morya:** The embodiment of Abraham, "father of many nations."

- **Yogananda:** The Indian yogi who founded the Self-Realization Fellowship in 1920 based in Los Angeles. He also introduced kriya yoga to the West.

There have been reports of each of these Ascended Masters visiting people on their deathbeds, which actually supports the argument for wish fulfillment at the end of one's life. But could it also be that there's only one Supreme Being, and he or she comes to us in the form we're expecting? No one will ever know for sure—at least not in this lifetime.

Brief Accounts of Deathbed Visions

I've collected accounts of deathbed statements from those in the medical profession, hospice workers, and other people kind enough to share their information.

Here are some examples of last words from the dying:

◆ "Oh look—Grandpa isn't sick anymore."

◆ "You're so bright."

◆ "It's beautiful."

◆ "Wow, this is fantastic!"

◆ "You're all here … nice."

◆ "Daddy, how are you?"

◆ "I can't see, but I think that's Lewis."

◆ "That angel's big."

◆ "May, is that you? You look good."

◆ "Well, I'll be darned!"

◆ "What a feeling!"

◆ "The pain's gone."

◆ "Are you here for me?"

◆ "I'm light as a feather."

◆ "I'm ready to go now."

◆ "I knew it … I just knew it!"

◆ "I thought you'd never get here."

It should be noted that the relatives who are referred to in these quotes had already passed on. But in any event, *who's* bright, and *what's* so beautiful? Again, these are questions that will only be answered when it's our turn to cross over, but it sure does make you wonder.

Death is certainly a serious matter. Regardless, when one actually hears a loved one having a conversation or seeing visions of spiritual beings, beauty, and peace, the knowledge that there is an afterlife to which they'll now transcend is a relief and takes our own fears away.

The Least You Need to Know

- One of the most common deathbed visions includes seeing deceased family members.

- Researchers have studied deathbed visions; many feel the evidence suggests that they are not drug-induced or caused by hallucinations.

- Children who are prematurely near the end of their lives sometimes see other children playing and beautiful scenery.

- Other visions include religious figures, beautiful landscapes, or angels.

Chapter 9

Pathways to the Other Side

In This Chapter

- ◆ Pointing the dead in the right direction
- ◆ Can you see a soul leave the body?
- ◆ The souls who don't make it
- ◆ How you can help a lost soul find its way into the afterlife

When the soul leaves the body of the newly departed, does it instinctively know where to go? Or does it float or flounder around until it finds some sort of mystical portal to the other side? You may have never considered these questions, but think about it—if someone has a terrible sense of direction in this lifetime, can they be confident that upon their death they'll suddenly be blessed with knowing which way leads to bliss? Might they end up in the wrong place? Could this be what happens to souls who end up as ghosts?

In this chapter, I'll talk about what happens when a soul passes and how it actually makes its way to the other side. (Rest assured, no road maps or GPS systems are required!)

Where's My Compass?

Not too many people think of a compass point when they think of the departed. They either imagine the spirit goes straight up or down (though in this modern age where we view the Supreme Being as a loving, forgiving spirit, the belief that we're sent to the underworld or hell is diminishing). Some people even think the soul takes off on an angle.

So in which direction does the soul make its departure, and does the direction it takes make a difference as to the dimension in which it will reside?

North, South, East, West

Many cultures, such as the ancient Egyptians, some Native American tribes, and Eastern cultures, honor the idea that certain types of energy emanate from different compass directions. These groups feel that certain directions offer a better frequency for certain things, including the soul's passing into the afterlife.

◆ **Go west, my soul … go west.** Many ancient religions believed the soul departed to the west. They assumed that because the sun set in the west and concluded the day, it would make sense that this was the doorway to the after-life. In this theory, west offers a conclusion, an ending.

◆ **East … the dawning of a new life.** The sun rises in the east, starting a new day; this represents new beginnings and opportunities. To early man, this made common sense—it was nature that told them this direction is all about start-ing anew. Many modern-day believers of the power of direction frequencies have taken this belief from the ancients and feel that the soul travels to the east, where it will begin a new and spiritual reality.

◆ **Northern lights.** North is a powerful direction. According to the winds of nature, most cold fronts come in from the north. It's believed to have the stron-gest energy, or push. Many feel the north is the only route strong enough to help pull the soul across to the other side.

◆ **Southbound for the afterlife.** South is a bearing that deals with human emo-tion and love. Warm winds come in from the south, as in "southern breezes." According to those who look to nature as part of their religion or spiritual beliefs, it seems reasonable that the dead are accompanied to the south by dead loved ones when they cross over.

Ethereal Potpourri _____

Many people believe if you're going to a negative place (like hell), your soul immediately goes into a downward spiral. This is most likely not true, as most people also believe that in some way, we have a life review after we die (see Chapter 22). So if you're headed somewhere that's not so pleasant (if that's even possible), it probably doesn't happen immediately after dying.

Just Floating Along ...

There are also other thoughts as to where the soul begins its journey to the next plane or dimension, which include ...

♦ Souls ascend straight up until they're out of this dimension, and then they simply know where to go.

♦ The soul only rises a few inches above the dead physical body and immediately slips into another dimension. In other words, it doesn't travel out of the body much before it takes off in no direction at all.

♦ The soul lingers around the physical body for a while to comfort relatives and loved ones. Then it takes off in one of the directional points as it's escorted to the other side.

This subject is obviously difficult to research, much like many other topics related to life after death. It's very rare to hear a firsthand account of someone who has actually seen a soul depart the body. However, there are accounts of people seeing something that could well be the spirit energy. We'll talk about this in the following section.

Soul In, Soul Out

Many people have been with friends or loved ones when they've died. Often, you'll hear that the deceased looked at peace in their final moments; you might even hear an account of a deathbed vision (see Chapter 8). However, you'll hardly ever hear someone say, "I saw Grandma's soul rise up out of her body and leave the room." Most people just don't see these things.

However, there are those who have had some sort of experience with a soul as it left this world. I've included some of those incidents in this section.

The Car Incident

I was driving on the interstate going south when I saw a car up ahead that was half on the road and half off. There was no fire or sign of smoke around the car. A police car had just pulled up and blocked the interstate, waiting for a tow truck to pull the car away. There was no ambulance present and the officer was basically just standing there waiting for assistance.

I waited in my car, thinking it might just be an abandoned car or that the driver had already been removed from the scene of the accident. But then I noticed a gray misty vapor come out of the driver's side window and float at a moderate pace to the east. I got chills when I saw it and the first thing I thought was, "I hope that wasn't a soul."

I was trying to convince myself there was no one in the car and it was just being pulled off the road so the traffic could pass. Unfortunately, an ambulance did arrive and a body was removed from the vehicle. Later that night, I heard on the news that a person had been killed on the interstate. Had I actually seen that soul depart? Was it a cloud of smoke from the car's exhaust? Had I been hallucinating? I really didn't know.

What Skeptics Say

Skeptics attribute mists, vapors, or anything one may think is a visual clue that the soul is leaving the body to atmospheric conditions, the observer's blurred vision due to stress, or something environmental such as car exhaust smoke.

Years later I started reading other people's accounts of what they believed to be a soul leaving a body. Many accounts were similar to mine—they thought they saw a grayish mist. As I investigated further, I found accounts of people seeing whitish, cloudy hazes and other colors emanating from bodies at the time of death.

The interesting thing is that it seems as though the majority of people see the soul leave on an angle. Most don't notice the direction (north, south, east, or west) initially, but upon recalling the incident, they can usually determine what the direction was. They also point out the mist traveled in an upward course, never down.

Souls Coming Back

By virtue of the fact that people may see souls leave others' bodies, if they're in the right place at the right time, I have to question if one can see the soul return.

In Chapter 7, I talked about the soul returning to the body but not the actual vision of this occurrence. So I started talking to people who had witnessed someone else having a near-death experience and asked what happened when the person came back.

One lady was with her son, a coma patient, when she thought she saw a flash of light coming down at her son on an angle. A few moments later, he woke up. He had no tales to tell of being dead and coming back. However, she felt confident that she had seen something unusual in the moments before he came out of the coma.

Another instance happened to a soldier during Desert Storm. He told me that a friend of his had been in a jeep accident. The jeep turned over and his friend was knocked unconscious. He lay there, still, and was thought to be dead. Suddenly, the soldier telling me this story said he saw a quick stream of light descend upon the fellow who lay motionless, and he snapped to.

Were these possible cases of souls returning to the body? We can never say for sure, but what is the likelihood of seeing a flash or stream of light come down on someone who is unconscious and the next thing you know they have awakened? It seems like more than mere coincidence.

Souls Stuck on Earth

It appears that most souls leave the body when the body dies and pass over to the other side. But what happens when something goes wrong and the soul doesn't make it up and out (or up or down, or to the north or south)? Is there a late bus or a morning train for souls that have been left behind?

Escorts Have Their Limits

In Chapter 8, I talked about dead relatives, friends, angels, or spiritual escorts who guide souls over to a new existence. So how can anyone get lost or not make it if they have someone guiding them along?

In cases like this, the soul often doesn't want to go because of plain stubbornness. In that state of consciousness, the soul may just be left until it can find its own way home. It's like someone going to a party with a group of friends. The group is leaving but that particular person decides he doesn't want to go just yet. The friends get fed up and say, "Okay, you can get yourself home!"

Stubbornness—the reluctance to leave this life behind—can be caused by several factors. The soul or spirit may feel it still has something to do here on earth. Perhaps the soul doesn't even know that the physical body is dead. In addition, the soul may have had some difficulty crossing over to the other side, so it chooses to stay to be with loved ones for a while until it can come to grips with the transition.

Eventually, the soul realizes there is nothing else it can do for those left on earth. When that "pull" or energy from the other side calls it, so to speak, and the call becomes irresistible, the soul gives way to crossing over.

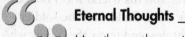

> **Eternal Thoughts**
>
> May the road ever rise to meet you,
> May the wind ever be at your back.
> May you safely be in heaven at least one hour before the devil knows you're gone;
> And may the good Lord always hold you in the hollow of his hand.
> —Gaelic toast

Sudden Death

In cases of sudden and unexpected death, the soul may linger, as it hadn't expected to make the transition to the other side so soon. Therefore, it may take a little time for the soul to find its own way to eternal life, or it may have to wait for a guide or guardian to take the soul to its new location.

That doesn't mean this happens in all cases of sudden death. If someone you know met with an unexpected demise, don't assume this happened to them. I think souls who get stuck on Earth are rare.

Often people will say, "I just have a feeling he has not passed over. Is his spirit bewildered?" Is this an intuitive thought of the living, or is it just a negative feeling they have?

In events like this these, souls don't become ghosts and haunt places and scare people. They're just a little confused, a little lost. They actually want to go, but don't know how to find their way to the next life—yet. The souls of people who are totally dysfunctional here are on Earth are sometimes the ones who remain as ghosts. It's as though when they pass quickly they still are keeping their "living" personalities and simply don't understand they should follow the light or path to the other side. Not all souls are like this; often, when someone who is dysfunctional passes, he or she immediately understands their problems, are healed, and cross over happy and balanced.

Send Them Home

I think souls who are stubborn and don't want to make the transition for one reason or another at the time of the body's death may be left here to learn one more lesson. And part of their lesson is to go when you get the call. (It's a lesson worth learning, don't you think?)

So what's to be done for these tardy spirits? If you feel a spirit may have been abandoned on Earth without transportation or guides to get them to the other side, don't give up hope. Show an act of kindness. You may be able to ever-so-gently intervene.

Are you interfering with lessons they have to learn? No. If a time comes when you feel a departed person is calling out to you for help because they're confused, I think you have permission from your higher power to give them a little assistance; otherwise, you wouldn't have been able to receive this telepathic thought in the first place.

A few ideas for giving the departed a direction—some old methods and some new ones, too—are included in this section.

Prayers

I've always believed in the power of prayer. I think upon hearing of someone's death, it's wise to say a little prayer for the safety of the soul into the afterlife, either by using traditional words of your religious faith or your own personal appeal to the divine.

If, weeks or months after the death (or if you sense that a spirit has lingered for much longer), you sense that a soul hasn't moved on to the other side, you may want to take a few minutes every day and pray that they make the transition.

Sensing is pure intuition. It's when you just know what you know, but you can't explain it. "Gut feelings" are just another name

Ethereal Potpourri

Those who practice organized religion may feel more comfortable talking to a religious figure from their church or spiritual organization about a soul that hasn't transitioned into the next life. Some religions have special prayers for the dead.

for it. You may feel a presence lingering near you or around you. Possibly, you "pick up" that they want to make contact once more before passing. If this is the case, I suggest taking a few minutes to see if you can intuit what the entity wants. (I show you specific methods using visualization a little later in this chapter.)

Candles

When they hear that someone has died, many people light a candle for the safe and speedy passage of the spirit. Usually white is the color of choice, as its vibration is that of peace, purity, and newness.

A candle represents the three levels of existence:

- ◆ Wax: The physical body
- ◆ Wick: The mind
- ◆ Flame: The soul or spirit

Ethereal Potpourri

There's no reason to burn a large candle all the way down. Just snuff it out when you feel that the soul has completed its journey. Any size candle can be used, but discard it when you're through with it. Its intention was for one person, so don't save it for other uses.

As the smoke from the candle rises, so does the soul. Therefore, as you light a candle for a departed soul's journey, think about their soul going to its ultimate destination.

Some people also burn purple (associated with intuition, independence, and wisdom) and blue (associated with peace, tranquility, and protection) candles along with white, or even in place of it.

You might even consider taking a toothpick and carving the person's name or initials on the top of the candle as a way of clarifying your intention that this person's spirit find his way to the tranquil beyond.

Visualization Techniques

Another approach to lending a hand to those who are earthbound is to use visualization methods. Here's one you might try:

1. Sit comfortably in a chair with your feet flat on the ground. Place your hands, palms up, on your thighs or knees.

2. Say a prayer or affirmation that you want the soul of this particular person (use her name—first name is good enough) to make the transition to the afterlife in a composed and willing manner. You might say something such as, "Ann, look to the light and just let go of the fear. When you let go, you will be free to advance to a superior dimension or place."

3. Visualize the individual's soul or, if you need to, see her physical body ascending to the universe.

4. After you're done, wash your hands as a form of cleansing, and relax.

If you feel this isn't working, you may want to try another time or another approach.

The Angel Swat Team

If you feel nothing you do is making a difference for this poor soul, you may want to try this method. Basically, you'll be calling in angels to take that stubborn soul over to the other side. Once it gets to the passageway, a higher source will take it from there.

1. Make yourself comfortable in a chair.

2. Say prayers or affirmations for the transport of the spirit.

3. Visualize angels (one or several) taking the hand of the earthbound soul and escorting it to the entry to the other side.

4. Once you visualize the angels dropping off the soul, you've done your job.

Naturally, you can make any variation on this method or any others. I'm only presenting some general starting ideas. But think about how happy *you* would be if you were lost or stuck somewhere and a kind person took the time to help you find your way. Maybe, as a result, you'll have someone on the other side looking out for you.

The Least You Need to Know

◆ Some people believe the soul needs to travel to the afterlife in a specific direction.

◆ People have seen souls leave and/or come back into the body.

◆ Some souls are stubborn and get left behind in this dimension.

◆ In cases of sudden death, a soul can get confused.

◆ There are methods to help souls who are lost on Earth and bewildered.

10

Tunnels, Corridors, and White Light

In This Chapter

- ◆ Pathways to the beyond
- ◆ Do men and women have different experiences?
- ◆ Children entering the afterlife
- ◆ Seeing—and hearing—the light

In Chapter 7, I discussed what happens in a near-death experience (NDE). Some mystic travelers see themselves approaching a white light, while others suddenly appear in front of a divine presence surrounded by bright light. In this chapter, I'll expound more on the actual pathways these people have taken while approaching their final destination, or the source of the light.

Additionally, I'll talk about whether men's, women's, and children's experiences tie into their gender and age when traveling the road to another dimension. Are special considerations given to specific groups?

Entrances to the Beyond

When entering into the next life, there typically seems to be some type of transition. Not all people are given a chance to adjust to this new dimension, but most are. Apparently, a good way to do this is to allow the person to go from point A to point B via a walk toward a distant end. According to those who have walked those trails, there are many different ways to reach that end.

Corridors and Doorways

Several versions of NDEs talk about walking through corridors that lead to other doors. Also, a maze may be encountered, leading to a final door that opens into a beautiful garden, a distant city, or something similarly peaceful and beautiful.

Those who have been through these corridors or doorways say they aren't confusing or chaotic. They intuitively knew exactly which door to open or which hall to take. There is no guessing.

Perhaps the reason for all of the doors or corridors is to allow us to slowly start to adjust to the detachment from the body and to keep us occupied at a moment that could otherwise be very frightening.

Bridges

Some versions of NDEs report the crossing of bridges. Now, depending on how you feel about bridges—some people have a real fear of them—they can appear to be treacherous or they can be beautiful.

Ethereal Potpourri _____

Animal communicators tell us animals that have died cross over the Rainbow Bridge, so called because of its various colors. It is a place right before entering the other side. Our pets play, eat and drink, and wait for us until we make the transition and then we cross together. The pets are restored to good health, regardless whether they were hurt or injured upon dying.

Most of the people who speak of bridges in their NDE thought of them in a positive manner before their brush with death. Some report the bridges in the afterlife are radiant, shimmering mists crossing a beautiful body of water or piece of land.

No matter what the appearance of the bridge, the feeling of safety while crossing is always present and a new life of peace on the other side appears to be a given.

Tunnels

Tunnels are a common theme in NDEs. By definition, a tunnel is an underground passage, but most people think of a tunnel as being any sort of closed passageway. NDE tunnels are not *always* dark, like a railway tunnel or a subway station, but mysterious tunnels like these do seem to crop up more often than not in recollections of traveling to the beyond. Thankfully, it's typically only a few seconds before the traveler sees the light offering comfort at the end of the passageway.

Besides these "black-hole tunnels," there are many different types of NDE tunnels. People have reported strolling through tunnels of trees that arch from one side to the other, forming a trail that encompasses them in nature and serenity. Light tunnels with blue, yellow, and bright light also have been the foundation for the walk to the other side. Crystal tunnels, adorned with quartz-looking clusters and large crystals—the size of large trees—have also been noted.

Some miscellaneous notes on passageways:

Ethereal Potpourri

In my research, I've heard stories of tunnels of stars that souls swoosh through at high speeds, like one would see in a science-fiction movie!

- ◆ Stairways to heaven, as some would call the afterlife, or to the cosmos, as others describe it, are said to be made of marble, crystal, silver, gold, or other elements that are illuminated yet not known to this world.

- ◆ Some stairs spiral and some ascend straight up. The rails are dazzling and radiant. Some hear angelic music as they ascend through a peaceful misty white haze, and rise up the stairs with no effort—they practically float and feel more at peace with every step.

- ◆ Boat rides, flying through the planet, and train rides into the clouds have been reported.

It seems as though the soul knows no limits when it comes to traveling into the next life. Perhaps our means of travel is based on what we're most comfortable with in this lifetime. Only time will tell, of course.

Exact Change, Please!

Some cultures believe that the passage to the next life involves the assistance of a ferryman, who transports the living across a river to the land of the dead or the other side. This concept comes from Greek mythology, where this ferryman was called Charon. He took the recently dead from one side of the river Acheron, which means the "river of woe," to the afterlife. However, the dead had to have a coin to pay for the ride. Therefore, in ancient Greece, the recently deceased were buried with a coin underneath their tongues—so they could pay Charon. Those who couldn't pay for the journey were left to wander the banks of the Acheron for 100 years. (Which is decidedly worse than being stranded at a bus stop or train station when you find yourself short of cash on the trip home from work!)

Other cultures had the same general concept and put coins on the eyes of the dead or in the tombs or coffins.

What's Your Idea of Adult Paradise?

When referring to adults, we could technically be talking about someone who is 18 years of age or someone who is 94 years of age, so it's fair to ask whether the elderly have near-death experiences that differ from those of young adults. From the accounts of near-death experience that have been researched worldwide, it appears that the experiences are still basically the same. The elderly do not pass more calmly than the teenager, for example.

When the soul leaves the body, *it* is not 18 or 94 years old; it's developed spiritually to a certain level (or age) that we aren't aware of while here on earth. So the soul of an elderly person isn't necessarily wiser or more experienced (or more jaded) than the soul of a young adult. The best proof we have of this is that all souls seem to experience the same sense of awe when they cross over. However, the way an *individual* relays information about the experience is different, and largely depends on the person's *life* experiences.

A middle-aged woman who reads romance novels, for example, might describe her near-death experience like this: "I saw beautiful gardens with sweet-smelling flowers that were exotic and colorful, with hues of purple and blue. And as I walked farther through the tunnel of trees, which seem to shimmer with lacy leaves, I could feel a gentle breeze that felt soothing and relaxing.

Then, unexpectedly, I saw a tall, dark, muscular man with broad shoulders and a smile that was in itself heaven. As I came closer, my heart began pounding like a drum, even though I didn't have one anymore—a heart, not a drum. I knew it was my departed lover, Julio. I rushed to him and he opened his arms and embraced me. I knew this was where I wanted to be."

On the other hand, an 18-year-young adult might report on his near-death experience by saying this: "Yeah, it was neat. There were these really pretty flowers and stuff. Some lady who looked like my grandmother gave me a hug at the end of the road. That was cool."

Although we have all accepted the fact that men are surely different than women, the dying experiences of both genders seem to be generally the same. I haven't heard stories of the females of this planet seeing boutiques filled with ribbons and pearls while walking toward the light, even though many of us would consider this type of vision the ultimate paradise.

Of course, not all women are into ribbons and pearls; many women might find it more comforting to see objects connected with their favorite hobby, like golf, kayaking, or chess—whatever they do for recreation—on their way to the afterlife.

On the other side of the gender scale, I haven't heard one story of a male seeing fishing poles, bowling bags, or girly magazines mounted on a tunnel wall. (Sorry, guys.) To be fair, though, we haven't heard about every single encounter, and these might be visions that someone doesn't want to talk about.

Now, I'm not making light of the topic, but as we walk a road that is supposed to make us feel welcome, I wonder why we don't see things that we associate with being on our way to the ultimate spot for rest and relaxation. I suppose the answer could be that what so many people report seeing in their NDEs are visions more beautiful than anything we could ever imagine in this earthly dimension. (And, yes, I would guess that the experience is also far more exciting than a shoe sale at the mall or a round of golf!)

Children, Have No Fear

I've talked about the common experiences adults have when they face death. Do children share these same visions, or is someone looking out for these tender souls, which may be more fearful than the souls of grown-ups?

In NDEs, children experience going through gates, garden arbors, and doorways more often than adults do. No one can ever know why this is, but perhaps it's because kids can relate to these things in life more so than dark tunnels and other pathways that would simply be scary to them. A tunnel might terrify a child, while a garden path is probably a much more welcoming sight.

> **Eternal Thoughts** _____
>
> Men fear death as children fear to go into the dark; and as that natural fear in children is increased with tales, so is the other.
>
> —Francis Bacon, English philosopher and statesman

"Playmates" Help Ease the Transition

Because young children have little information about life after death—as well as few general life experiences behind them—it's interesting to hear what they encounter in NDEs. Children report remarkably similar experiences of what they've seen, heard, and felt when recounting what's happened to them in death.

If a pathway of any type is involved, children tend to see other children playing at the end of a walkway. Perhaps this is a way to comfort them; encountering playmates is less frightening than running into a Supreme Being at the very onset. The other children draw them into a place that looks fun and inviting, after all.

What Happens Next?

What happens after children meet with other children on the path is only left to speculation. The trouble with gathering information on NDEs from children is that many of them naturally aren't able to express themselves very well. They simply aren't articulate enough to give a full account of what has happened. (On the flip side, this also usually means that whatever information we get from them is free from exaggeration.)

Since few children report being terrified in NDEs, it's safe to say that their experiences are most likely filled with love and tranquility. I am sure as they walk the path those feelings intensify as they draw closer to their final target.

Light of Love

No matter how many people talk about the diverse ideas of crossing over to the other side, they all seem to have one thing in common: they all report seeing a bright light (which is described by some as simply a white light).

Those who have experienced an NDE say the light starts like a pinpoint. As you walk along, it gradually gets brighter until you're encompassed by the light. You feel the passion and the purity of love from your divine source. The light suddenly flows right through you.

> **Eternal Thoughts**
>
> I would rather live and love where death is king than have eternal life where love is not.
>
> —Robert G. Ingersoll, American politician and lecturer known for his adamant support of scientific and humanistic rationalism

> **Ethereal Potpourri**
>
> I've tried to make the distinction between "bright" and "white" in my interviews with people who've crossed over and returned to this life. It may seem like a small distinction, but my curiosity always gets the better of me, and I want to get the full picture. Almost always, the person who had the experience says, "It was more of a bright translucent light." Regardless of the use of "bright" or "white," they experience this light surrounding them with love.

Sound of the Light

Some people have also described hearing music or musical chords during their NDEs. I haven't heard it said that the sounds are voices of angels, like you might see in the movies, but just gentle, soothing musical frequencies. People who've experienced this say it's a great comfort, as the tones are meditative. For those who've heard these sounds, they felt it was an indication that there was something or someone waiting for them at the end of their journey.

In some instances, the sounds vibrated with shimmering light. The light and the sound drew them closer. Is this the sound of light? Although we can't experience the sound of light here on Earth, maybe it exists outside of our understanding.

Ethereal Potpourri _____

In a 2006 Gallup Poll, 72 percent of Americans say they are certain there is a God and have no doubts, while another 14 percent think that God probably exists and have only a few doubts. Only 3 percent feel certain that God does not exist. There are no significant differences in belief in God by age. Men, those living in the East and West, those who are college graduates, and those with high incomes are less likely to believe in God than others.

Could It Be Coincidence?

How is it that so many people—of different cultures and religious backgrounds—report seeing the same type of light in their NDE? Skeptics say that we now have computers, television, and books that talk about experiences from the beyond and that could explain this ... but these reports have been around for a long time, *way* before the mass proliferation of information. I believe that this is a genuine experience people have as they cross over; the stories are just too similar to dismiss it as anything else.

One question was posed to me about seeing a bright light: How about people who were blind or color-blind while they were alive? How could they identify a light as bright or white? One theory is that when a person leaves their body they have no pain and all their senses and facilities are returned. Therefore, their vision would be restored. The restoration to a perfect body form in the afterlife is discussed in more detail in Chapter 16.

What Skeptics Say _____

Skeptics have plenty to say on the matter of the bright or white light. According to research done at the University of Kentucky in Lexington, the impression of having visited the afterlife may be due to a neurological condition called REM (rapid eye movement) intrusion, which can lead to sleep paralysis upon waking or falling asleep.

The researchers' findings showed that the majority of people who report "seeing the light" in an NDE have also experienced REM intrusion at some point prior to their NDE. Additionally, skeptics believe that the white light effect may be because of oxygen deprivation. (However, since oxygen deprivation usually results in brain damage—and brain damage is not something that commonly affects those who report having near-death experiences—this doesn't seem to be a reasonable explanation.)

We associate light with a higher level of consciousness; we say things like "seeing the light" and "finding the light." Light guides us, and as with the sun, it helps us grow. Perhaps it's a universal symbol or sign or a higher level of understanding and existence.

The Least You Need to Know

- There are many different passageways to the afterlife.

- Men and women do not appear to have different experiences because of their gender.

- Children's stories of NDE seem to have gentler entrances to the other side, with "playmates" often present to ease the transition.

- Reports of seeing a bright light of some kind are common among those who have crossed over and returned.

Chapter 11

Ghostly Categories

In This Chapter

- So many ghosts, so few categories
- Is it a ghost, or is it a place memory?
- Without a shadow of a doubt: shadow people
- Possessed by a ghost
- Ghost detection equipment and methods
- Who ya gonna call?

For most of us, the very mention of the word "ghost" brings to mind misty figures, cemeteries, and hauntings. Picture a Scottish castle on a foggy night with vaporous beings in the window peering down at those who pass. (You're getting chills, aren't you?)

When it comes to specters, there are different categories. There are also circumstances that may appear to be hauntings but really aren't. Can a ghost take over a living person's body? And if so, how does it choose that person?

There are real-life ghost busters, but does ghost busting really work? There is ghost hunting equipment available for little cost; is it a worthwhile purchase or not? Should you attempt to do your own ghost busting? It's not easy to send them packing. We'll consider all of these things in this chapter.

Ghostly Classifications

If you have a fear of ghosts, you'll probably be surprised to learn that the more you know, the less frightened you'll be. Knowledge is power, after all. If you take the time to learn about ghosts, you'll have a better understanding of what you saw or what you're dealing with if you ever happen to encounter one.

The presence of ghosts is difficult to prove. The different types of ghosts that I'll talk about in this chapter represent theories and explanations that I've gathered through the years by physical researchers, parapsychologists, and ghost busters—all of these people are "experts" in the business!

For further clarification, you may want to check out *The Complete Idiot's Guide to Ghosts and Hauntings, Second Edition*, by Tom Ogden (see Appendix B).

> **Eternal Thoughts**
>
> There are an infinite number of universes existing side by side and through which our consciousnesses constantly pass. In these universes, all possibilities exist. You are alive in some, long dead in others, and never existed in still others. Many of our "ghosts" could indeed be visions of people going about their business in a parallel universe or another time—or both.
>
> —Paul F. Eno, *Faces at the Window* (New River Press, 1998)

Apparitions

Apparitions are what we typically think of when we hear the word "ghost." They appear suddenly and in a recognizable form, whether it's a human or an animal. They demonstrate consciousness, meaning that they are alert and thinking with intellect and aware of their surroundings. They are able to do certain things with intent. They also interact with the environment.

Apparitions of departed individuals or animals most often emerge suddenly and very clearly, as if that person or pet is there in real life. An apparition can also surface in a vague form. In this case, you might still be able to determine who it is, but the person may not totally appear as they did in life. Those who've seen apparitions also tell us that these nonliving forms can move through walls, doors, or other solid objects.

It's been said that when these ghosts are present, the temperature of a room will suddenly plummet. (We'll talk more about dropping temperatures a little later in this chapter.)

Apparitions are typically considered harmless and have an "in-and-out" attitude. They don't make themselves at home on the sofa or sit down to have a snack with you. They also don't rattle chains or moan and groan. They appear only for a few seconds and don't mean to create fear or havoc.

Often, people who've recently experienced the death of a loved one will see an apparition of the newly departed. This may be a way for them to say one last good-bye; they're letting us know they're fine before moving on to another dimension. Those who see apparitions of these types are usually not afraid. They feel it is a farewell and are comforted that there is life after death.

Orbs

Orbs are small balls or spheres of energy that are said to be the onset of an apparition. They can't be seen by the naked eye but can appear in videos or photographs. The more credible orbs sport tails of light whisking from them, making that type of orb a little more plausible. (A speck of dust or a piece of dirt doesn't show a tail. It's just a dot). However, all orbs are extremely controversial.

Is this one area where the skeptics and the believers agree? Not necessarily. There are still professionals who feel orbs may have some value, as they think that it's unlikely that all orbs are simply specs of dirt or dust. Therefore, even if the majority are dirt particles, there's a good chance that at least some are spirit energies appearing as small balls of light.

> **? What Skeptics Say**
>
> Even believers concede that it's difficult to distinguish between genuine orbs and specs of dirt, dust, general camera equipment flaws, or insects darting about. And many psychic researchers *cringe* at the idea of orbs.

Drops in temperature can be detected with infrared thermometers, which don't have to be in contact with an object. So if you were pointing the thermometer at a door and all of a sudden the temperature drops 10 degrees or more and there is no living person in that area, it could be that a ghost is present. It is thought by paranormal investigators that spirits may use the heat energy in the air to manifest. If this theory is true, it would explain cold spots in certain places or why cold air is often experienced during ghost investigations. The energy (which may be what orbs are) that encompasses the entity or ghost could be what creates these cold spots.

Get out your camera at a supposedly haunted location or go on a ghost-hunting excursion and see what you think.

Poltergeists

The word poltergeist means "noisy ghost" and refers to energy that creates havoc in a certain location. But is it really a ghost, or the result of a human condition?

In a poltergeist haunting, observers think that a ghost is giving them a difficult time by moving chairs or other items, making things fly off shelves, or relocating objects in order to scare them away from the location or simply to be malicious. However, some researchers feel that poltergeists are nonexistent, at least as separate entities. Experts believe that poltergeists are actually the manifestation of negative energy (such as stress) and not a true haunting.

def•i•ni•tion

Psychokinesis is also referred to as telekinesis. These two words are used interchangeably and indicate a mind-over-matter situation. This theory tells us that our own thoughts can sometimes unconsciously be used to move objects and/or to misshape them, usually when an individual is experiencing great anxiety and tension.

According to many parapsychologists, including Al Rauber (an expert in Electronic Voice Phenomena whom you'll read more about in Chapter 18), a poltergeist is a projected energy from a living person under stress. It's an unconscious release of energy. The term is *psychokinesis*. This happens intermittently with all people on some level. When it happens over and over again, it is referred to as Recurrent Spontaneous Psychokinesis or RSPK. This is what a poltergeist-type "haunting" or infestation is. Therefore, many authorities in ghost investigation don't believe in the existence of a poltergeist as someone who is dead and returning to create havoc.

Poltergeist activity is often found in homes where there are teenagers going through puberty or where there are huge amounts of stress within the household or any building. So if you suspect you have a poltergeist, I have some simple advice for you: relax. Get rid of the stress and you get rid of the poltergeist!

That's No Ghost ... Just a Cosmic Video

When I first learned about a *place memory* (which is sometimes referred to as a place haunting), I sure slept better at night when staying in presumably haunted hotels.

So what was the knowledge that freed me from insomnia in these spirited locales? I learned that place memories are much like a cosmic video that doesn't need a battery or outlet. The simplest way to describe a place memory is to say that it's akin to a recording of an event or noises or sounds from the past that keeps replaying itself.

def•i•ni•tion

A **place memory** refers to a ghostly voice or image that has burned itself into the atmosphere of a home or area.

Place memories are past situations that have imprinted themselves on the environment. Some people call these "residual hauntings," but they *aren't* hauntings, at least not in the classic sense of the word, because there is no consciousness involved. It is a "psychic record" of a person or sounds of days gone by.

In addition to sounds and voices, likenesses can become impressed upon a certain location and keep replaying themselves, just like a movie would continue to replay. For example, when people say ghosts are seen in the same window of the same house, always wearing the same thing, and even doing the same thing, it could very well be a place memory.

It's important to understand the distinction between a ghost and a place memory. Place memories are the repetition of an identical image doing the same thing each time, or identical sounds repeated over and over. This is far different than seeing ghosts, who have a consciousness and are therefore able to partake in different activities.

It's been suggested that changing the environment—by painting or changing furniture placement or redecorating—may put an end to the place memory because you're shifting the "energy" of the surroundings. One woman I interviewed was picking up voices from a window air conditioner—and it wasn't just the sound of the AC. Since this technically didn't involve a space, she painted the air conditioner and put a crystal above it. Poof! She didn't hear the place memory anymore. Add something, take away something, just make changes and the place memory may come to a screeching halt.

If you have a chance to see a place memory on a ghost tour or excursion, don't discount it because you don't think it's not an actual haunting. Any sort of energy from another dimension is worth investigating! I discuss place memories in more detail in Chapter 18.

Shadow People or Beings

Every once in a while, you may be working at your desk or fixing yourself a snack when you're surprised to see something darting across the room. Are your eyes playing tricks on you, or did you just see a shadowy figure whizzing past? No more late-night anchovies for you!

We often question what we see. We dismiss things we don't understand out of fear or skepticism. But let's forget about all of that. What's the *truth* behind these figures?

def•i•ni•tion

Shadow people are sometimes also called *shadow figures* or *shadow beings*. They are seen out of the corner of our eye for just a second or two and look like a fleeting shadow of a person but are not recognizable.

There's been a new emergence about what are said to be *shadow people*. Other cultures and belief systems have long taken notice of menacing shadows. The idea of shadow people dates back to Cherokee mythology, where they thought these creatures were evil and could go as far as to steal the souls of the dead or seriously ill. So the concept is not new, but as the interest in ghosts and spirits seems to evolve, the interest in these shadows is becoming more prevalent.

Shadow people are simply outlines, and though they may look like a human or some type of entity, they have no details about them. People typically have a negative feeling when encountering this supernatural phenomenon. That does not mean it is necessarily a premonition of something negative happening. It could still be a ghost form or someone picking up negative psychic energy that has somehow entered that area for a moment in time and then moves on.

So what are these fast-moving silhouettes? Are they visiting from the other side trying to let us know there is existence after death, or is it something else?

There are five basic beliefs to explain them:

◆ Some believe that alien beings pass in and out of our lives camouflaged within the forms of shadows.

◆ Others believe shadow people are astral bodies—images of people having out-of-body experiences and flashing by us.

◆ Because these visions are dark, shadowy, and without detailed characteristics, some people believe they're demons.

♦ There's a belief that shadow people may be interdimensional beings. Simply put, this belief tells us that there are other dimensions and those who inhabit these have discovered a way to cross over into our dimension, becoming only slightly visible.

♦ Some people believe that shadow people are time travelers observing our lives with just a passing glance.

Shadow people used to be seen only out of the corner of one's eye, but now it seems people are claiming to see them right in plain view, so here's something to consider: what if certain vibrational levels or frequencies are shifting, and we're simply becoming more in tune with other dimensions? Maybe we're seeing these things because we're getting closer to them on an energetic level. Maybe this is a line of communication from the other side that's just beginning to reveal itself!

What Skeptics Say

What do skeptics think of shadow people? Imagination, imagination, imagination! They believe these glimpses can be anything from a bird flying by to car headlights to a flash of lightning—and I agree in some cases. But is this the case for *all* of these sightings? The skeptics say of course not! It could also be poor vision, fatigue, hallucinations, or too many beers!

Taking Possession

We often hear about ghosts, demons, or entities of some type temporarily taking over a living person's body. When this happens to people, they are no longer "themselves," so to speak. Their behavior changes. Their faces may become distorted or not look normal. Their voices may change and their body language is not the natural attitude you're used to seeing from them, to say the least. For example, if the person is always calm and smiling, he may become jittery and have a look of discontent on his face. He may walk differently, or exhibit a different posture. This person has fallen victim to a possession by some type of spirit. This is also sometimes also called a "spirit possession," as it's the spirit of an entity that makes its way into the body.

The spirit uses the person's voice box to talk, and the human body of the person who is being overtaken has no way to defend herself. She has become an empty shell for the force to use to its own satisfaction or needs.

Knock, Knock! Let Me In!

It is speculated that human beings in a weakened state of physical health or mental health may be susceptible to spirit possession. The entities are always looking for the "weak link."

People sometimes unconsciously open themselves up through the use of drugs, excessive alcohol, depression, or general ill health. Weakness of body, mind, or both is like an open doorway for a dysfunctional entity to try to take over.

On the flip side, not all possessions are evil. There are mediums who allow entities to take over their bodies for the purpose of communication between the dead and the living. Some people feel under no circumstance should a medium (or anyone, for that matter) allow this because you don't know what will happen—what if the soul doesn't want to leave the body, for example? Also, the physical body of the person who allows the spirit "in" may become drained and exhausted after this occurrence.

How to Stop a Possession

If you or someone you know is in a weakened state and you're concerned about possession, the keys to safeguarding yourself are daily prayer, affirmations, meditating on strength, and positivity. Also, as I wrote in my book *White Light: The Complete Guide to Spells and Rituals for Psychic Protection* (see Appendix B), you may want to incorporate techniques for protecting yourself every night with a circle of white light to keep negativity away.

The best thing to do is to not allow possession to occur in the first place; however, if you feel you or someone you know has become possessed, I would seek advice from a psychologist, professional counselor, or spiritual professional. With the help of these professionals, you should be able to resolve this situation.

What Skeptics Say

Most skeptics maintain possession does not exist and is the result of sudden brain disorders such as epilepsy, hysteria, or schizophrenia. It appears that once the idea of mental illness was acknowledged and understood around the seventeenth century, the idea of demonic possession was somewhat set to rest, or at least was not as prevalent.

The Ghost Investigation Tools, Rules, and Equipment

If you're interested in investigating ghosts or hauntings on your own, I highly recommend working first with a professional ghost tour, organization, or someone who has investigative experience so that you don't waste your time and/or money. In these cases, you'll often get a taste of what it's really like to investigate spirits (and realize whether you enjoy it or not), and you'll also often be able to use someone else's equipment.

Now, I realize that people often conduct their own research or take ghost investigation into their own hands. You'll need to do your own research and figure out what works best for you. There is nothing written in stone when it comes to making contact with these entities who have survived life after death, so you'll have to find out on your own what works in terms of contacting them ... and what doesn't.

Your Paranormal Tool Kit

There are a few pieces of basic equipment that you'll need. Buy yourself a carrying case or tote in which to keep all of your tools. Staying organized will create less chaos, and you need to be focused. Basics items you should consider are as follows:

♦ A notebook or some type of journal, and a pen or pencil. You may want to write down times, weather conditions, and any other sights or sounds you think are noteworthy.

♦ A flashlight, since you'll usually be working in dark places.

♦ Extra batteries—not only for the flashlight but for all of your electronic equipment.

♦ A tape recorder with an external microphone to pick up EVP recordings. (We'll discuss this in detail in Chapter 18.)

♦ A compass. It's said that the pointer begins to spin when the energy field changes, which may indicate the presence of a ghost. A compass can also be used to detect the direction from which noises or images are heard or appear.

♦ A 35mm camera to photograph anything of interest. Digital cameras can be used but professionals in the field of ghost tracking don't necessarily hold high-tech gear in the highest esteem. It's just too easy to alter the images.

You may already have these things in your home. And if you don't have them handy, they're easy enough to find and relatively inexpensive. Each item is a must for your investigative toolbox (or tote).

Electromagnetic Field Meters (EMF)

If you want take your investigations a step further, you might consider purchasing some electronic equipment to help you along your path. The most popular and common device used by modern-day ghost hunters is an electromagnetic field meter, also referred to as an EMF. These are considered by the experts to be a reliable way to track ghosts.

Researchers give credence to the idea that ghosts are electromagnetic energy. The energy that emanates from these spirits—whether they have a type or consciousness or are place memories—causes a disruption in the magnetic field of the area. Therefore, they may become detectable if you use a device to measure these frequencies and any changes in them.

Ethereal Potpourri

When using any type of equipment, it must be noted that other things can influence the meter—things that are not paranormal. Therefore, it's important to experiment with your devices before using them so that you have an understanding of what's normal for the area and what isn't. The abnormal readings are what you're looking for, as they indicate a change in the atmosphere that may indicate a ghost has decided to drop in for a visit!

EMF prices range from $20 up into the thousands of dollars. When you're just getting the feel for this kind of work, you might start with an inexpensive unit to see if this is something you're actually interested in before you invest a whole lot of money in your equipment. Naturally, the less expensive models are going to give you poorer accuracy. For this reason, some people feel that it's worth it just to spend the extra money to purchase a device that gives you a rock-solid reading. I say to each his own.

Other Equipment

There are several additional types of equipment used to detect ghosts. Everyone has their own opinion as to whether these devices work or not, but I say if you're interested in any one of these methods, why not give it a shot? (Like the electromagnetic field meter, some of this stuff is pretty high tech and can be expensive, so again, make sure you're interested before making the investment.)

- Temperature-sensing devices, such as an infrared thermometer. These are used for detecting sudden temperature changes in a room. It has been said that when a ghost manifests itself, it must use the energy from a particular area of a room or location. When this happens, the shift in energy creates a "cold spot."

- Geiger counters can help you pick up unusual or inconsistent activity, like the existence of a ghost who is walking around or who is stationary but present.

- Night vision binoculars will allow you to see images at a distance without shining a flashlight.

- Video cameras are for the obvious reason of getting those apparitions on film!

Ethereal Potpourri

If money is an issue, look for used equipment. Some people lose interest in ghost hunting and are happy to unload their pricey supplies at a fraction of the original cost. (This is why you might want to start out with cheaper equipment—so that you don't become the person taking a loss on it!) Internet auction sites are a great place to start looking for used equipment. If you don't have access to the Internet, call a ghost tour business; they can most likely direct you to a satisfactory source.

Your Ghost-Hunting Excursion

If you decide to conduct your own investigation, be practical. Don't go breaking into boarded-up buildings or trespassing on someone else's property or you may end up investigating the paranormal activity in jail!

Other things to keep in mind:

- Cemeteries don't have as much paranormal activity as you might think. Spirits don't linger near their graves; they tend to move on fairly quickly. (See Chapter 18 for more.)

- If you're in a public area, be discreet. Some people are afraid of ghosts, so don't walk into a public building and announce that you're there to investigate a haunting.

◆ Dress comfortably, and if you'll be walking through a town or city, don't forget comfy shoes. You'd hate to have to quit your work early because you're too hot, too cold, or your toes are pinched!

Eternal Thoughts

Absence of evidence is not evidence of absence.
—Sir Martin Rees, astronomer

◆ If you're nervous, take someone with you for support and assistance.

◆ Don't tire yourself out. Allow an amount of time that seems comfortable to you. You don't want to overdo things and/or bore yourself your first time out. If you don't pick up anything, try again at a later date or pick a different location.

Remember, when using equipment, you must practice and become comfortable with its purpose. Additionally, arm yourself with as much information as possible. Learn the history of the area you're investigating; read what other paranormal researchers have found there. This type of knowledge can help to explain any confusing signs if and when they arise.

Ghost Busting?

Finding a ghost is one thing; getting rid of it is quite another. If you happen to encounter a ghost in your basement, for example, can you really coax him or her out of there by yourself? Some psychic researchers say if a ghost doesn't want to go, it's not going. Others say that some ghosts try to get in touch with us because they need directions on how to get to the other side. They're like lost tourists; they don't mean us any harm.

The good-guy ghosts may just need a map and a boost, but the bad-guy spirits may be entities to be reckoned with. If you've found yourself a troublesome ghost (or it's found *you*), talk to credible parapsychologists, established psychical researchers, or ghost research organizations that are respected in their fields. These professionals can help you gain insight as to whether it's really a ghost or not, and what to do. Spiritual counselors can also be of help.

Send That Ghost on Its Way!

You can find professional ghost riders all over on the Internet, in magazines, and by word of mouth. Many of these people are mediums or psychics who claim to have the power to show a ghost the way to the other side. Some are spiritual people who have a flair for releasing these troubled souls; others are religious figures who have an understanding of such things. Some are none of the above, but have developed methods to deliver these phantoms to the other side. And, of course, some are simply fakes and charlatans looking to take your money and run.

To avoid falling prey to fake ghost busters, follow these tips:

◆ Check their location and see if they have been in town for any length of time, or talk to them to prequalify their experience.

◆ Ask for referrals. If they have nothing to hide, they won't mind.

◆ Ask about their methods and use your own intuition or go with your gut feeling. If their methods don't sit right with you, move on.

Ethereal Potpourri _____

If you have a fear of ghosts or hauntings in your home or building, try putting a dash of salt in the four corners of a room or within the four farthest interior corners of the house. Salt is believed to prevent the entrance of ghosts. When the salt evaporates or is vacuumed away, a new amount doesn't have to be applied. The energy remains. (However, a yearly application can't hurt, provided it doesn't damage your floors.)

On a Wing and a Prayer

Sometimes people who run into "ghosts" feel they're experiencing a gentle presence that is simply lost here on Earth. If you think you can lend a hand, sometimes a couple of simple methods can help.

You can simply say any prayer of your choice or make up your own words to the god of your understanding that this soul be taken over. Often, people will simply tell the spirit, "Follow the light." Another method you might employ is calling in the angels and asking them to guide the soul over.

You can also light a white candle and put it on your stove for about an hour. As you light the candle, imagine the soul making its ascent to the dimension where it's meant to be.

These are only ideas to consider. Remember, your intention is everything.

The Least You Need to Know

♦ There are different categories of ghosts, including apparitions, which generally don't linger, and poltergeists, which can appear to be more malicious but are basically created by a living individual due to stress.

♦ A place memory is not a classic ghost with a consciousness, but more like a movie about an event replaying itself.

♦ Shadow people are most likely not ghosts.

♦ People can be possessed by dysfunctional entities when they are at a weakened state of their life.

♦ If you're going to hunt for ghosts, you'll need some basic (and some not-so-basic) equipment.

♦ Don't attempt to do your own ghost busting; call in a professional organization or parapsychologist. Of course, a prayer and a candle most likely won't hurt.

12

Let Them Be for a While ... Then Make Contact

In This Chapter

- ◆ Waiting to make contact
- ◆ Dreaming of the dead
- ◆ Using tools of divination
- ◆ Say, let's have a séance!
- ◆ Finding a professional spiritual communicator

There are diverse theories regarding how long it takes a soul to cross over to the next life. Some religious and spiritual groups believe the dead can make the transition in the speed of light, while others believe the journey may take a few days.

One question remains the same, however: Once a loved one is gone, when and how can we make contact with them? Can you do it yourself, should you use some type of psychic tool, or are you better off consulting a professional medium who talks to people who have crossed over?

This may not be up everyone's alley—in fact, if you tell someone you're planning on making contact with a deceased friend or relative, you might get a strange look—but I think if you're interested in reaching out to the other side, you should go ahead and give it a try. You might just find some comfort in knowing that your loved one is safe and sound in the next life.

When to Make Contact

Often, people will feel desperate to make contact immediately following a loved one's death. Goodness, they just died! Maybe we should give them a break!

If we accept that the newly departed need a transition time before we can contact them, the question remains, how long a time? A day? A week? Years? In this section, I'll talk about the reasons why everyone is better off delaying contact for a certain period of time.

Thoughts from George Anderson

On his website (www.georgeanderson.com), psychic medium George Anderson discusses this very issue:

"The right time to make communication with a loved one who passed on is after some time and perspective. We receive many desperate calls from people who feel they must make communication right away, but there needs to be some acceptance and understanding of the passing first. There are many wonderful things that happen as a result of a session, but the session will not keep your loved one on the earth. Once acceptance of loss has taken place and you feel strong enough emotionally, you can begin the process of understanding and learning about loss, both from those around you and your loved ones passed on."

In other words, you need to move through the mourning and healing process before making contact with a deceased loved one. Otherwise, you may misinterpret your communication and see and hear things that aren't real. That isn't good for anyone!

> **" Eternal Thoughts**
>
> The souls are able to communicate immediately. There is no time of adjustment needed for the souls to reach out, and very often they are as eager to reach out to us at those first critical hours as we are to hear from them. The issue is not with the souls, but rather with the bereaved.
>
> —George Anderson, from his website

Use Your Gut Feeling to Make That Decision

Anderson's way is one way to think of it, and a good one at that. Here's another way: trust your gut. Go with the intuitive feeling that it's time to make contact—whether it's been a week or a year since a loved one has died. Just don't confuse intuition with your own needs or desires, or else your judgment—and your perception of any contact made—could be clouded.

If the deceased person hasn't made a complete transition to the other side yet, no harm will come from you trying to contact him; you simply won't be able to connect. It's like calling someone on the telephone. If they aren't home, they just don't pick up the receiver, but if you try at a different time, you may well get in touch with them.

Above all else, remember to be patient, take your time, and don't get discouraged if at first you don't succeed. Contacting the dead isn't an easy endeavor—if it were, people would be talking with the departed all day long, and proof of life after death would no longer be an issue!

Was That a Dream?

There are several methods people use to try to contact the dead ... but sometimes these expired souls just show up.

Frequently, people will say that they dreamt of a departed friend or relative. Occasionally the deceased person will talk; other times you might simply experience their presence. Every now and then, you might even feel a physical touch.

People who have these experiences tend to have varying reactions to them. It all depends on the dreamer and how they interpret what they saw in their dream state. One person may think she's being warned of impending doom, while another person may see this contact as a form of communication that allows him to know that the deceased has made his or her way to the next life and that all is well on the other side.

When you see a loved one in a dream, concentrate on her appearance. This will let you know whether she's dropping by to bring a warning, to send her love, or to just say, "Hey, how're you doing?"

> **Eternal Thoughts**
>
> Dreams are answers to questions we haven't yet figured out how to ask.
> —From the TV show *The X-Files*

The following interpretations are a cumulative summary of the many stories I've collected from dreamers; the focus is on how the deceased person looks and what happened after he made an appearance in a dream. This is not a professional study!

◆ If the dead person looks healthy and happy, sometimes younger than she was at the time of her death, this is a good sign. This message is, "I'm here and doing fine. No reason to worry about me. I'm fantastic and there is life after death … a good life, too."

◆ If the person looks sorrowful, sad, or stressed, it doesn't necessarily translate that the departed soul is unhappy. But he might be conveying to you by facial expressions that you need to take care of some issues in *your* life. It could be that the new guy you're dating isn't for you or that you should start looking for a new job.

◆ If the person has a concerned expression, it may mean someone is trying to tell you he is sorry for something. This type of dream happened to a lady I know. Her father had not been particularly understanding or affectionate when he was alive. She said about 10 years after he died, he came back to her in a dream and kissed her on her cheek. When she awoke, she could still feel it. She felt he had learned his lessons wherever he was and wanted to let her know that he understood how it would have made a difference had he been more loving when she was a child. This brought her comfort and she was happy for him.

Ethereal Potpourri

Some dream interpretation books tell us that any dreams about the dead are a bad omen. This is not a blanket belief, however, especially according to those who've had wonderful experiences dreaming of the dead. Some people believe that dreaming of the dead may mean they are coming to take you with them to the other side. I have interviewed many people and have dreamt of the dead myself throughout the years. No one I know who's reported dreaming of the dead has made the journey to the other side yet, and obviously, I'm still here, too! This doesn't mean it can't *ever* happen, however, but I don't think this is an accurate theory.

Pay attention to the expressions and attitude of the person you dream about. These may contain a wealth of information. Keeping a dream journal is helpful when experiencing unusual dreams about the dead. Take notes upon waking and then document the events in the next few days and draw your own conclusions. Was it a warning or a good sign?

In Chapter 18, I'll talk about how the deceased *sound* in your dreams and what that might mean.

Tools of the Trade

When people want to know what their departed friend is doing on the other side and whether they in fact still exist, they often use tools of divination. These are items that one can use to predict the future, look into the past, or examine the present. They are forms of fortune telling and are used as a medium between you and a higher force or source where information may dwell.

I've listed a few tools of divination here— but keep in mind, there are many more. I've chosen to tell you about these because they're tools that can be used by one person. In other words, you don't have to enlist the help of anyone else in order to make use of these communication tools:

> **Eternal Thoughts**
>
> If you hear 3 knocks and no one is there, it may mean someone you know has died. This belief has been called "the 3 knocks of death."
>
> —Superstition

- **Tarot cards** are a deck of 78 cards with illustrations. You ask a question and receive answers by defining the card meanings. You could, for example, ask if someone on the other side is okay and what it's like over there for them. By a few turns of the cards and putting together a story from the definitions, you should be able to interpret an answer.

- A **pendulum** is a weighted object hung by a chain or string. You ask yes or no questions while focusing on spirits of the departed. To start out, you have to ask the pendulum a question that you already know the answer to, such as, "Is my name Diane?" It will swing up and down or left and right to determine the answer "yes" for that day. That's right—the yes and no directions will change each day, because energy shifts daily. Once you know the direction of the swing for "yes," you can ask other questions.

- **Crystal balls** or **spheres** are made of clear quartz crystal and can be used for scrying, or gazing into a reflective object and seeing impressions as in day-dreaming. With practice and concentration, you may be able to see the image of the departed person you're looking for. You might also be able to telepathically receive messages from the other side or catch a glimpse into the goings-on of life after death.

When you're working with any new technique, it behooves you to do your research so that you know what to expect and what you should and shouldn't do. For a complete look at these tools of divination and several others, read my book *The Complete Idiot's Guide to Fortune Telling* (see Appendix B).

Holding a Séance

In Chapter 4, I discussed séances in terms of how skeptics and debunkers feel about them. Here, I get into the details of setting up a séance for the purpose of talking with a departed soul.

How to Conduct a Séance

So how do you begin a séance—and why? Well, séances aren't for your spiritual enlightenment. In other words, it's not like meditating or practicing yoga. Séances are used for the express purpose of contacting a deceased person.

Ethereal Potpourri

There may be a fear factor to conjuring up spirits in your dining room if you've never done it before, so if this really spooks you, just don't do it. On the other hand, if you think your concentration is good enough and your paranormal IQ is high enough, give it a try!

Do you have to hire a medium to lead a séance? Not necessarily. If you're brave, organized, and have a few open-minded friends who are interested in joining you, you might be able to do it yourself.

If you decide you're up for the challenge, there are a few things you should do before you begin. This is an easy technique that can be very successful when coupled with strong minds and good intentions.

First, choose a time. Most people like evenings because there is less chaos and the veil of energy that separates us from the other side is thinner. You will need at least three people—and that can include yourself. Don't go over a total of 12, including yourself. It is important that the people you choose are serious about this and are at the very least open-minded. (They can be skeptical, but they should be "open-minded skeptics." See Chapter 4 for more information on what makes a skeptic tick.)

Someone needs to be appointed the medium for this session. If you know someone who has experience in leading a séance or seems to have above-average intuitive skills, ask that person, even if he or she isn't a "professional" medium. Otherwise, appoint someone who is the most willing and excited about the thought of connecting with the other side.

Intention and believing are powerful. Make sure there are no disturbances: cell phones, faxes, radios, televisions, or anything that makes noise should be turned off. Turn off the lights and light a candle, if you like.

Now, begin:

1. Sit at a table in a circle, or as close as you can come to forming a circle. You can also sit on the floor, if you're limber enough. It's most important that everyone is comfortable.

2. Everyone should join hands.

3. The medium should lead or say (or both—there's no such thing as too much protection!) a prayer for protection from negative entities. Here's an example: "Protect all those here today from any negativity." Then end by saying, "And so it is," "Amen," or "Bless us all." Be creative here. There's no standard rule.

4. Everyone gathered should visualize a protective cloud of white light surrounding all the participants and the table.

5. The medium should attempt to relax everyone by asking them to slowly breathe through their nose and exhale through their mouth three times. (If there is a different relaxation method the medium would like to do, that's fine.)

6. Everyone and/or only the medium should say three times, "[Name of spirit you are trying to contact], we ask that you communicate with us now. We come in peace."

7. Wait for a response. It might be a sound, a drop in room temperature, or someone feeling a touch. (Yikes!)

8. If there's no response, the medium should take over and ask again for a sign. The medium can repeat himself as many times as he deems necessary.

If nothing happens still, wait for another day and try again. If you do get a response, continue on ....

Séance, Phase Two

Picking up a response from the other side can be exciting, unnerving, or terrifying! What happens next? Well, don't panic, scream, or even say anything. Stay calm and keep holding hands (even though everyone's palms might be getting sweaty by now).

1. To make sure you've contacted the correct spirit, ask point-blank for verification. Ask for a rap or some type of response if you are, indeed, communicating with your intended target. If you don't get the response you've asked for, you might have a lost soul on your hands.

2. If it's not the soul you were looking for, ask if it would be willing to help you.

3. If you get a response that seems negative, the medium should tell the spirit to go away in love and peace. Drop hands and turn on the light. (Whew!)

4. If you continue on, ask only yes or no questions, using a rap-response method: one rap for yes; two raps for no; or "Knock three times on the ceiling if you love me … Twice on the pipes, if the answer is no." (But only if you suspect the spirit is a fan of '70s music.)

5. The medium may be able to telepathically communicate with the spirit, which is fine as well. In this case, you'll receive messages that are more involved than "yes" or "no." However, no inexperienced medium should invite a spirit into her body in order to answer questions! Telepathy works just fine.

6. When the medium decides she's getting drained or losing energy, she should thank the spirit and tell it to go in love and light. At this point, everyone should drop hands and turn on the lights.

Ethereal Potpourri _____

When you're conducting a séance, there should be no joking, like yelling, "Boo!" No one should tap their foot on the floor to be cute or create drama, either. Ghostly friends are sensitive. Don't make fun of them! Record the events of the séance in a book or journal, including the opinions and reflections of each person present.

Not Small, Not Large ... How 'bout a Medium?

So you say there's no way you're going to conjure up a spirit by yourself? Too spooky? Give yourself credit for recognizing your boundaries!

If you're interested in contacting a deceased loved one but you're too jittery to actually do it yourself, you'll need a professional to step in and help you. Now, I've already mentioned that there are phonies out there who will charge you an arm and a leg for their "services." You obviously want to hook up with someone who's genuine and talented. How can you find this medium?

You've no doubt heard of the famous and popular television psychic mediums or survival evidence mediums, as they're often called, such as John Edward, James Van Praagh, George Anderson, and Allison Dubois. Due to cost and waiting time, obtaining the services of any of these professionals is not easy for the average person. So what are your options?

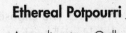

Ethereal Potpourri

According to a Gallup Poll, those who believe that some people or psychics can actually hear and communicate with the dead increased from 10 percent to 26 percent from approximately 1996 to 2001.

Finding a Medium

When selecting a psychic medium or spirit medium, it's best to rely on word of mouth and testimonials from people who've had firsthand accounts with good intuitives. This, I admit, is not an easy task. It's simply not something most people talk to their casual acquaintances—or even their family members—about. The number of people who visit mediums is not necessarily large, and people who do use mediums often keep that information to themselves until they think you're like-minded or at least nonjudgmental. Hence, referrals are not easy to come by.

If you can't find anyone who can give you a personal recommendation, find a local New Age or metaphysical store and inquire there. You can be fairly certain that the establishment isn't going to recommend someone who's a phony—after all, the shop's reputation is on the line, too.

The most important thing when looking for a good medium is to take your time, do your research, and don't grab anyone just because you feel desperate.

Eternal Thoughts

The three eternal questions: Who am I? What am I doing here? Where am I going ... and will I get frequent flier miles (and if so, how will I redeem them)?

—Horace J. Digby, winner of the Robert Benchley Society Award for Humor

What to Ask

Whoever you choose shouldn't ask you too many questions about anything, but should stick to the topic at hand, which in this case is your deceased loved one. If he's really a psychic telephone to the other side, he should be able to tap into the energy of that spirit and go from there.

Always ask for cost and how much time you'll be given. You don't want any surprises at the end. Some mediums charge each person attending or the host or hostess splits the cost. Communicating with spirits is a draining situation for the medium, so don't be surprised if he or she comes in with a high figure. Some might charge hundreds. It's really difficult to put an average on the amount. A typical price range for a medium who isn't famous may run from $75 and up.

If your time goes over the agreed-upon limit, ask in advance what the charge will be for additional time. Like the cost, the time varies. The medium may tell you he or she will continue with the session until the spirit leaves—and no one ever really knows when that will be.

Also remember, *no* spiritual medium has a 100 percent success rate—but some are far more intuitive than others. You must be open-minded at the outset and if you don't have a successful session, you shouldn't expect a refund. This is the chance you take as a seeker. Remember, although this is a gift and a calling for the readers, it's also a business.

> ### What Skeptics Say
>
> Surprise, surprise! I'll be playing the part of the skeptic here! If you're looking for a medium on the Internet, please reconsider and try to find someone through a personal recommendation. I have nothing against the Internet, but you'll literally find thousands of psychic mediums there—how will you find the right one for you?
>
> Also, there are many out there who will take your money and run. I'm *not* suggesting that all Internet psychics are charlatans; I *am* saying it's easier and possibly safer to find an honorable and gifted medium through a personal reference. And those 900 numbers? Well, you can get some good readers occasionally, believe it or not, but you just don't know who is going to pick up the phone on any given day. So beware!

Think about it this way: if you went to a doctor and decided at the end of your visit that the guy was a quack, do you think he would give you your money back? No way! But you also wouldn't go back to him the next time you needed medical advice. That's why genuine, talented professionals in any field—whether it's spirituality, medicine, law, or whatever—tend to do well, and those who aren't so gifted usually deserve the bad reputations they've earned. (Another reason I urge you to try to find someone based on a personal recommendation!)

The Least You Need to Know

- Take the time to grieve a loved one's death before attempting to contact him or her.

- Sometimes the dead come to us in the form of a dream; paying attention to how they look can give you a clue as to the message they're imparting.

- You can use tools of divination to attempt to contact those who have crossed over.

- You can conduct your own séance with other participants if you are serious and up to the challenge.

- When hiring a spiritual or psychic medium, it's best to go with a personal recommendation.

Part 3

What Do Dead People Do?

Perhaps you've always believed that life after death is a lot like a resort vacation: you plan on spending eternity relaxing, listening to beautiful music, and hitting the buffet every couple of hours. (If this is paradise, after all, there *must* be a buffet!) Well, guess what? Some theories of the afterlife have us *working!* In these chapters, you'll learn what everyday "life" might be like on the other side. You'll also read about some of the most controversial theories about life after death, including the soul's journey to other planets.

13

I'm Here ... Where Is Everybody?

In This Chapter

- Starting life on the other side
- How you might look and feel
- I forgot all about the time!
- Love conquers all?
- Death is everything you can imagine

When you pass over to the other side and arrive as the new kid on the universal block, it can be very overwhelming. You may see people you've forgotten about, and you may be bombarded with questions from spirits wanting to hear what's happening back on Earth.

What's more, the people who greet you—most of them deceased loved ones—may look years younger than you had expected!

In this chapter, we'll talk about what happens as you enter into the afterlife—who you'll see, how you might feel, what kinds of thoughts might be racing through your mind. Thankfully, it seems as though the entities in the next life have done all they can to make us feel welcome and relaxed!

Hail, Hail, the Gang's All Here!

The information in this section is based on the accounts of people who have had near-death experiences and the visions of mystic mediums. Their stories suggest that when you make the transition from this life to the next plane, there will be departed loved ones waiting for you at the end of the passageway between the two worlds.

But at the moment you let go of this life and move on to the next one, who will you see? Will they recognize you? Will *you* recognize *them?*

For Appearances' Sake ...

Maybe you have a loved one who passed away years and years ago. How will you recognize him when he presents himself to you at the time of your death? Will he look the same, or will he have aged normally? If the person died in some sort of accident, will he bear the scars of his injuries, or will he be restored to perfection?

> **Ethereal Potpourri**
>
> Not only will she look hale and hearty, but Grandma may also be sporting a slimmer physique when you see her on the other side! (Restoration of the body to near perfection is just one perk of life after death.)

People who have been at the crossing-over point report that dead loved ones often appear pretty much the way you remember them when they were healthy and looking happy. That could be at any age you remember them at their best.

The effects of illness or injuries are corrected, and sometimes they will appear younger than when they passed, but they're always recognizable to you. So although your grandmother may have been wracked with disease when she died, when you meet her on the other side, she'll appear healthy and alert.

This makes sense, if you think about it. Although you'd probably be happy to see her again no matter what she looked like, who wants to be reminded of the pain and suffering she went through—especially when both of you are supposedly in a better place now?

There are different thoughts about how children may appear, though. Some say you'll see them grown and others say they will appear as they were when they passed on. If a child was an infant at the time of her death, you may see a relative or friend holding her.

Essentially, when you cross over, you'll see your friends and loved ones in good health in their earthly bodies. They won't have wings, as humans don't transform into angels. (For more information on angels, read Chapter 5.) The blind will see; the deaf will hear; the sick are cured.

Now, you might be asking, "If this transformation to the next life is so wonderful, then why are people stuck in their human form?" The answer is that they probably aren't. They appear to you in this way to ease *your* transition into death. For them to appear in any other form might shock you. (Of course, it couldn't shock you *to death* anymore, but still, it's more comforting to make a gentle, slow transition.)

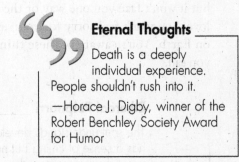

Eternal Thoughts

Death is a deeply individual experience. People shouldn't rush into it.

—Horace J. Digby, winner of the Robert Benchley Society Award for Humor

Think about this: would you rather see a recognizable figure at this time, or the orb of light containing your loved one's soul? Sure, a soul is a soul and your loved one's essence is what's most important, but until you're comfortable in your new dimension, it's best for you to see a few familiar faces—and bodies.

But I Don't Know Anyone Who's Died!

We all assume that everyone knows people who have passed and when you make the final journey from Earth you will have a big welcome party.

But if you die at an early age, or if you just never happened to have a friend or loved one pass on before you, who meets you on the other side? Will you be all alone, or will someone else's family come to greet you—sort of like you're a foreign exchange student?

In this case, you're surrounded by spirit guides who look just like regular people, and the volunteer welcome community of souls who just want to help. These souls welcome a reason to be needed. These spirit guides will have loving and kind faces. You may have even known some of them from your life on Earth but forgotten about them.

So you will never be alone or unwelcome in your transition to the next life. *Everybody* gets a welcome committee.

What Time Did I Arrive?

When you first enter the next life, you'll have no concern about time. The present is all there is.

On the first level of entrance into the spirit world, you'll have recollection of the past but it won't faze you one way or the other. You won't miss being with people you love. You won't feel sorry for yourself for the trials and tribulations you encountered on Earth. You're aware of these things but numb to the fact that they should make you sad.

Ethereal Potpourri

> The soul understands development, but not time. So in that regard, the soul has a sense of timing but not in the way we think of it. This is another reason it's sometimes difficult to contact the dead. They might show up five days after a séance, not knowing that a lot of time has elapsed from when they were called upon to when they made their appearance.

In the next life, you still love those people you loved on Earth but you don't long for them, which is a blessing in disguise. If you spent all your time mourning the fact that you couldn't be with your family anymore, you'd just be miserable, and that's not what the afterlife is all about. In the traditional sense of the word, you are always happy in the next life. This is why when psychic mediums contact the dead, these souls are usually cheerful and tell us not to agonize over their passing.

Your expired friends, relatives, co-workers, and acquaintances aren't mourning the fact that they're not with you, because those feelings of sadness simply do not exist in their minds. They still feel love for you, but they don't yearn for your presence with them. The deceased feel no length of time from the time they leave their loved ones to the time the loved ones come sauntering down the pathway of death. To them it seems like a second and suddenly you, too, have passed over and you're back together!

Ethereal Potpourri _____

In a 2005 Gallup Poll, 85 percent of Americans say they would want their life support removed if they were in a persistent vegetative state with no hope of recovery. The majority of Americans—even those who attend church weekly—say doctors should be allowed to end the life of a person with a terminal illness.

What's the Latest on Earth?

When you first disembark from your life on Earth and enter into the fleet of other departed souls, you'll feel an immense amount of love. It's said that this love is so comforting and beautiful it actually overwhelms you until you get used to it.

But once you adjust to the overflow of love and settle in a bit, you may be faced with a lot of questions from souls who've been waiting for news from the living!

Fill Me In!

Your welcome group will guide you along your way to the right guides and entities that will help you transition. However, on your way to meet those individuals, your dead friends may have lots of questions.

Because of the numerous theories that the dead know exactly what's going on on Earth, you may wonder why the heck they're so curious about their home planet—why, you were hoping they could fill *you* in on some of life's mysteries!

Eternal Thoughts _____

Death ends a life, not a relationship.

—Jack Lemmon, actor

This just isn't the case. Perhaps the dead don't follow the news from Earth (or even care about it most of the time) because they have their own lives, so to speak, and interests on the other side.

"All right," you say, "so why do they want the news from Earth at all if they're so content with the afterlife?" It would be like if you moved out of town next week: you'd want to keep in touch and find out what was going on in the old neighborhood every now and then, but in order to be happy, you'd also have to concentrate on making a new life in your new place.

So when you arrive, the dead may want the latest scoop from Earth out of curiosity, but not necessarily out of want or need.

What Skeptics Say _____

Of course, skeptics feel that the dead aren't interested in our lives back here on Earth because they ceased to have a consciousness when they died. If you have no consciousness, you can't really be interested in anything! This issue is the main difference between skeptics and believers in life after death.

The Contradiction

Although some people have come to the conclusion that the dead don't necessarily take much interest in life on Earth, you do have to wonder about the signs and symbols and forms of contact that we talked about in Chapter 18, where I told you that sometimes the dead try to contact us via dreams or just stop by to say hello in other forms such as apparitions at a bedside.

Some people would ask—and rightly so—if the dead aren't interested in this dimension anymore, then why do they pop in every now and then? Well, there's a school of thought that tells us that the dead can find out what we're doing if they want to … but they don't necessarily want to, except on occasion. Hence, the occasional visits from some souls and not from others.

If they don't check in, does it mean they no longer care about us? Of course not. Perhaps it's just that they're absorbed in their new lives and what used to be important to them on Earth isn't as significant as what they are doing now. This is a good thing for them—remember, we don't want anyone on the other side sitting and mourning for their past life—so try to be happy for a deceased loved one who isn't stopping by to say hello. It probably means he or she is busy and happy!

Did Houdini Lose Interest?

Lack of interest in the goings-on on Earth can be an explanation for why someone like Harry Houdini (1874–1926), who was a famous escape artist, magician, and debunker of Spiritualists, failed to make good on a deal he made with his wife to contact her from the afterlife.

Houdini was afraid that after he died the psychic mediums or Spiritualists, whom he generally detested, would take advantage of his fame and pretend they were in contact with him via a séance or other form of paranormal communication. If this were to happen, the Spiritualist could financially benefit, not to mention gain their own source of fame.

To prevent this from happening, Houdini came up with the idea to choose a code that was known only to his wife, Bess, as a sign that there was life after death. In the event of his death, he would contact her from the other side and relay the coded message. In the spirit of trying to contact him, Bess held séances on Halloween, the anniversary of his death, every year for 10 years. Unfortunately, Houdini never made an appearance.

Ethereal Potpourri _____

Houdini's secret code was made up of 10 words chosen at random from a letter from his former friend, Arthur Conan Doyle (author of the Sherlock Holmes stories). As opposed to Houdini, Doyle was a believer in Spiritualism. It's said that when Houdini began to debunk Spiritualists with a passion, their friendship took a nosedive and eventually ended.

However, for those who believe in life after death, this isn't conclusive evidence that the afterlife doesn't exist. Perhaps once Houdini made the transition, this simply wasn't important to him anymore. His consciousness may have evolved. Maybe he asked himself, "What was I thinking when I said I would let Bess know that I was still alive to try to prove something?"

This could just be another example of the deceased living in the present and not being too concerned about promises of the past or any other earthly matters.

Anything You Want, You've Got It

Another theory about of what goes on in your new life after death includes the idea that you can be or do anything you want just by thinking it.

Poof! Whatever you want will materialize.

If you want a mansion, you have one. If you want to live on an alien planet, you can. If you want to have a movie star—living or dead—fall in love with you, then so be it. (In Chapter 15, I talk about the aspects of relationship in this mind-set.)

Fantasy

You may wonder where the spiritual growth is within this theory. If you can have whatever you want, whenever you want ... what the heck are you learning from that?

It's thought that the fantasy part of death happens at the beginning, when you first cross over, in order to give you rest from the drudgery of life on Earth. Even if you had a great life, it's still relaxing to be totally blissful. Think of it as a day at the spa. Sure, it's great, and yes, you could get used to this kind of living, but you know eventually it's going to come to an end. (Keep reading ....)

Pushed Forward by Boredom

Eventually, you may become bored with having anything you want just by dreaming it up. At that time, you may want to move on to another unknown existence where you'll again find newness and intriguing knowledge.

When boredom sets in, you ask your higher power to move you on to a higher and more complex level, as you no longer take joy in only what you knew to be real on Earth. In other words, a graduation takes place by your desire to learn more about things not of an earthly realm.

However, I imagine there are those who enjoy this fantasy state of being so much that they decide to stay in this illusional domain for years or decades. The time you stay in this elusive state is determined by how spiritually evolved you are when you die. You may be an old soul who has been incarnated many times and learned many lessons, or you could be a new soul who's only been dead a time or two before!

> **Eternal Thoughts**
>
> Boredom is the feeling that everything is a waste of time; serenity, that nothing is.
>
> —Dr. Thomas Szasz, author and critic of the foundations of psychiatry

The old souls don't have the interest in waiting too long, enjoying material pleasures, but the new souls embrace it. I say to each his own. It all works itself out on the other side in due time.

The Least You Need to Know

◆ Friends and relatives will be waiting for you at the end of a tunnel when you die. They'll basically look the same as they did before they died, with minor improvements.

◆ The dead have little concept of time. They live in the present but have an unemotional recollection of the past in.

◆ The departed still love those on Earth, but are sometimes caught up in their own existence.

◆ Another view of entering the afterlife is we can conjure up anything we want and stay in that place for a long period of time.

14

Let's Get Physical

In This Chapter

- ◆ No pain, lots of gain
- ◆ I had to die to get the body of a swimsuit model?!
- ◆ Tuning in to a person's aura
- ◆ How to read an aura: what do all the colors mean?
- ◆ Body, soul, and matter all have a vibrational level

There are numerous religious and spiritual beliefs that stem from the idea of the soul continuing on without a body, and other beliefs that tell us the soul reconnects with a better "body," one which has the virtual characteristics of a human body, but functions on other planes or dimensions, living in an existence similar to that on Earth, but without any negativity.

Yet what about bodies that were deformed, or limbs that were severed, and the mentally challenged? Are they suddenly whole and perfect in the next life?

It's amazing how many people want to know what they might look like after death and whether the physical body can somehow follow the freed soul and materialize later once the soul reaches its destination. Forget what you've seen on those makeover shows—*this* transformation is *truly* extreme!

Free of Pain at Last

It's generally believed that suffering of any kind—whether it's physical or emotional— doesn't exist in the next life. According to psychic mediums, soul travelers, those who've had NDEs, and many spiritual leaders, we are free of pain, disfigurements, and psychological disorders upon death and sometimes in the moments leading up to death.

Some Spiritualists and religious advocates feel that even when someone is not totally dead, the soul actually leaves the body before the life force is discontinued, especially if the person is in severe pain, or experiencing any type of torment.

For example, if someone were in a catastrophe and experiencing great anguish, they're taken out of the body before they die. Thus their pain is ended. They may not have suffered the horrific fate you feared they did. This gives great comfort to those who've seen or assumed loved ones endured agony prior to death.

The mentally challenged become sharp as tacks when they're free of the perils of Earth.

Ethereal Potpourri

"Bless his heart, Great-Grandpa looks funny with no hair, those big ears, and all those tubes in him." Watch what you say to Great-Grandpa who has Alzheimer's, because when he passes on, he'll remember everything that was said and even thought! It all comes back like a dam bursting open. Unkind or insensitive comments in the days leading up to a loved one's death may put up a wall between the two of you that's stronger and more permanent than death. (If you ever want to contact this person, why would he or she want to talk to you?)

I Want to Be a Deceased Hottie: Shallow or Fun?

Finally, you're a size 0 with a 24-inch waist and no belly fat. Love handles? What love handles? You left those on Earth with your thighs that resembled holiday cheese balls covered with cashews. Is death the only way to lose that extra weight that you've been carrying around since childhood?

On a shallow level, maybe being dead isn't that bad when it comes to cosmic fashion. But once we're dead we're not supposed to *be* shallow anymore, right? Well ... not necessarily. Some think balance is the key to eternal happiness. So a lot of spiritual awareness and a little bit of earthly pleasure makes for a happy dead person.

I Look *Way* Better in This Life!

In Chapter 16, I mention the idea that some people feel we have the ability to live an existence in the afterlife that's similar to the one we have on Earth, only better. In some belief systems, this includes all earthly pleasures, like eating, drinking, sex, and so on, so why wouldn't fashion be included as well?

If this is your take on life after death, it could be rather fun. And why shouldn't it be? Everyone will be looking good so the competition is deadly! Except there is no competition. You *want* everyone to look good because you look good, too.

> **Eternal Thoughts**
>
> Some people, no matter how old they get, never lose their beauty—they merely move it from their faces into their hearts.
>
> —Martin Buxbaum, author

The More Christian View of Clothing

We like to think of those in heaven as being clothed, whether they're wearing clothing we would recognize as modern or clothing from the time they lived on Earth.

What's interesting to note is that in the Bible, "clothing" (if you want to call fig leaves clothing) came about after Adam and Eve disobeyed God. Clothing was a result of their shame. Prior to that, they were naked and just fine and dandy with it. So it's fair to wonder why we would wear clothing in heaven. Shouldn't we be beyond shame after death? Well, the theory goes that once we're redeemed (after death), nothing is shameful, including clothes.

So if you enjoy being a fashion plate and simply like to "dress," you can—and no one can *ever* make you feel shallow about it!

Your Hair Looks Great

In the next life, you never have a bad hair day. And gentlemen, any hair you've lost comes back. Guys don't have to shave and women never worry about waxing. All you do is think about the hairstyle you want and it appears!

If you don't like it, just rethink it. (All that thinking might make you tired, but it sure beats going to a stylist twice in one day to get the color just right.) Just check your heavenly mirror; if you don't like what you see, change it.

Let's not forget that when you first cross over, you have to get hip to the fashions and trends in the ethereal realms. It's like moving to Paris from a tiny town in the Midwest. So you might look like a cosmic geek for a while, but there are those who will direct you to looking good.

As far as others recognizing you when they pass over after you, they'll intuitively know it's you. The connection will be between your souls.

Eternal Thoughts

I'm not worried about life after death. I'd just like to know if I'll be able to get a decent haircut.

—Horace J. Digby, winner of the Robert Benchley Society Award for Humor

It may sound like I'm making light of a serious transition, but this is not about humor. People who have had near-death experiences (see Chapter 7) say they've seen civilizations that are akin to Earth, but better. The spirits in these civilizations are all what we would call "the beautiful people" here on Earth—in other words, they're as close to perfect as you can imagine. I have an idea we'll all be looking like we're on the cosmic red carpet at the Universal Awards. (Just be sure to wear your comfy astral shoes.)

The Aura That Surrounds You

The word *aura* comes from the Greek language and means "air" or "breath." You can't touch it; it's an essence (like a smell or the feeling of vapor on your skin) that comes from and surrounds a person. Some people describe it as an energy field that encompasses each living thing on the planet. Even though it isn't a physical object, it has an impact on our physical being.

Interestingly, if you've ever seen a portrait of one of the Ascended Masters, such as Jesus Christ or Buddha, you'll note that the artist most likely has surrounded their figure with a glow—that's the person's aura.

Small children are able to see auras easily, since they haven't yet learned to suppress their spiritual instincts. Sometimes you'll see a toddler screaming and crying in the presence of an adult who's doing their best to make the kid laugh or smile. Everyone around is wondering what this child is seeing in this adult that's so terrifying. It could be that the child doesn't like the adult's aura!

def•i•ni•tion

An **aura** is an energy field that surrounds each living thing. Auras appear in different colors, depending on the person's state of health mentally and physically.

I Can See Clearly Now

If you're able to see a person's aura, you have the ability to know their feelings, thoughts, intentions, or state of health before they even speak! If we could tune in to each other's auras, think of the possibilities! You'd know when someone was lying, you'd know when someone was ill, you'd know whether a person had the best of intentions—in any situation.

How, you ask? A bright, clear energy field means that a person is kind, balanced, and spiritually strong. A gray or dark aura indicates that the person has some serious issues going on and you need to be on the lookout for some underhanded moves from them.

Seeing auras isn't as difficult as you might think. It's not a skill you're either born with or not. Of course, there are people who are naturals at this—they've always been able to see auras and always will be able to. But you can see them, too. Learning to see auras takes practice, concentration, and positive intention.

How to Read an Aura

Edgar Cayce, America's best-documented psychic, also known as the Sleeping Prophet (as most of his readings where done in a sleep state), was always aware of people's auras. He once said, "Ever since I can remember, I have seen colors in connection with people. It was a long time before I realized that other people did not see these colors. I do not ever think of people except in connection with their auras; I see them change in my friends and loved ones, as time goes by—sickness, defection, love, fulfillment— these are all reflected in the aura, and for me the aura is the weathervane of the soul. It shows which way the winds of destiny are blowing."

There are a few different ways to view auras. One way is to simply look at a person (or plant or animal—remember, all living things have an aura). Eventually, you'll see a light or glow around the person. For some observers, this takes only a few minutes; for others, it takes longer. Be patient and have an open mind. It's there; you just have to let your eyes adjust to this level of sight.

Here's how to observe another person's aura:

1. Choose a time when there are few distractions and you are comfortable with your surroundings. Find a willing subject to observe.

2. Situate the person in front of a plain white background, such as a soft white wall, drape, or sheet. Focus on the middle of their forehead.

3. After approximately 30 seconds, analyze the area with your peripheral vision. Remember to keep your focus on the spot in the center of their forehead.

4. Don't look around the room. Maintain your concentration. Eventually, you'll see the background directly behind the individual is brighter and different than the backdrop actually behind them. This is the aura. It will become clearer with more focus. You may sense several colors or just one or two at first.

To sense your own aura, stand or sit in front of a large mirror and follow the same procedure.

What Skeptics Say _____

Skeptics have another explanation for the colors that surround a person. They suggest that if a person stares at another person (or even an object) in front of a white background in a room with low lighting, the haze around a person—or what might be described as an aura—may be due to retinal fatigue.

Is This My Color?

Most people have one or two colors that dominate their aura, but it's not unusual to see combinations of colors and/or flashes of colors. The colors of our auras change frequently, depending on our health and moods. Each color has its own meaning:

◆ *White* (bright light) will always have a positive vibration. We should strive for bright light, not white (the color). In the hours leading up to death, it's not unusual for a person's aura to become larger and brighter.

- *Red* represents the physical body and indicates force, energy, and stamina. This color might surround a self-centered, materialistic, athletic, or sexual person. Deeper shades of red have a negative connotation.

- *Orange* represents thoughtfulness, self-control, and optimism. An individual with orange in their aura usually has some interesting insights to share.

- *Yellow* in the golden tones shows well-being and deep wisdom. If the yellow is pale, the person tends to be timid and may be looking to start life all over again in a new direction. Regardless, yellow is essentially a positive color.

- *Green* in a person's aura indicates a good listener who's interested in healing the self and others. Green is nature's color; it provides peace and harmony, which means this person is helpful but not domineering. A green aura that borders on becoming yellow, though, can imply deceit and indecisiveness.

- *Blue* auras indicate spirit, meditation, and truth. All shades of blue are positive. Artistic people are apt to have blue in their auras, even though they may be a bit melancholy.

- *Purple* is the most mystical of all the colors. It encompasses spirituality, intuitive nature, and seekers. Purple auras tend to be fleeting—they won't hang around too long and they don't appear in a strong hue. Often a purple aura will settle into a deep shade of blue. But when you do see it, it signifies that the person it surrounds has spiritual thoughts and strong insights at the time.

Colors mirror the body, mind, and spirit. Pay attention to them in yourself and others. Nature provides us with the tools to see auras. All you have to do is make a conscious effort to see and the knowledge is yours!

Ethereal Potpourri

Colors connected to auras are very important because they connect with the vibrational energy of a person. It's interesting to note how we relate color to emotions: We say, "I was green with envy," or "She's feeling blue," or, "He was so angry, he saw red!" You probably already know, feel, and see more than you realize about color and auras.

What Happens to Our Aura When We Die?

In the hours leading up to death, a person's aura may become larger and also turn white or bright. But other thoughts about dying and the aura tell us that the aura pulls in and decreases.

So which is it? In or out? Bigger or smaller? Light or dark? And what does that mean for our energy field?

Actually, these are the same concepts worded differently. While the colors may initially increase in the moments leading up to death, upon dying the colors of the aura diminish, therefore "pulling in." Some will say they go completely dark, as they are no longer present.

As for our energy field, it ceases at the moment of death—at least in this plane—which is why the aura pulls in. Do we take our aura with us into the next life? We'll talk about this in the next section.

The End of the Physical Journey, the Beginning of Something New

Everything in existence is energy and functions at a certain level of vibration. The body and the soul have a vibration unique unto themselves: The soul vibrates at a higher level while the body is more mundane, acting as a shelter for the soul.

Now, remember, the aura is connected to this vibrational energy; that's why different people have different-colored auras. The color reflects that person's vibrational energy.

When the aura retracts into the body at the moment of death, it journeys *with* the soul in the astral body, which is a spiritual or mystical concept of a second body (discussed in detail in Chapter 16) or a soul-body that isn't physical but may look like light or colors of light. The astral body takes the consciousness or the personality of the person—the aura of the person—with it.

The place our soul travels to in the afterlife also has a vibration, whether it's a planet or an entirely new dimension. The different levels of heaven, Nirvana, or Paradise will also each have their own vibration.

This is a rather complicated concept, I know, so if you don't want to sit and pick it apart, that's fine. Just know that your body and soul are connected to an energy that continues on well after your physical being ceases to exist!

The Least You Need to Know

- Upon crossing over to the next life, your mental and physical facilities are fully restored.

- Some theories believe that the soul leaves the body before physical death in cases of extreme mental or physical anguish.

- You can't touch a person's aura; it's more like an essence that comes from and surrounds a person.

- Beauty is redefined in the afterlife according to individual preferences.

- The aura of a person pulls in at death.

- The soul has a higher level of vibration than the body. After the body dies, the soul continues to vibrate on another plane.

15

The Others Who Crossed Over Ahead

In This Chapter

- ◆ Not all my soul mates in the same place
- ◆ Cosmic relationships
- ◆ Dead and still ducking the in-laws!
- ◆ Sex and life after death
- ◆ Will I see my pet on the other side?

We all have so many soul mates and so many lifetimes! When you enter into the next life, you might just need to learn to juggle all those past loves of your lives. How will you do this? Will you have to sneak around, or are these souls so open-minded that you can all be one big happy dead family?

If your soul mates don't keep you busy in the hereafter, your dead relatives will. But what about the relatives you didn't like? Does paradise have a hideout you can duck into when you see them floating your way?

Relationships continue on the other side on all different levels of understanding. The bad news is that once you cross over, you aren't automatically accepting of those you didn't care for on Earth; the good news is that in time, you will be.

Soul Mates and Life After Death

One of the good things about dying is that you'll get to see your soul mate if he or she dies before you, right? Back in love, back in their arms (if they have any)!

But how does it all work? We have so many lifetimes and so many soul mates—do we only get to hook up with the one true love of our many lives after we die? And what if you never were fortunate enough to have ever found your soul mate? Surely, you can't be destined to spend eternity alone … or can you?

> **Eternal Thoughts**
>
> We choose those we like; with those we love, we have no say in the matter.
>
> —Mignon McLaughlin, *The Neurotic's Notebook* (Bobbs-Merrill, 1963)

Some people use the term "soul mate" to describe someone they feel is the perfect mate, or to use the old-fashioned lingo, "the one and only love of [your] life." Romance writers, self-help authors, and dating sites use the term often. The good news is that each of us has more than one soul mate. The tricky part is finding that person across the expanse of space, time, and different lives.

Counting Soul Mates Like Railroad Cars

For those who believe in reincarnation (the theory that when we die our souls come back into another physical body to learn lessons before it eventually resides in a higher realm; discussed in Chapter 22) a question arises: who's our real soul mate and will we be with her or him after death?

For example, let's say you've incarnated back and forth to the planet 20 times and each time, or even half the time, you've met someone who you thought was your soul mate. Then you would have quite a few soul mates on the other side when you finally arrived for good. What's a soul to do?

Don't panic and try to back your way out of the tunnel. Surely those souls also had the same problem you did when they first made the transition and found all of *their* soul mates waiting. (You didn't think you were their one and only, did you?)

Meeting a soul mate after death is not much more than meeting an old friend. When you meet all those soul mates of yours there's no desire, jealousy, or wanting. It won't matter if they were the soul mates of 100 others. It's just a platonic type understanding and love.

It's like meeting an ex-husband or, as I like to call them, "wasband," who you were once very much in love with and remain friendly with, wishing him all the love and joy he can find … as long as it's not with you.

Dull Souls?

So, you can have numerous soul mates through time and soul travel, but surprisingly, soul mates are *not* the hot and heavy romances of the planet. They're people with whom you share similar goals, ideas, and an attraction, but not always of a physical nature. Soul mates typically march to the beat of the same drummer, so to speak.

This is why some people will say, "I love my husband, but I'm not really in love with him in the romantic and passionate way you find in romance novels." (Of course, you can insert "wife" into that sentence, as well!) This might *still* be a soul mate relationship! This doesn't mean that soul mate partnerships aren't passionate or erotic—they can be. But soul mates see the bigger picture and don't rely on the entire relationship to be an intimate whirlwind.

These relationships seem to flow, are balanced and enjoyable, and both parties are healthy and happy. Therefore, when you die don't think you are going to catch up with your soul mate or someone you deemed a soul mate in a perfect heavenly relationship.

Signs That This Person Is Not Your Soul Mate

Many people feel we have many soul mates who walk the planet at the same time we do. Hence, there's more like a "soul clan" of compatible spirits for each person to choose from. This could also mean that soul mates don't really exist and we just gravitate toward certain people who we may have known in a past life but were not necessarily our perfect soul mates.

Past lives may explain why we may be drawn to men or women who we know in this lifetime but who clearly are not for us. Unfortunately, when this happens we can end up in dysfunctional relationships because of pure stubbornness.

? What Skeptics Say _____

Skeptics, of course, don't believe in a connection between two souls (because they don't believe in souls at all). They would say that most people who say they are soul mates typically go through the same trials and tribulations as two people who don't believe in soul mates. Skeptics also think that what people refer to as soul mates are simply two people who are like-minded with an attraction. Naysayers downplay spiritual bonding from another dimension or lifetime as a romantic notion for authors, seminar facilitators, and matchmaking sites to make money.

Because you feel an affection or have a kindred spirit with someone doesn't mean you should force a relationship that is not workable. Sure, you may have been a soul mate with this person in another lifetime, but now you have to move on to someone else.

If you're feeling torn in a relationship—you really feel that this person is your soul mate, and yet the two of you just can't make things work—check out this list and ask yourself if you fall into any of these categories:

◆ There is an immediate physical attraction but later you find you have no common ground. Everyday living just doesn't work for the two of you, but you can't let go of the sexual part.

◆ You get along on a daily basis with the same interests and goals, but the physical side is not present. You hope it will eventually come into being because you get along on every other level.

◆ You have a need to take care of someone no matter what they've done wrong or how they treat you. (Can we say co-dependent?)

◆ A psychic reader or medium tells you someone you just met is your soul mate, and even though you don't have those feelings for the person in question, you try to make it come true. This is not a karmic relationship, soul mate, or twin flame (which I'll discuss in a moment). It could just be an error by the reader. No one's perfect!

◆ Your new love seems familiar to you in some way or you saw him or her in a dream or while having an out-of-body experience. Feeling as though you have known someone for a long time could indicate you knew that person in a past life, but it doesn't necessarily mean that he or she is your long-lost love. He or she could have been a friend in Atlantis. And if you met during an out-of-body experience, that might merely mean you were traveling the galaxy at the same time.

◆ You're attracted to someone who is married or not available for a relationship. And even though that is not normally your practice as a moral person, you have an affair anyway, because you just can't help yourself. Is it a past-life thing?

Any of these points are indications that this person is *not* your soul mate. Now, don't get discouraged at the thought of soul mates not existing. I'm not implying they don't exist. However, there is also another philosophy that should be considered regarding the existence of a spiritual companion for life, and it's an intriguing one.

True Relationship Concepts for Wholeness

Looking for your soul mate is, in essence, searching for a way to become whole. Many authors have written about soul mates. Among my favorites is Edgar Cayce, an American *psychic* who was known as the Sleeping Prophet, as he would put himself into a trance state and *channel* information to his clients. Once in a reading he said, "But know, the soul is rather the soul mate of the universal consciousness than of an individual entity."

I think that's a lovely idea, that our souls are first and foremost bound to a greater consciousness than to another person's soul. While this kind of kills the notion of romantic soul mates, there are other theories that talk about how souls part ways and meet up again.

def•i•ni•tion

Channeling means receiving information from a spirit, higher power, or other supernatural source that is not of the mind of the channeler or the person who is receiving the information.

Twin Flames

In her book *Soul Mates & Twin Flames: The Spiritual Dimension of Love & Relationships* (Summit University Press, 1999), Elizabeth Clare Prophet brings up a fascinating concept called Twin Flames. This is the idea of a oneness that was once split and is looking for that other half to become once again whole.

The philosophy of the twin flames is basically that in the beginning there was a single element, egg, or unit of some type that had a flaming or fiery quality. This entity was separated into two separate positions of existence, one masculine and the other feminine. Each unit had the design of spiritual sameness although there was physical differentiation.

These twin flames eventually came to Earth and sometimes live lifetime after lifetime looking for each other, but rarely finding one another. In some lifetimes they'll miss each other completely and in other lifetimes they'll have a brush with each other—if they're lucky, they may marry.

Whether they meet up on Earth or not, their connection is eternal. When they reach an elevated consciousness, they'll be united for eternity on a different plane that vibrates at a high frequency.

This may sound like the epitome of romance, but it really isn't romantic at all—it's a cosmic connection where both divisions learn and grow and then reunite, creating a powerful understanding of the universal flow.

> **Ethereal Potpourri**
>
> Elizabeth Clare Prophet was the leader of a New Age religious movement, The Summit Lighthouse, an organization encompassing the branches of Church Universal and Triumphant. Their followers believe that they are messengers of the Ascended Masters.

Karmic Relationships

Now we're talking passion! In karmic partnerships, two people are usually very attracted to each other from the beginning and are drawn to each other in a powerful union.

Why? It's not their hair or body; it's more. It's the interest of karmic balance.

Their souls see a key to freedom if they team up; meaning that with each other they can pay off karmic debts or balance those karmic scales.

> **Ethereal Potpourri**
>
> It's said that in our lifetimes, we all experience karmic relationships and learn from all of them. This type of education is expensive (literally and figuratively), but it's something that needs to take place for the evolution of our soul.

These relationships, though often passionate, can be rocky, abusive, and leave you wondering why you make wrong choices when it comes to romantic companionship. Many will have a feeling of loneliness in such a relationship because it's not about being with that person for peace, love, and harmony, but more about learning or paying back a debt for something you did in this lifetime or a past lifetime.

Yes, you may have chosen your present girlfriend, boyfriend, husband, or wife because you were bad in a past life and this is the punishment you suffer. Sounds comedic, but it's true.

The good news is if you grow and see where you made mistakes, you can free yourself of these relationships and move on to a better type of partnership. Hopefully, that occurs before the two of you marry, but the reality is that it doesn't always work that way.

So *someday* you'll join with your twin flame and be at peace and whole again. But that doesn't mean it will happen the minute you walk through the gates of your new celestial home after death. Even in death you may have to master lessons and slowly work your way up the levels of spiritual evolution. So that flame can still be a *long* way off.

Meeting Up with Friends and Foes

Once you're dead, you still keep your basic personality until you seriously evolve in spiritual awareness (which can take centuries of incarnating—or learning, if you don't believe in reincarnation). That's why some ghosts are tricksters and others are sweet and kind. The personality remains consistent until you evolve more.

Upon dying you don't become the perfect soul who loves everyone and forgives everyone for their wrongdoings. No, it takes time for you to grow and learn and accept other souls for who they are at this point and who they were at another point in time.

You're Here?

As I discussed in Chapter 7, people who've had near-death experiences (NDEs) often report that once you transition to the other side, relatives and loved ones gather at the gate, so to speak, to welcome you to your new life.

But you may wonder about those who you don't want to ever see again. According to mediums, mystics, and the near-death experiences of many people, you simply don't encounter those people unless you choose to. This makes perfect sense. After all, your life after death is supposed to be peaceful, not bring you stress or pain. If your neighbor has created havoc in your life, then you can take great pleasure in knowing that you won't have to see him or her again once you cross over!

Later, as you begin to understand mistakes you made on Earth, you may change your mind about the folks you've been avoiding, and there may be a joint desire between you and the person with whom you had a misunderstanding (or worse) to get past the disagreement. At this point, you both may want to forgive and forget. There is no pressure to do this, but to truly evolve, you have to experience forgiving and accepting why people did things and acted certain ways on Earth.

Make New Friends but Keep the Old

Just as you see old friends, acquaintances, and loved ones in the afterlife, you also make new alliances, just as you would on Earth.

You may gravitate to someone who you feel is a kindred soul or someone who had interests similar to your own on Earth. They may even be children you don't recognize, as they've grown well past the age they were at the time of their death. Children grow to approximately the age of 22 in the dimensions or cities of the afterlife (although newcomers to the afterlife may initially see children as they were when they left this planet). Therefore, when you see them you may recognize the soul but not the body.

Sex in the Afterlife

Until you get to the level where physical intimacy is unnecessary for your evolution, you can still have intimate relationships in the process in the afterlife.

It's more or less your option and often has to do with your attachment to things that gave you pleasure: if you loved eating, for example, you can continue to eat. If you enjoyed working out in the gym, you can still get buff. If you loved to prepare meals, you'll be able to cook to your heart's content. And, of course, if you enjoyed sex, you can continue doing so. There will be many willing participants who feel the same way, so you'll have lots of partners for dinner, dancing, and you know what else!

The interesting thing is that as you grow in spirit and knowledge and start to lose attachment to this life, eating, cooking, and sexual intercourse may not seem important anymore. In fact, you may someday in the afterlife look at these things and think, "What's the point when there is so much more to the universe?"

You may slowly let go of certain things, keeping others. You might be able to dwell in this state of begging without the food but not without the sex, or vice versa. But eventually, you'll detach from what you think are pleasures right now and tune in to another level of your higher self.

People wonder if they'll have to be monogamous on the other side. The consensus is that there is no jealousy in the afterlife, so monogamy is not an issue. Marriage is also a choice. If you want to be married you can be, and if you don't you don't have to. Again, there will be plenty of souls who think the way you do.

Ethereal Potpourri

Some people who've described out-of-body experiences say they've encountered what we'll call astral sex, or having sex as a union of souls as opposed to the physical touching we understand. The souls unite in a form of affection for each other and merge in whirls of light and feelings that aren't comparable to anything we can feel here on Earth.

Pets and Life After Death

The question of whether animals also cross over comes up often. After a pet's death, some people think they see the ghost of their cat running through the house or their dog still jumping in the backyard. It comes down to a question of whether they have souls.

Many spirit mediums feel that pets *do* have souls and can live with us in the afterlife. However, not all pets or animals make the transition like humans. Animals who may not have had owners who reared them like children may not have the spiritual awareness of love as some other animals. Therefore, the animals who did not grow, learn, and feel loved don't evolve like the others.

In this case their souls are said to go back into a type of collective "soul pool" and a new soul is born and comes back in a different animal form.

So in a nutshell, if you had a loyal pet who you fed, cared for, and treated with respect, you helped that animal to evolve and you will most likely meet again in the afterlife. I'll talk more about animals and life after death in Chapter 21.

The Least You Need to Know

- You don't have to interact with those on the other side whom you don't care to see.

- Monogamy in different dimensions is not necessary unless you really want it. There is no jealousy in the afterlife, just love.

- After a while, the earthly desires pertaining to the flesh will become less and less important.

- If a pet was well loved and cared for during its life, chances are the pet will be reunited with its owner in the afterlife.

Living Arrangements: Dimensions, Planets, and Cosmic Vagabonds

In This Chapter

◆ Far-out ideas about life after death

◆ Life after death on other planets

◆ Taking a soulful journey

◆ Becoming a drifter in the cosmos

Many religious and spiritual traditions are governed by the belief that there's a special place for those of us who have been "good" in this life on Earth, and a really negative place to which we're doomed if we've led a less-than-stellar lifestyle. Some teachings allow for an in-between state: a place where we learn and grow before we go on to anther level of existence. And of course, there's the whole idea of reincarnation; but the question still arises as to what happens when you don't have to incarnate anymore. Where does the soul ultimately end up?

In this chapter, I'm going to discuss some ideas about life after death that you may find to be really "out there." Most of these are centered on the belief that after death, the soul simply exists in a consciousness that we can't comprehend—but I'm going to try to explain it to the best of my ability.

I give you fair warning: the idea that our soul travels to different planets or galaxies and meets up with alien life forms is included in this chapter. Now, I know that not everyone will agree with these concepts, but since there are groups who theorize that this is what happens upon our physical death, I would be remiss in my duties if I didn't present this information here. So now let us explore these concepts, as unusual as they may seem.

Cities and Places of the Afterlife

One of many concepts of life after death is that one actually resides in a city of sorts on another plane where day-to-day activities are the norm. As you'll read in a moment, the cities' appearances are quite different, but they share a common element—there is no pain, no depression, no hunger, no anger.

I will present a few general notions of life in these cosmic counties. You can decide if any of them sound like an ideal place to rest your spiritual bones.

Like Home, Only Better

Some people have reported afterlife cities with a similar existence to earth, but more evolved. I have heard about locations having buildings constructed of some sort of laminated material found on Earth. As for entering into these cities, you simply arrive after you cross over and have your life review. One moment you're watching the story of your life and the next—poof! There you are!

> **Eternal Thoughts**
>
> The fact of a pre-Earth life crystallized in my mind, and I saw that death was actually a "rebirth" into a greater life ... that stretched forward and backward through time.
>
> —Betty J. Eadie, *Embraced by the Light*

In her book *Embraced by the Light* (see Appendix B), author Betty J. Eadie tells of a near-death experience in which she was taken to a place where there were beautiful gardens and beings weaving clothing for the newly dead. These spiritual beings, both male and female, seemed to be enjoying their tasks. Eadie also mentions that in the afterlife city she visited, one could go to a library without actually making the trip to the building. By just focusing on the fact that you wanted to gain knowledge on a subject, the information would automatically be transferred into one's mind, and that knowledge would be totally clear.

Crystal Palaces

Perhaps this will sound like a fantasy movie or a writer's overactive imagination, but crystal palaces and communities of dazzling structures and nature at its finest are said to be alive and well in other dimensions. These theories are derived from people who have had near-death experiences and experienced out-of-body journeys.

In these places, the soul can continue to learn and grow and has a life of sorts, but deals with different surroundings. There's no furniture—it's not needed because there is no longer a body housing the soul. You drift into different chambers and meet with other souls to discuss and learn. Eating and drinking are not an option— again, they aren't needed. There are beautiful gardens filled with foliage and flowers that don't exist in this life, as well as rivers of light and beaches of fine crystal instead of water and sand. The skies are filled with colors so beautiful they can't be described.

Body *and* Soul

There are a few places where the spirit resides that are very much like Earth—with a few minor changes. Think of these as planes where you have some choices. If you want a body and choose to eat and drink, you can. The body you're given is the one you had in your early 20s, which may sound great to many of us—but if by chance you had physical problems at that age, they're all removed. Weight, by the way, is never a problem. (This *is* paradise, after all!) In other words, the body you're given on this plane is perfect. If you hadn't reached your early 20s before you died, then you would be allowed to grow to that age, being cared for by other souls.

Sex and intimacy are also part of the lifestyle but the issue of monogamy doesn't exist on some planes, as there's no jealousy or anger. In other dimensions, you can choose to stay with one other soul if you like.

What about shopping? Now, this is one topic I haven't heard much about, but I would imagine there would be the opportunity to buy and sell goods, but I'm doubtful there would be anything resembling money. I would see a fair exchange of energy instead, meaning *I help you and you help me.*

Afterlife on Other Planets

Some theories have our souls traveling to other planets or galaxies where they reside with alien beings. People who subscribe to these ideas often believe that the cosmic area we return to after our physical death is actually the place we *came* from.

Many people think that this theory of originating from other planets is far-fetched, but we all have a right to think and believe what feels right for us. And hey, it was once believed that the world was flat, remember? Who knows which theories about life after death are really true?

Cities of Gold

Some people who've been there describe outer space's afterlife cities as cities of gold, though these golden cities may not be constructed of the same gold we know here on Earth. It's said that these cities have no grass, no trees, no vegetation. The buildings appear to be modern construction and travel is done via air as opposed to automobiles. By air travel, I mean that a flying device of some type—like a saucer or jet—transports beings from one location to another. Other people who've been there and back report that no transportation is needed. Your mere thought transports you from one location to another.

Ethereal Potpourri

Pleiades is a cluster of seven stars, six of which are visible to the naked eye or with binoculars. Some people believe there is alien life living in and around this cluster, and that we join their world after we die. What makes *this* cluster so special, when there are millions of others? The ancients spoke often of this cluster, and some ancient drawings from the aborigines and other cultures depicted people from this star cluster. Also, people who claim they have had experiences with alien beings refer to this grouping often ... but that's *another* story!

Daily Life (After Death)

As I mentioned earlier, reports of afterlife cities come from people who have had near-death experiences, people who soul travel, and some mediums who can contact the dead. These folks say that in these cities, dead souls exist with the life forms already there. You become a type of light being with a form similar to humans.

Life in these cities includes work, relationships, family, and leisure times, just like on our own planet. The difference is that this planet is evolved to the point that wars, killing, and negativity are not part of the mix. However, there are different social structures. There are beings who have more than others, but it depends on your work ethic and if material goods are important to you. No one goes hungry or is jealous. It's your choice as to what you have and don't have.

You might say it's an ideal version of life on Earth, only better.

The basic afterlife-style includes ...

♦ Entities work, but enjoy what they do.

♦ You love all, but you connect better with some beings than others; these beings become your friends.

♦ Intimacy is part of the existence, but it's soul to soul. It's not physical.

♦ There can be commitment to another soul, but not what we call marriage.

♦ Children exist and souls of young children who have died are allowed to grow to adulthood.

♦ Death doesn't exist. However, if you tire of your location, you can relocate to another planet. (Yes, it's like cosmic real estate.)

♦ Knowledge and education are provided and all entities are always learning.

♦ Food and liquids are not necessary and not a part of this life, but if you choose to eat you can.

♦ There are days and nights, but there's generally more light than darkness.

♦ In the darkness, there are ways and means to generate light, similar to electricity.

All of this is certainly food for thought, isn't it?

From the sound of it, this is a happy, working community—not the afterlife of total relaxation and peace that many of us are expecting. Maybe *this* afterlife is for those souls who are still looking for a little action, who aren't content to drift around on a cloud all day.

Soul Traveling

Some people have out-of-body experiences and conduct *soul travel* (also called *astral travel*) to explore these places of wonder and amazement. Soul travel occurs when we can leave the physical body and allow our *second body*, or our *astral body*, to travel to another dimension. This is not an NDE but an intentional voyage into the unknown with a clear intention of returning. In this altered state, one is said to be able to visit communities of the afterlife and commune with beings we can't even comprehend while trapped in the physical body.

def•i•ni•tion

Soul travel (or astral travel) involves intentionally putting oneself into a trance for the purpose of visiting other dimensions of the universe and planes of the afterlife. In soul travel, your body departs from itself to explore various areas of the universe and/or afterlife. The body that's sent out on the journey is called the **second body** or **astral body**.

Up, Up, and Away

So how does one pack up one's soul and send it on a trip? Very carefully.

Before you start your astral trip, think about where you want to go and what you want to achieve. Do you want to visit planets and planes of the afterlife? Do you want to see the cities and palaces where the souls of the dead reside? Want to ask Grandpa where he hid that gold watch he promised you? There are no limits. Just have a basic idea of what and who you want to encounter. If you can think it, you can find it.

If you decide to attempt it, begin by taking a shower. Visualize all the negativity of your life and the day washing down the drain. Within 45 minutes of showering (so as to not get too many dirt particles back on the body), lie on your bed or somewhere you can recline and relax. Since the physical body can get cold during this process, cover yourself with a blanket or sheet.

If you believe in prayers, say a favorite prayer or make an appeal to your higher power to keep you safe while soul traveling.

Now, close your eyes and follow these steps:

1. Visualize a white light coming up from the bottom of your feet to the top of your head. This light will protect you from anything you may not even know exists out there. Visualizing it coming up your body should put you into an altered state of consciousness, which is where you need to be before your astral flight.

2. Some experts recommend that you visualize a silver cord attached to your body as a type of safety net. Some see it connected to the solar plexus or stomach or navel, others see it connected at the heart. Connect it where you like. The purpose of this is that while you are out there exploring in your second body, your soul can't detach from your physical body and you always have a way home.

3. Visualize yourself leaving your physical body in a second body that looks just like you. This body can be wearing whatever kind of clothing you want; if you feel more comfortable having it in a "natural state," that's okay, too.

4. See your second body rising out of your physical body, toward the ceiling. You should rise to the ceiling and go directly through the ceiling until you are looking down at your roof. It's common on the first attempts to be unable to see yourself getting through the ceiling. If this is the case, make it easy on yourself and picture your astral body leaving through a window or door.

5. Once you're outside, ascend straight up into the outer limits of our atmosphere. Rain, snow, or sleet won't impede you. You're spirit now, and these elements have no effect on your travel.

Once you're in outer space, you'll simply know which direction to follow. In essence, you'll be flying of your own accord through the limits of time and space.

Coming in for a Landing

Eventually you'll be drawn to land in an area that should be what you were looking for. If you didn't have a particular destination but just wanted to see what was out there … well, you'll end up somewhere interesting, that's for sure!

Keep in mind you'll never visit a negative place if you make that your intention from the beginning. If you visit a place of the afterlife that you enjoy, remember it so you can go back again.

You can always opt to end your soul travel by simply thinking, "I am going home." When reentering, come down gently, back through the roof, window, or door and back into your body. After this experience you should fall into a peaceful sleep. The journey may take practice but is worth the effort.

Ethereal Potpourri

Once you're confident that you can go back and forth between dimensions, you can ask questions of and give messages to loved ones who've passed over.

Keeping Fear in Check

Many people are fearful of soul traveling. If that's the case, I have a perfect solution: don't even consider doing it! If you're bent on going on a soulful trip but have just a little bit of fear, here are a few tips to keep in mind:

- Remember that the silver cord will always guide you home.

- Always say a little prayer or affirmation before the trip to ensure safe passage.

- Do this when no one is around. If you have someone else in the bed next to you (this includes pets) and they roll over or push you, your second body will come crashing down. If your second body were to come crashing down for any reason, you won't get hurt, but it will startle you—and you don't need extra excitement on this trip!

Cosmic Drifter

Some believe that that when the soul is free of the body and lessons to be learned, it doesn't have to dwell in one location. It's free to travel from galaxy to galaxy, dimension to dimension, plane to plane. It's pure energy that is exploring. In other words, at this point, the spirit has earned the right of total freedom. It can visit anyone and anything it wants to—no spaceship needed. You need only your intention to launch you from point A to point B.

Because this is a state of consciousness and there is no body or resemblance of body included, food, work, and play are not necessary. The soul can jet around quickly or simply float in a bliss that we can't comprehend, free from any attachments. It needs nothing to exist. It exists as a form of peace and love.

Now, some of us on Earth may think this sounds awfully boring, but it's important to remember that the afterlife likely includes feelings we can't comprehend. In any event, total freedom of the universe and what it has to offer sounds pretty good to me!

A Solo Journey?

Bear in mind that cosmic trekking isn't like traveling abroad on Earth. It's a consciousness in a nonphysical existence *without* the burdens of other people's influences or ideas.

So … will we see our loved ones on our journeys? I believe that perhaps we can connect with other space voyagers in the afterlife, but it would only be for a short time. When the soul is free, it needs to continue its freedom. Dealing with another soul's objectives isn't being true to thine own self. Therefore, as I mentioned earlier in this chapter, you might visit with another soul, you might explore together for a time, but you aren't chained to someone else's path.

Eternal Thoughts

It's life, Jim, but not as we know it.

—Mr. Spock speaking to Captain Kirk, from the TV show *Star Trek*

Going Back

So there you are, a cosmic drifter, just a floating orb of love and light, free of attachment and needing nothing to exist in ecstasy. You're simply in a state of being. With that consciousness, you wouldn't think of anything else, would you?

Once the soul has achieved this highest level of being, can it go back to a lesser level? It can if it wills it. When you've evolved to such an existence, you're given the right to do whatever you like. By "lesser level," I don't mean returning to Earth, but going back to a different dimension such as a city of gold. The soul still has the opportunity to explore, if only for seconds at a time, and then go back to its state of being.

In this instance, think of the soul as a retiree. That person usually doesn't want to go back to the workaday life, but now and then, he or she might think that it would be interesting to work at the old job again—just for an hour or so, just to remember how it felt.

Some would say that if consciousness had *really* evolved there would be no desire for this comeback. But then again, perhaps this is what keeps the soul in this state of exhilaration—the rare trip back.

The Least You Need to Know

- Mediums, soul travelers, people who have had near-death experiences, and stories of the ancients have formed many ideas of the afterlife cities and locations.

- Some people believe life after death consists of cities of gold, crystal palaces, and beautiful gardens.

- While alive, you can do your own soul traveling.

- Cosmic travel without limitations may be possible in the afterlife.

Chapter 17

You Can't Rush Meeting Your Higher Power

In This Chapter

◆ Upsetting the natural balance

◆ If you leave early, you're still coming back again

◆ The soul and suicide

◆ Turning off life support: does the soul live on?

I've discussed what happens to the soul when the body dies by natural causes, accidents, or illnesses—events that we usually try to avoid, as most of us try to hang on to this life for as long as possible. We think, act, make laws, and have systems in every aspect of life to preserve and enforce the sanctity of life. But what happens when we interrupt the natural order of life and cosmic law?

Those who believe in reincarnation believe that we are here to learn lessons that will help our spiritual growth and allow us to gain knowledge. So ending your own life is like dropping out of school. Does the shortcut help or hurt? And even if you who don't believe in reincarnation, do you think your higher power won't notice you slipped past him before it was your natural time to go?

In this chapter, we'll talk about what might happen to the soul when it enters the next world before its time, whether a person makes that decision for themselves or for another person.

We Try So Hard to Live!

At most given moments we do everything we can to preserve our life. We try to stay in shape, we take medications to keep us alive, we attempt to eat right (some people even cut out bacon and butter sandwiches—except for me) and typically, even if we don't live the perfect life, most of us want to stay in the realm of the living. Therefore, is it a reasonable thought to expect no consequences to the ending of a life when all rational humans make the efforts we do to preserve it? In a universe that demands law and order everywhere, what makes us think that any unnatural interference would go unnoticed?

We're here to grow as souls within this lifetime. We should be striving to awaken our sleeping spirit and allow it to reach a higher nature while we're here on Earth. If we could just drop out of life whenever we felt like it, we'd have to ask what the purpose of that would be. If indeed there is a purpose for each of us on Earth, then it makes sense that the unnatural ending of a life upsets the balance of life as a whole. And if you believe in reincarnation, this balance is really knocked out of whack—souls arrive for a life review way before they're supposed to, and then they have to be sent right back to Earth (we'll get to this in the following section).

Ethereal Potpourri

We tend to think of how suicide affects the emotional health of those left behind. But think about this: each soul is here to learn lessons. When a loved one leaves this life too soon, it affects the growth of *their* loved ones' souls.

Each soul has a purpose. We are *all* here for spiritual growth, and this growth takes time and opportunity. So whether you clean fish for a living or you perform brain surgery, you're part of the balance of life. You can't jump ship too soon, or it rocks the entire boat, so to speak.

You Can't Fool Reincarnation

Do the methods by which we experience death of the physical body have an effect on what the soul experiences after death? According to some theories, it certainly does!

The opportunity of the soul to incarnate, to live and express through a divine plan set in place at conception, is thrown away when a person commits suicide. It's like saying to God or your higher power that life is worthless.

So You Think Life's Not Fair

Sometimes when people are considering ending their lives prematurely, they say, "Well, life's not fair. All of these terrible things happen to me and not to anyone else!"

In this way, we try to reconcile the seeming injustices of life. But there are those who would say that bad luck or life not turning out the way you want is nothing more than your paying off bad karma. This is the "what goes around comes around" theory. You're just making amends for things you've done either in this lifetime or a past lifetime. And as you do this, your soul is learning and growing!

Make Your Own Path

The seeming injustices of life *can* be reconciled. God or the Supreme Being doesn't reward or punish; we reward and/or punish ourselves by our own actions. Our failures teach us some things and our successes teach us other things—I assure you, almost everything in life is a learning experience!

All of this learning brings us right back to the reincarnation theory. If you end your life, then you haven't learned all the lessons your soul needs to learn. How do we know this? Because you were supposed to have more time on this Earth, during which you would have learned more lessons. So you're coming right back to learn those lessons. And again, you won't get credit for suffering through *some* of those learning experiences already—you'll restart life at the very beginning.

> **Eternal Thoughts**
>
> Life is better than death, I believe, if only because it is less boring, and because it has fresh peaches in it.
> —Alice Walker, American author

Life After Suicide

Suicide breaks the natural order of things; the going out and coming in of the soul are both interrupted. But it's even more than that. In addition, the soul can't go to the next level of incarnation, because it has to turn around and reenter the same type of situation it prematurely relinquished.

"What?!" you ask. "How can *that* happen?" Well, you read what I wrote, and I wrote what I meant: the soul of a person who has committed suicide has to turn right around and come back in and live out the life it left. It won't be the same *exact* life, obviously, but it will be a very similar situation—only not as good. In fact, the life that was abandoned is always a better situation than the new one you're preordained to relive and experience. (You know that saying "you don't know what you have until it's gone"? Well, it applies to this situation perfectly!)

The soul's evolution is realized through the physical life, so it's senseless to end it prematurely. Think of it this way: life is like a race. If you quit too soon, you have to go right back to the starting line, and any progress you made is canceled out. It's best to stay the course and finish the race, no matter what obstacles are in your way.

As our thoughts, deeds, and actions of the past affect the here and now and the future, the actions we set into motion *now* affect the future. If life is ended abruptly and intentionally, do our thoughts, deeds, and actions just disappear? Are they forgiven? Why would they be? Why should they be?

Is a world that operates within the law of cause and effect going to change because we think we can *create* the effects we want? Probably not ….

Don't Lose That Universal Balance

Any disruption to the laws of harmony and balance by actions that are controlled by free will but that work against harmony and nature—and therefore, the soul's evolution—throws nature *and* man out of balance.

Cosmic law operates to restore balance and harmony and strives to maintain it. It's the law of cause and effect. Man's ignorance of the law is no excuse. The effects of our actions will happen whether we realize they will or not.

def•i•ni•tion

Cosmic law is a universal law or a sense of awareness that gives people on Earth the insight of the basic principle of self-preservation against harming themselves or others. It is a principle that defines right from wrong regarding the moral value of life.

No Paradise for You!

When you make the decision to exit planet Earth prematurely, you'll still have the same experiences as those who die naturally. The hook is that eventually, you'll come to a place where the souls become stratified according to their learning experiences. Some souls will be headed for paradise, having learned all of their lessons, and others will be headed back to Earth to learn more. You won't exactly be at the top of the ladder in this situation. You won't come back into a higher life form; as I said before, you'll start back at the beginning.

Perhaps this is the reason some people have such difficult lives. They may be suffering the consequences of mistakes or choices they made in past lives.

The life taken by suicide is one that affects many, but none more profoundly than the person who committed the act. The sacred experience of the soul's opportunity to work out or unfold his immortal invisible self is unnaturally terminated and has consequences beyond the conceivable.

Many ancient doctrines stress what they refer to as the evils of suicide and explain that there is a profound mystery concerning this crime against the soul.

Do Suicide Attempts Count Against Your Soul?

If you attempted suicide but didn't die as a result, that doesn't mean that upon death you're going to a low level of existence.

As long as you realize that attempting to take your own life was a bad choice and you've made your life better as a result, then you've made progress. Your soul has grown. In fact, your higher power may be proud that you saw the light of this situation. As a result, you'll see the *divine* light of love and peacefulness.

In other words, a failed attempt at taking your life could be a great big learning experience for the soul. Does that give you permission to try taking your life? No! If you think about self-destruction but realize you need help and never attempt it, that's even *better*.

Turning Off Life Support

There are many religious, spiritual, and moral issues about turning off life support on someone who may be brain dead, or has been described as a "vegetable."

The issue, for the purposes of this book, is what happens to the soul that is alive in a body that's comatose. Even though the body isn't functioning, is the soul somehow still learning lessons by observing those around it or in other ways we do not understand? Or has it already taken off for a better place while loved ones and medical

personnel keep a spiritless shell alive for no purpose other than the possible guilt of
loved ones or the lack of understanding in order to make a decision?

Whose Soul Is Most Affected?

We're talking about a decision to end the physical life of an individual, and it shouldn't
be taken lightly. We should begin to understand that no matter what religious belief
one may subscribe to, there are universal laws and principles that operate equally and
are not suspended but can be overcome by self-mastery, by ceasing the opportunity to
live out a full life.

But when it comes down to a choice between letting a loved one linger and turning
off life support, how can you know what's right—and maybe more importantly, what's
best for the person lying in the bed and his or her soul's existence?

The true potential for trouble lies with the person who may be chosen to have to
make that decision.

This is a tough responsibility, and the wrong choice could have karmic consequences.
That said, it's imperative to form an intelligent philosophy of life regarding the existence of the soul and its purpose before one is put into a position to make the decision.

There are those who say that when there is no brain
activity the soul has already left the body.

> **Ethereal Potpourri**
>
> When a loved one is
> declared to be in a
> "vegetative state," some people
> rely on their intuition or gut feel-
> ing as to whether the soul of
> this person has already crossed
> over. Others attempt to telepathi-
> cally communicate with the spirit
> of the person and get a sense of
> where he or she is, cosmically.

If someone is being kept alive by artificial means but
there *is* brain activity and his or her wishes are not
to be kept alive artificially, in many people's philosophies, this would not be suicide. This is why it is often
important to talk to people about this topic so if the
time arises one knows what action to take—so that
they're clear on your wishes, and you're clear on theirs.
In any event, it's good to search your heart and form
some type of philosophy on this topic, so you're comfortable with your own belief system and know you're
doing the right thing.

Dialing for Help

A chaplain once told me a very fascinating story that applies to this very subject. There was a man who had been in a coma for years. His family had become exhausted and financially depleted from keeping him alive on a life-support system.

At the point of giving up, they asked the chaplain for his advice. The chaplain felt that this wasn't something he could really advise them on, since he didn't know them well. However, since they were obviously in anguish over this decision, he told them he would meet with them that evening. The chaplain went back to his home to take a break and to think about what he would tell this family when he spoke to them later that night.

As the chaplain sat with his thoughts about this family, the police arrived at his door, responding to two 911 calls that had been placed from the chaplain's phone. The chaplain told them that it must have been a mistake; he was the only person who lived there and he had not made the calls; in fact, he hadn't used the phone at all that day. They asked whether he'd had trouble with his phone lines in the past; the chaplain assured them that he hadn't. As a precaution, the police took a look around the house. They saw nothing suspicious and left.

Suddenly, the chaplain thought of the man in the coma.

If you could not communicate using your body, could a soul possibly do something to send a message that it wanted to live? He immediately went to the hospital.

He told the man's family what had happened to him; he told them he thought it was a cry for help—a cry for life. The family didn't turn off the life support. A few days later the man came out of his coma and went on to live a normal and healthy life!

Now, I'll admit this is by no means a normal occurrence, and you can take it any way you wish. Skeptics will tell you it was just a coincidence, but those of us who believe in signs, signals, and communication beyond our comprehension will say that this guy was good at making cosmic phone calls for help. So why didn't he call earlier? Well, some people believe that a soul learns lessons while the body is in a coma; perhaps it took this man this long to gain the knowledge to communicate with the outside world.

Of course, not everyone will be so lucky as to receive a cosmic message from a loved one who's hovering between two worlds. For these people, I say you must be comfortable with your own belief system and make decisions based on what you know to be true. If you do this, then any decision you make will sit well with you.

The Least You Need to Know

◆ According to the rules of reincarnation, if you commit suicide you have to come back and start all over—and it may be a worse existence than you have now.

◆ If a soul is sent to another dimension before its time because of a decision by a family member or loved one, it goes to the same place it would have had it died in a natural way.

◆ One should form a philosophy and a type of game plan with loved ones as to what should happen in a case of no brain activity or a life that is supported by artificial means.

◆ It's possible a soul can communicate through signs and signals.

18

Voices from Nowhere Here on Earth

In This Chapter

- ◆ Tracking voices that come from nowhere
- ◆ Electronic Voice Phenomena (EVP)
- ◆ Setting up a recording
- ◆ Chitchat in the cemetery
- ◆ Listening in your dreams

Hearing voices in the middle of the night or in an empty room might seem shocking, but it's amazing how many people hear things on occasion. Now, you may be thinking, "I don't know anyone who hears voices," but hearing someone call your name when there's no one around is the type of incident that many people don't want to admit, either for fear of being thought of as "crazy" or because they just don't know how to handle it.

And what about those dreams where departed loved ones speak to you and tell you everything's all right? These incidents can't be real—or can they? And how would you know, in any event? Is there some way to prove that what you're hearing is really coming from the other side?

In this chapter, I'll talk about what voices from the afterlife might mean, and how, when, and why you might go about capturing and/or interpreting these eternal voices.

Yoo-Hoo! Where Are You?

It's evening and you're lying in bed or reading in a chair. Suddenly, you hear music or voices and think you left the radio or television on. You get up to check and find that no, you didn't. Maybe the neighbors have their radio or television turned up way too high. You lean an ear out the window for verification of this, but no, that's not where the sound is coming from, either.

Suddenly, you hear it again—laughing, shuffling, and glasses clinking. Why, it sounds like a party! (And no one invited you?!) Now it's driving you nuts. *Where are those voices coming from?*

Perhaps you track the noise down and quietly approach the room you think the voices are coming from. If you don't hear the voices behind a door, it might be down a stairwell or in another ill-defined area of the house. The sounds become louder and louder as you approach. Feeling brave, you gently turn the door knob and ease open the door.

The voices and sounds abruptly stop, and the room is silent—and empty. You're left wondering if this sort of thing has ever happened to anyone else and why this is happening at all. You are not alone! The following section contains two stories about real-life encounters with ghostly visitors.

Ghost Parties

Rest assured, you're not the only person to hear mysterious voices. The story of the Walker Plantation is an especially compelling account of ghostly noises. In the article "Party Ghosts Once Inhabited the Walker Plantation House" from the *Fayette County Review* (Somerville, Tennessee) dated July 21, 2004, writer Nancy Brannon tells the story of Kathryn and Walter Foster, owners of the Walker Plantation, who repeatedly heard strange noises in their home.

Kathryn says, "I was in the bedroom and I heard a noise that sounded like someone had left the radio or TV on. It sounded like voices with some nondescript music playing in the background. When I would go into the other room, the sound would stop."

In fact, all the members of the Foster family heard the noises (as did a painter doing some work at the home) but never discussed it with each other until their teenage daughter asked her mother if she ever heard people talking in the house. They all agreed they did, but when they would walk into the room, the voices would stop.

A similar account of a ghostly get-together is that of the Novak family in Seattle, Washington.

When the family moved into their 97-year-old home, they were excited about the project and the possibilities. After a busy day of moving, the family ordered take-out and sat on their unpacked boxes in the living room to eat and celebrate their new home. Unexpectedly, all of them heard music and laughter coming from their front porch. "Oh no, not noisy neighbors," Mr. Novak said. However, they thought it might be a welcome committee at the entranceway and decided to investigate.

When they opened the front door to the porch, the sounds ceased! They went back to their living room, sat down, and the murmur started again. Mrs. Novak went to the door again; after opening it just a few inches, the voices stopped. Immediately, Mrs. Novak proceeded to set up a set of wind chimes she had unpacked earlier outside her front door. She told me she had read in an article that the sound and movement of wind chimes would disperse any bad vibrations or, better yet, ghosts. It seemed to work, as the family never had a problem again.

Did the wind chimes *really* get rid of ghostly visitors? You decide. To this day, wind chimes still sing at the entrance of this old but charming home.

> **Ethereal Potpourri**
>
> Some funeral processions sometimes take a different route home from the gravesite as opposed to the one they took there. This is believed to confuse the spirit of the departed so it cannot follow anyone home!

Why Doesn't Everyone Hear Ghosts Talking?

You'd think that if it were this easy for people in the afterlife to communicate with the living, we'd all be sitting around having conversations with our dead friends and relatives. Obviously, this isn't the case. Noises like those described here are typically heard in specific areas by specific people. (This isn't to say that you can't try to listen in; I'll talk about using Electronic Voice Phenomena for this purpose in the next section.) There are various theories that may help to explain these types of episodes.

According to several ghost authorities, these sounds could be a place memory. As explained in detail in Chapter 11, a place memory is an image or a voice from the past that has imprinted itself into the atmosphere. This could also explain why the moment someone enters the room or opens a door, the voices stop. The conditions of that area (the atmosphere where the memory "lives") immediately change with the disruption.

def•i•ni•tion

Telepathy is the aptitude of a person to communicate with others, alive or dead, from one mind to another. No tools or equipment are needed. They simply "hear" in their mind.

Further research led me to some interesting concepts about hearing these voices. I was told by numerous paranormal investigators that people who hear voices without any digital equipment (provided they're mentally stable, of course) are typically sensitive or have a sixth sense—whether they know it or not. These special people may pick up sounds or voices the average person cannot. They also may have the gift of *telepathy* and are able to send and receive messages from those on the other side.

Electronic Voice Phenomenon (EVP)

How would you like to communicate with someone who has passed over? According to many paranormal researchers, you can. Using a method called EVP, or Electronic Voice Phenomena, voices from beyond the grave can be preserved on a tape recorder or video camera.

You might be asking yourself, "Why would I want to go to all the trouble of setting up a tape recorder or video camera? If I really want to remember what I heard, I'll just take notes." Ah, but there's the catch! In order to hear the voices, you have to play back what you've recorded. In other words, the voices aren't audible to you unless they're heard via the tape. In fact, it is thought by EVP enthusiasts that the drone of the tape allows those on the other side to rearrange sounds, hence forming audible words.

Talking with the EVP Experts

To learn more about EVP, I contacted two accomplished paranormal researchers. These men provided me with a wealth of engaging information about Electronic Voice Phenomena, including tips for setting up your own EVP experiment, which I'll discuss a little later in this section.

First, a bit about their backgrounds:

- **Al Rauber** has 37 years of experience tracking paranormal activity. He's worked as a consultant on many media projects, including the television shows *Unsolved Mysteries*, *The Other Side*, and *Sightings*. He's considered an expert on the topic of hauntings.

- **Garrett Husveth** is a forensics examiner whose expertise is in digital media. He is a media consultant on the topic of the paranormal, working on projects such as the History Channel's *Haunted History* series. Currently, his work focuses on using the most current technological advances to capture EVP.

When investigating a site and using EVP, this team sets up equipment for an audio and video analysis. Husveth says that they use VHS surveillance tapes, which are useful because you can see that no one was in the area or you can also verify that no one spoke.

Listening to the tapes after the session is completed can be time-consuming and monotonous. (Husveth doesn't recommend it, but says some people read a book or work on their computers while listening for evidence of EVP.) Husveth discounts anything that is questionable or may have come from voices of the living in the given area.

Sometimes after the long wait to pick up voices you may get just one or two words, but they can be very exciting. For example, if you ask a question such as "Are you a male or female?" you might get a one-word answer, "Male." Or something might be added like "the basement," which would mean you should perhaps look in the basement for something.

Visit their website at www.hauntednewjersey.com for detailed accounts of their paranormal investigations!

Ethereal Potpourri

If you're interested in capturing a voice from the next life but wonder if you're qualified to do so, rest assured. You don't have to be a noted paranormal researcher with an extensive background and expensive experiment to do your own recordings. Start out small, with inexpensive equipment and a lot of patience. If you're successful and/or interested enough to continue, then you can spend a little more money on better equipment.

Basic Equipment for Beginners

I talked to several EVP researchers and they all have excellent processes that work for them. Because I can't provide each individual method, I'll give you a general overview of the simplest ways and means to record EVP.

Here's what you'll need:

♦ **A tape recorder.** Try to use one that has a counter so that you can easily note any areas of the tape where you think you've heard a voice or an unusual sound. Recorders using magnetic tapes have been used for years, but digital equipment is fast becoming the tool of choice.

♦ **Name-brand tapes.** If you're trying to capture voices from another dimension, go ahead and splurge on better-quality tapes. Less expensive tapes may have blemishes that could be mistaken for EVP upon playback. If you're asking spirits specific questions, you can purchase a shorter tape (30 minutes), but if you're monitoring a room, you'll have to run a longer tape (60 to 90 minutes).

♦ **An external microphone.** It's important to note that ghostly voices have been reported on telephone answering machines or other recording devices that don't have an external microphone. Many of these sounds are actually caused by the internal workings of the machinery. An external microphone, by contrast, records sounds in the room. The exception to this is when you're using digital equipment.

Ethereal Potpourri

Digital equipment produces what's called a lower sample rate, which results in the noises experts believe dead people use to create their own sounds. Since digital recorders don't produce internal noise, you also won't need an external microphone.

The Actual Recording

Spirit communication can happen anywhere—why not start your EVP experiments in your own residence? If you prefer to go to a location where you think there is para-normal activity, that's fine as well. (Cemeteries are not recommended, for reasons I'll discuss a little later in this chapter.)

You can attempt to do an EVP in your home by setting up your equipment and simply asking a spirit to identify itself. The place you record doesn't necessarily have to be known for having spirit or ghost activity, but you should be constant in your location and the time of day you try to connect for best results. In other words, if you don't succeed try, try again, but do it in the same place and at the same time. Paranormal researcher Al Rauber says the reason for this is because those on the other side will then understand there is some type of consistency or an open channel from that area. This will develop a relationship with these spirits and a level of trust.

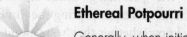

Ethereal Potpourri

Generally, when initiating an EVP experiment, you can ask if there's anyone out there who wants to communicate. It doesn't have to be anyone specific.

As you would expect, you should keep background noise to a minimum. Close the windows. Turn off phones, fax machines, and anything else that could be picked up as EVP, including noisy air-conditioning units or creaky ceiling fans. However, as I stated earlier, Rauber says that *some* types of background noises can actually enhance EVPs. EVP researchers believe those who have crossed over use white noise (which is a drone or a hum as opposed to a clinking or a clattering) to rearrange the sounds into words. I suggest trying the recording both ways—with no background noise, and with a low, steady background noise.

To begin the recording, set up your equipment on a solid, stationary surface like a desk or table, and turn on the recorder. State your intentions: "I am attempting to communicate with dead Uncle Winston. Uncle Winston, this is Jodi. I am attempting an experiment to record your voice. Is there anything you would like to say?"

Do *not* start out with "Uncle Winston, where is that safety deposit box you had?" Give the spirit a chance to get comfortable with this setup and to allow the initial communication to come through. (The big message here is that they all *want* to come through.)

Once you identify yourself and establish an open channel of communication, sit quietly and let the recorder continue recording for approximately 30 to 60 seconds after each question. This gives the spirit an opportunity to respond. At this time, you won't hear anything and you shouldn't *say* anything. Remember: *the voices are heard when you play the tape back, not while you are recording.*

For example, "Uncle Winston, it's your niece Jodi trying to get in touch with you. Can you give me any indication you can hear me?"

Later, you might try, "Uncle Winston, I am trying to make contact using recording devices. Can you manage to make any type of sound so I know you are here? A 'yes' or 'no' would be great."

After pausing, go ahead and ask another question to someone else or the same spirit. Do *not* keep repeating the same question because while you're recording, you won't know whether they've responded or not. (How would you like it if someone kept asking you, "Are you there? ... Are you there? ... Are you there?" Even dead people can get annoyed!)

When the recording time is over, play the tape back to see if you've recorded anything.

Tips from the Pros

Paranormal researchers Rauber and Husveth offer the following tips for a good EVP session:

♦ If other people are present, have each person state his or her name on the tape. This way, you'll have a sample of everyone's voice, which will help to differentiate between their voices and voices from the other side.

♦ State the purpose of your experiment (such as "Uncle Winston, I'm trying to contact you ..."). Let the spirits know your intentions, and you might just get a better result.

♦ When you're recording and a car passes, for example, or a cat meows, it's important to note on the tape what has just happened (by saying aloud, "My stomach just rumbled") so you don't forget what was heard. Additionally, if anyone else is listening to the tape and they weren't present for the recording, they'll recognize that what they're hearing is not EVP.

♦ There should be no whispering among attendees or it could be mistaken for EVP.

♦ Record on only one side of the tape to prevent a bleed-through from the other side.

♦ Timing is important. Usually no one comes through if you're in mourning over someone's recent passing. The person trying to communicate may want it so badly that they may not be realistic about what they're hearing. However, EVPers do tell us on occasion those who just passed do communicate, but it is rare.

♦ Voices will typically form two- or three-word messages, although with more practice you may be able to pick up longer correspondence.

You may also want to keep a journal noting the date, time, and place of the recording. Some experts believe that the weather and phases of the moon can also have an effect on EVP experiments, so you'll want to make note of those conditions as well. Also make a note of the recorder's counter measurements where you suspect you've picked up EVP so that you can easily refer to it later.

How do you evaluate the tape? In other words, how do you know where and when to tune in and pay close attention? When using analog tape, what you are looking for is a change in the pattern or cadence of the tape. All tapes have a rhythm to them. Where there is a break in the rhythm is usually where you find a voice.

> ### Eternal Thoughts
>
> Al Rauber has some interesting insights about the spirits who communicate through EVP. He says that many spirits will take the personalities they exhibited while they were alive into the next world. Therefore, some spirit voices will have a sense of humor, some will be sarcastic, some will be loving, and some will be slightly offensive or threatening.

Can EVP Be Harmful?

Can you put yourself in a dangerous situation by experimenting with EVP? In other words, might you open a door to another dimension where evil ghosts and ghouls are waiting to harm you in some way?

I posed this question to Lisa and Tom Butler, the directors of the American Association of Electronic Voice Phenomena (AA-EVP), a group dedicated to helping others in their pursuit of EVP and Instrumental TransCommunication (ITC). Their names may be familiar to you moviegoers, as they were seen in the bonus feature of the 2005 movie *White Noise*, a suspense thriller starring Michael Keaton that explores communication with the dead using EVP. The Butlers also assisted in marketing the film after the movie was completed.

The movie focuses on a frightening series of communications between Keaton's character and his dead wife. In the bonus feature of the movie, it's stated that one out of every twelve EVP recordings is of a negative nature (meaning that an evil spirit of some sort rears its head or that a terrifying experience will come of the communication). The Butlers say that this is simply not true and that there is no proof to support that statement.

Tom Butler says that when he's asked about the possible dangers associated with EVP, he asks the questioner where they're getting their information from. Was it the movie, church, or a friend who influenced them to think this way? Lisa adds, "If you're easily scared and you want to be, then you might be." Both Butlers say that in all of their years of research, they've never known an instance where anyone was harmed via EVP.

I think it's true that if you're looking to be scared about something, you may create it within your own mind. I'm going to tell you what my mother used to tell me: "Don't worry about the dead ones—worry about the live ones."

Ethereal Potpourri

Some people conduct EVP experiments for the thrill of it, while others are more scientific in nature, looking for evidence of the other side or wanting to seriously communicate with loved ones who have passed on. Perhaps your state of mind at the outset of the experiment has a lot to do with whether you end up being frightened by the results!

Satisfying the Skeptics

Here are a few questions that skeptics typically ask about EVP:

- **Why do ghosts only seem to whisper on the EVP recordings?** This just isn't true. Although some voices may be soft, entities can come through as a person talking in a normal tone of voice.

- **Why do you have to have some type of noise in the background to pick up the voices?** The entities rearrange the sound to form words as a way of communication. Background noise may be helpful, but not necessary.

- **Why are the voices always heard in the language that the listener happens to understand?** According to Rauber, "You have to remember that you're dealing with an intelligence here." In other words, entities understand that we need to be spoken to in a language we can understand; this is possible since entities are on a higher plane of intelligence than we are. When a message comes through in a different language, it's because the person taping understands the language. They don't just use different languages randomly.

Chitchat in the Graveyard?

When we think about communicating with the dead, many of us envision calling out to a deceased loved one at their gravesite. In fact, many people claim to hear voices in cemeteries. Is it possible that these are the voices of those who have passed?

Anything's possible, but it's unlikely that you'll have much luck communicating with a dead family member in a graveyard. There are so many sounds of nature and outside interferences that it's difficult to tell what's what, even when you're listening closely.

Those who are mourning a recent death may think they're hearing voices because they want to or need to. The general consensus among ghost hunters, parapsychologists, and paranormal investigators is that voices are rarely heard in graveyards. The paranormal researchers I spoke with agreed that if you're looking for ghosts you most likely won't find them in the cemetery, unless they just happen to be passing (no pun intended).

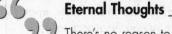

Eternal Thoughts

There's no reason to be the richest man in the cemetery. You can't do any business from there.

—Colonel Sanders, founder of Kentucky Fried Chicken

Think about it: why would a dead person hang around a cemetery when there are so many other things to do and places to go? Those who have just recently passed and are buried may stay close to their remains for just a few days (some religious groups say three days; others say seven) while adjusting to being free of their body, but they don't stay much longer than that. As Rauber says, "These entities don't haunt places where they died or are buried. They come back to places where they have lived and experience life and the processes of living."

Dream Communication from Beyond

People often hear or see dead loved ones while in a dream state. This type of communication is nothing to be alarmed about. The dead are always using different ways to try to communicate with the living.

Actually, I think it is almost polite of deceased loved ones to talk to us in a dream state. This way, we aren't frightened and we can always have peace of mind, thinking "It was just a dream." Regardless, when you're in an altered state of consciousness, just before you are falling asleep or waking up, your intuitive sense is more open. Therefore, voices you hear may be very real. Sometimes people will say, "I was almost asleep and I thought I heard my great-grandfather calling my name." Well, guess what? He may have been trying to.

Documenting Dreams About the Dead

Pay attention to any voice communication you hear in a dream state. Write it down the next morning when you're fully awake. If it happens often, keep a journal of what

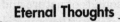

> **Eternal Thoughts**
>
> Probably a dozen times since their death I've heard my mother or father, in an ordinary conversational tone of voice, call my name. They had called my name often during my life with them.... It doesn't seem strange to me.
>
> —Carl Sagan, American astronomer and astrobiologist

was said. You may even want to talk back telepathically and see what kind of results you receive.

After dreaming/hearing the voice of someone who has passed, you should attempt to remember the tone of the voice. Note different voice inflections, such as …

- Calm
- Generally pleasant
- High pitched
- Excited
- Weepy

Differentiating between emotions may help you to pinpoint the message behind the voice. For example, dream interpreters will tell you that if the voice is pleasant and happy, good news awaits. If the voice is excited and anxious, it could be a warning from the other side that something negative will happen. I believe if you're given a warning in a dream via a voice tone you can do something to prevent a situation that hasn't taken place.

And just remember, voices in your dreams don't have to be precognitive. A spirit from the other side might just be dropping in to say a quick hello.

Go Away—I'm Sleeping!

If you're not interested in hearing utterances in a dream state, you can stop it from happening. Before you fall asleep, say to yourself or out loud that you want to block the communication from the other side. You can say something like, "I do not allow the presence from the other side to come into my dreams at night," or, "I don't want to hear from any dead people. Thank you!"

If it doesn't work, keep trying. They'll get the message. Your thoughts and actions are stronger than you think.

The Least You Need to Know

- Hearing noises that sound like parties or groups of people could be an impression from the past that has imprinted itself into the atmosphere.

- EVP is Electronic Voice Phenomena, the practice of recording spirit voices from the afterlife on blank tapes.

- Reports of ghosts or spirits in graveyards are overrated. They don't stay close to their remains for long periods of time if at all.

- Hearing the departed talk to you in a dream could well be real, but you have control over whether to allow the communication or not.

Part 4

The Return to the Planet

Ever wonder if you've been here before, in some other body, in another place and time? You're not alone. Reincarnation—the thought that the soul reaches the other side, only to turn around and come back at some point—is central to many belief systems. In these chapters, you'll read how the process of reincarnation works, whether you might someday come back as an animal, and how to explore your past lives.

Chapter 19

Guided by Spiritual Helpers

In This Chapter

- ◆ Working as a spirit guide
- ◆ Methods for contacting your main guide
- ◆ What do guides look like?
- ◆ Different guides for different needs

Life after death isn't just about floating in a heavenly realm, relaxing, and soaking up bliss. Some spirits feel compelled to help those who are still struggling on Earth. And I don't mean that they just pop in from time to time to see who needs a hand—these spirits actually *work* as spirit guides.

Granted, this isn't exactly like working in the rat race; in fact, this type of work is probably more enjoyable than we can imagine. The spirits who sign on for this job are following a vocation, a calling—doesn't that sound like someone you'd like to have on your side when you need advice?

In this chapter, I'll tell you who your main spirit guide may be, and how she or he came to be your helper. I'll let you in on how to contact him or her and how to find other sources of spirit help, too!

What's a Spirit Guide?

In Chapter 5, I talked about the theory that "normal" dead people don't become angels. Angels were created by God and never had a physical form. I think some misunderstanding occurs because the departed can become spirit guides, which are what many of us think of as angels. I know, it can be confusing. I promise, I'll clear everything up in this chapter!

def•i•ni•tion _____

Spirit guides are deceased individuals who offer counsel to still-living people.

A *spirit guide* is someone who lived on Earth, died, and has been chosen to come back from the other side to help and counsel those on Earth. The difference between an angel and a spirit guide is that angels are beings that have never lived on Earth. They have only had an existence in another dimension.

Keep in mind that we're talking about spirit guides who once existed on Earth. There are other types of spirit guides, such as:

- Spiritual beings of advanced intelligence with the capacity for space travel, who come from other planets to aid us individually and give us assistance for the betterment of our spiritual progress.

- Entities from another dimension who were never human, who can phase in and out of our lives, offering advice with only a thought—no transportation needed.

- Ascended Masters, such as Jesus Christ, Buddha, and Kuan Yin, the compassionate deity of the Eastern culture, to name a few. (To learn more about Ascended Masters, turn to Chapter 8.)

- In some instances, angels can act as guides in the form of protection.

I include these here so that you have a complete overview of spirit guides, but for the rest of this chapter, we'll only be talking about guides who have existed in *this* plane of reality.

When I'm Dead, I'm Getting Work as a Spirit Guide

So you want to know what else you can do once you cross over to the other side, other than being blissfully happy?

Well, you might want to come back to work on Earth—and that, too, can bring blissful happiness. The pay is zero, but the satisfaction is tremendous—and besides, you won't have any bills to pay on the other side anyway. (But oh! Those ethereal points you'll earn in your work will do wonders if you are looking to climb the spiritual ladder.)

Yes, you can be a spirit guide when you die. However, you can't just walk into the Supreme Being's office and say, "I'm ready! Send me out there!" You'll need to qualify to land this job.

Spirit guides come in all different forms, even though (or maybe because) they're dead. But there are a few things they all have in common:

- ◆ They've passed over to the other side successfully.

- ◆ They're willing to help guide and teach those on Earth who have asked for help.

- ◆ They only deal within their own expertise or experiences they learned on Earth.

- ◆ They strongly assist the living in looking at their options but they don't necessarily tell the living what to do.

- ◆ They recognize their limitations and don't give false hope to the living person they're counseling.

> **Eternal Thoughts**
>
> Spirit guides come in all shapes and sizes, and are from all different cultures. They can assume any visage, but I assure you, they're trusted valued friends, who will never disappoint you. They have great wisdom and courage and you will hear from them if you're quiet and listen.
>
> —Sylvia Browne, *Contacting Your Spirit Guide*

Spirit guides operate at a higher vibrational level than we do here on Earth: they've already crossed over, went through a life review, and now have the option to stay on the other side, help counsel those on Earth, or incarnate and come back as volunteers for a special purpose.

In other words, they don't have more earthly lessons to learn; they don't even have to be here anymore! They've *chosen* to help guide others through this life.

Contacting Your Spiritual Counselor

Some people think that while we're waiting to incarnate back to Earth, we make arrangements with someone who's with us on the other side to act as our spirit guide. Following this theory, the spirit guide has to be someone who is already dead by the time we're born. So your main spirit guide, for example, can't be your Grandpa Homer, who passed away last year. You couldn't have known him while you were waiting to come back to this life—he was already *here!*

However, some people believe that our main spirit guide can have a helper or two, in which case Grandpa Homer might be a guide for us but in a lesser form.

We contact our spiritual helpers because life is much easier with assistance from a higher source who has more knowledge of our future than we have ourselves. You can call upon as many spirit guides as you like. There are different spirit guides for different things. However, you have one main guide who acts as your general attendant.

There are several ways of getting in touch with your spirit guide. Try them out and see which one works best for you.

Dream a Little Dream of Your Guide

In order to contact your spirit guide, you must decide to do so before you go to sleep. In fact, the day you attempt this dream method of contacting your guide, remind yourself beginning in the morning and periodically throughout the day that *this* is the evening you'll attempt to discover your main spirit guide. Follow these steps:

1. Before you go to sleep, take a shower and wash your hair. As you shower, visualize any negativity from the day washing down the drain. (If you prefer to take a bath, that's okay as well. However, because you ultimately sit in your own dirt, you should end by rinsing off with a quick shower.)

2. Relax your body by breathing in through the nose and blowing out through your mouth three times or any other method that relaxes you.

3. Lie in bed. Silently ask your higher being to give your main spirit guide permission to make itself present in your dream state. An example you can use is, "I give my spirit guide permission to show him- or herself to me tonight in my dream."

4. Go about your bedtime routine as usual. Read a book; turn on the TV; prepare your grocery list for tomorrow. You've already put out the message and now you're just waiting for sleep. It's like planting a seed and going about your normal business until it starts to grow.

5. Hopefully, you'll have a dream where you encounter your guide. This initial contact may be fleeting, but since you're aware you're attempting to communicate, you'll know intuitively in your dream state that this is your spirit guide. This is actually a form of *lucid dreaming*, which means the dreamer *knows* that he is dreaming.

def•i•ni•tion

Lucid dreaming is the conscious understanding that you're in a dream state. As the result of this consciousness, you have the ability to control the process and the makeup of the dream. This gives you the ability to talk to people or entities in your dream, such as spirit guides.

If you can achieve this state, you can actually start to ask your guide questions while dreaming.

This process may take time, even weeks or months, for some to master, while others will hit on it the first time. Bear in mind that you may not achieve a level of lucidity on your first few attempts, but I highly recommend that you continue to try, as the results are extraordinary.

When you awake, jot down information about your dream. And remember: the more you contact your guide through lucid dreaming, the more you can ask questions and receive guidance.

Without permission or an invitation, spirit guides are reluctant to come through to us. However, there are many reported cases of guides trying to make contact with someone who has no understanding of what's happening. Therefore, sometimes people have recurring dreams about strangers trying to deliver a message. The dreamers don't know who the messengers are or why they've appeared.

I'll Meet You Halfway

Contacting your spirit guide in an astral meeting, or on another level of existence, involves inducing an *out-of-body experience*. Attempting to contact your guide in this manner can make the entire trip down to Earth easier for the spirit guide.

def•i•ni•tion

An **out-of-body experience** usually involves the sense that you're leaving your physical body and a second body—exactly like your physical body—is *floating* outside of it. The second body can move through solid objects and travel anywhere it wants to go. It can go to another location on Earth or travel beyond earthly planes. It can also look down on your physical body.

Out-of-body experiences can be used for many reasons, but for our purposes, I'm going to focus solely on contact with those who passed over or with spirit guides.

In this form of interaction, you must first learn how to carry out an out-of-body experience. The method I've included here is fairly easy to master.

The time of day for an out-of-body experience doesn't matter, but some feel night-time is better, as the energy of the planet is more calm. As always, when you're doing any type of meditation or contemplation, the space you are in should be serene and free from any distractions (like phones and TVs).

Now, begin ...

1. Sit in a chair with your feel planted firmly on the ground or lie down on your bed, floor, sofa, or wherever you're most comfortable. Make sure you don't accidentally fall asleep! You're trying to achieve an *altered* state of consciousness.

2. Close your eyes. Visualize a white light of protection in the form of a cloud around your entire body. This is a protective device from negative energy coming into your space.

3. Now visualize your astral body, or second body, floating above you. It has the same clothing that you're wearing. It makes an exit through a door, window, right through the ceiling, or any way it chooses to leave the room. Your other body will remain exactly where it is.

4. Some people see a cord connected to the body in some area as a safety net so they can't go too far with no way of coming back home.

5. With the knowledge that you're going into outer space to meet your spirit guide, begin your ascent. See yourself floating into the universe. When you see a place, dimension, planet, or whatever you feel works, stop and wait for your guide to show up. Don't worry—he will.

6. When you spot your guide, you can ask his name, ask for messages, ask questions, or obtain any information you want. That's what they're there for!

7. Whenever you feel ready, give thanks and begin your descent back home and back into your body. Open your eyes, focus, and slowly get up.

8. Write down the information you obtained.

9. If this doesn't work the first time, try again.

There will come a time when you may doubt if you're really receiving messages from those who on the other side or if you're making it up. The only way to know for sure is to watch for the results of your visits, which is why writing down your experiences is so important. You might want to get a journal or notebook especially for this purpose.

Automatic Writing

Another technique of contacting those special souls who want to guide us to a happier state of being on this planet is through automatic writing. No dreaming, no out-of-body journeys, just a pen and paper and a lot of concentration.

Automatic writing involves putting yourself into an altered state of consciousness or a trance, asking questions of your spirit guide, and letting your fingers do the talking, so to speak. Your hand starts to write the message, but you won't be aware of what's being written at the moment. (If you are aware of it, it probably won't make sense until after the session.) The writing could be whole sentences or simple words or phrases.

Here's how to do automatic writing to contact your guide:

1. Pick a place that's quiet and free of diversions.

2. Have paper and a pen or pencil available.

3. Sitting at a table or desk is best. Close your eyes.

4. See yourself protected by a cloud of white light from over the top of your head to under your feet and at least 3 feet around your body.

5. To relax, inhale and exhale deeply. When you're relaxed or in an altered state, ask your spirit guide to tell you her name. Invite her into your room.

6. Start writing your first thoughts. Just go with the flow. If a name doesn't come up, just write whatever you are led to write.

7. Start asking questions, either silently or out loud, and write the answers down whether you think you're making them up or not. If you don't have any questions, just ask your guide if she has a message for you about anything you should know.

8. When you're done asking questions, stop.

Sometimes the messages or answers will be profound and other times the messages may appear to be gibberish. Regardless, keep the papers and review them at a later time to see if the information is clearer.

Guided Meditation

Another easier and interesting way to contact one of our partners on the other side is through another party here on Earth during what's called a *guided meditation*. In a guided meditation, a facilitator (who may be a psychic, spiritual medium, or seasoned meditation practitioner) might lead a group of people through a meditation technique for the purpose of contacting your spirit guides. All you have to do is sit there and do what he or she tells you to do. (This can also be a one-on-one experience.) Guided meditation is very relaxing and takes the stress of doing it all by yourself off of you.

def•i•ni•tion

Guided meditation is a term used to describe the process of a person or group being led into a trancelike state by a medium or another facilitator.

You can also find videos and audiotapes to conduct a guided meditation in the privacy of your own home (see Appendix B).

Private Meditation/Visualization

The last method I offer is one of the most commonly used, which doesn't necessarily mean that it'll be best for you. Try out different methods, or choose the one that sounds like it might work well for you.

This method starts in very much the same way as the out-of-body experience. Sit in a chair or lie down on a bed. Protect yourself by visualizing a cloud of white light around your body. When you feel you're in an altered state, invite your main spirit guide to make an appearance. Then just wait until you see a being in your mind.

And then …

1. When you see your spirit guide, ask for a name. Sometimes a name will be given—but sometimes not.

2. Once you make contact, you can communicate by asking questions and receiving answers telepathically.

3. When you end the session, which is whenever you feel the urge to, always give thanks to your spirit guide.

As with all the other approaches, this one takes practice. So try and try again if you must, but don't give up.

Now, you might be wondering how the spirit guide will appear to you. In your mind, you might see one walking toward you, or see one in a park, or suddenly find yourself next to a pyramid in Mexico where one appears. You may see yourself standing at a dock while a ship moors. Suddenly someone walks off the boat—and hey, it's your spirit guide.

How they present themselves and in what type of environment is up to the spirit guides. Be prepared to see anything and to go anywhere!

More About Spirit Guides

The methods discussed in this chapter are ways and means to get in touch with your main spirit guide. But you *do* have more than one guide—and I should warn you now, their appearance may startle you!

What Do They Look Like?

You must remember that some of these guides who once looked like any of us, although in different times or centuries, no longer have a body. Therefore, when they present themselves to you, they attempt to take the form of what they used to look like from hairstyles, to clothing, to race, size, and weight.

Normally, this isn't a problem. For instance, you might have a spirit guide from medieval times who presents herself in period clothing. Perhaps a Native American dressed in warrior attire will show his face—or an Egyptian princess complete with headdress and elaborate jewelry!

Eternal Thoughts

You can be reunited with loved ones in the after-life. You may also have run-ins with that playground bully from fourth grade.

—Horace J. Digby, winner of the Robert Benchley Society Award for Humor

Now, here's the trouble: not all guides can remember what they used to look like! I've heard many accounts of people who said their spirit guides were carrying their heads, or they looked like animals or were otherwise startling in their appearance. It's really not their fault, so don't get upset if yours are not the most attractive guides on the block. You'll get used to them after a while.

Remember, it's not the appearance of the spirit guide that's important, but the message he or she brings.

Lesser Guides

We've been discussing your main spirit guide, who can help you with general questions about your life plan or which direction you should be moving in; however, I also mentioned that you can have more than one guide. These "lesser" guides, as they're called, are available for specific questions that fall into the area of expertise they had while they were on Earth.

For example, if you're starting a business and would like some insights about whether you're doing the right thing, you might ask for help from a spirit guide who has direct knowledge of your endeavor. If you're in the accounting field, ask for a guide who had knowledge of math and numbers. If you work in fashion, ask for a guide who had a flair for clothing design.

Ethereal Potpourri

Don't assume that all spirit guides lived centuries ago. People die every day, after all, and there are plenty of modern-minded "helper" guides waiting to help. Computer problems? Ask for a computer whiz who passed on. Can't run the business dad left you after he passed on? Give him a cosmic call and have him come and guide you!

You don't have to ask for a specific person unless you want to. But remember, not all spirits have decided to help the living or are qualified to become spirit guides. That's why you may achieve more help if you let your higher power pull from the pool, so to speak. It's like going to a career counselor at a free agency and settling for whoever they give you. You might say something like, "I want to have an acting career. Who out there is willing to give me tips and guidance to achieve my dream?" You can have 20 spirit guides and call each one for different concerns.

If a lesser spirit guide isn't especially helpful, give them up. (You can't change your main guide—remember, you chose him or her before you came to this planet.) Always thank a lesser guide before moving on. It's just like here on Earth. You may go to a well-meaning counselor, but he or she just isn't the right person for you. If this is the case, try to find someone else.

What Skeptics Say

Skeptics often want to know why we can't conjure up spirit guides at a moment's notice. "If they're so willing to help, then where are they?" skeptics ask. Well, saying "talk to me," "appear to me," or "give me a sign" usually won't work. Guides are limited. They have insights beyond ours but they aren't of the supreme intelligence. It also helps to ask for help from spirit guides calmly and respectfully instead of demanding it.

The Least You Need to Know

- ◆ Spirit guides are deceased folks who once lived on Earth and are now available to guide the living.

- ◆ We each have one main spirit guide, but others are also available to us.

- ◆ We can contact our main guides through meditation, lucid dreaming, or automatic writing.

- ◆ There are "lesser" spirit guides for different specific needs in your life.

- ◆ If one lesser spirit guide doesn't work, give thanks and try someone else.

Chapter 20

Children Who See the Departed

In This Chapter

◆ Your child's imaginary friend?

◆ How to handle a child with a sixth sense

◆ Balancing extrasensory abilities and childhood

◆ The story of a child with spirit-world connections

◆ A five-year-old cosmic communicator

Children are beautiful, innocent spirits. They start out in life not knowing that they are restricted in their actions because of their human minds and bodies. In other words, until someone "sets them straight" about their "limitations," they believe anything is possible—and oftentimes, they're right!

With that said, children, especially preschoolers, may go beyond what's comfortable for adults to hear or think about. These youngsters may actually see dead people and think nothing of it. "Can't everyone see them?" they wonder. These children are simply in tune with their sixth sense—something we *all* have, by the way.

This, of course, goes hand-in-hand with psychic or intuitive ability that these children may possess. But what happens to this ability as these kids grow older? Should parents or guardians discourage it? Or do the little ones forget about it after it has been discouraged and pick it up later as adults? Are these special kids the mediums and psychics of the future, or do they just have overactive imaginations?

Imaginary Friends?

First, let's address the issue of imaginary friends so that we can differentiate between a normal phase of childhood and the extraordinary ability to speak to the dead.

It's very common for children to have imaginary friends. The majority of people tend to think that when a child is playing and talking with someone that no one else can see, it's just the result of the child using her imagination. Because it's not an unusual situation and most kids grow out of this phase on their own, adults don't pay too much attention to these friendships.

> **Eternal Thoughts**
>
> Childhood is measured out by sounds and smells and sights, before the dark hour of reason grows.
>
> —John Betjeman, British author and broadcaster

Parents really have nothing to worry about where imaginary friends are concerned. In fact, psychologists say that having an invisible friend is a good way for a bright child to get out of trouble: "It was my friend Peggy who messed up my room. Blame her, not me!" Having imaginary friends allows your child to express and learn about her emotions, as when she comforts the "friend" when the "friend" is hurt or scared, and also allows your child to learn about sharing.

In addition, the child never feels alone. She has a buddy who has the same interests and they investigate things as a team. Parenting experts suggest that a parent should neither contradict the child nor encourage the friend's presence. Saying things like, "Go tell Peggy we're ready to go to the park" might result in having Peggy hanging around for much longer than necessary.

So there are plenty of reasons that parents might welcome an imaginary friend or two—but what happens when your child tells you her new friend is a dead person?

"I See Dead People"

"I see dead people" is a catchphrase from the 1999 film *The Sixth Sense*. This excellent film makes you think about what children see, feel, and sense when it comes to life after death.

The reason this phrase still sticks with us after all these years is because it's so simple and so true when it comes to the way children express themselves about seeing the departed here on Earth. "I see dead people." What part of it don't you understand?

What's a Parent to Do?

Watching a movie about a child who talks to dead people is one thing. What do you do if your own child claims to have contact with the dearly departed? Should this relationship be encouraged or discouraged? That's a lot to think about. (Certainly, this is *very* different from the child having an imaginary friend, because the communication here is real!) On the one hand, you want to make sure the child is well and isn't suffering from some sort of psychiatric issue; on the other hand, you don't want to hinder the child's natural abilities to pick up communication from the other side—or do you?

What parents do in this situation usually depends on their beliefs. If you don't believe in the paranormal, a *sixth sense*, mediumship, or psychic abilities, you'd most likely try to discourage the child from believing in spirits. But what about parents who *do* believe that these types of communications are possible? What are they to do, encourage the child to talk to ghosts?

If the child continues to have these visions after five years of age or they develop later in childhood, you may be tempted to encourage your child, believing that he may be the next great television medium, he'll make millions, and he'll help people to boot. Not a bad career. But is it really the right thing to do?

> **def•i•ni•tion**
>
> A **sixth sense** refers to extrasensory perception, or ESP. This is the capacity to receive information by means that have nothing to do with your other five senses (taste, sight, touch, smell, and hearing). It involves sensing things that have not been proven by science. It's intuition; a knowing or an awareness of things around you that other people cannot sense.

I'm not implying parents will exploit gifted children. However, sometimes people get overly excited when they feel their offspring has a supernatural ability. And in that situation, it's easy to make poor choices. I think that no matter what parents decide in this situation, they need to proceed slowly and cautiously.

Testing: One, Two, Three ...

Perhaps the first thing a parent should do is to determine if the child is *really* able to speak to the dead or if she just has an overactive imagination. Without taxing the child and without letting her think anything special is going on, you might be able to ask a few simple questions to gain the proof you are looking for.

It's very difficult to test someone's sixth sense (or extrasensory skills). It's even more difficult with kids, because they don't appear to have much control over their powers.

? What Skeptics Say _____

Skeptics often want to know why children who supposedly talk to the dead can't get information from their deceased friends when they're asked to. The reason is that spirits typically appear to children at random; children can rarely bring them front and center at will. When they're under pressure to perform, they can't totally relax, hence accuracy in "seeing dead people" doesn't come easily. (This goes for adults, too!)

I don't encourage the testing of children. I feel it pressures them and makes them feel different than their peers. However, if you're curious as to whether your child's dead friend or friends are real, you could try this mini-experiment, which will give you a little bit of insight as to whether your child is using imagination or really picking up some otherworldly information:

1. Don't tell your child you're testing her.

2. Ask your child a question that you know the answer to that she wouldn't know. You could ask the date of your hairstylist's birthday or the date of someone's anniversary. Your child will most likely answer, "I don't know."

3. Next, ask your child to ask her imaginary friend if he or she could help with the answer. If you get the right response, then you have evidence that your child is in touch with some sort of intelligence. Be aware that it could take a while for the "friend" to come up with the answer, so if your child seems to be conferring with her pal, don't rush her.

4. If the child says the friend doesn't know, give your child a choice of 10 dates and then see if she comes up with the answer. (We can't assume the person from the other side is perfect.)

If the answer isn't even close after you've given the child a choice of 10, don't pursue it. But if the answer is accurate, you might say casually, "Well, that's right! What fun!" and make it sound like it's just a game.

Let Them Be Children

There are no statistics regarding how many children can really see ghosts or spirits and how many otherworldly "friends" are just the results of a creative child's imagination. However, these ultrasensitive kids may be more prominent than we know. With enough programming and discouragement from their parents and other elders, children may eventually close their *third eye* and actually stop their inborn sixth sense from coming forward.

def•i•ni•tion

The **third eye** is a concept in metaphysics: the idea that between our eyes, on our forehead, we have an invisible eye of sorts from which our intuitive impressions stem. Some people refer to it as the *mind's eye*. Those who have their third eye "open" would have psychic abilities or a level of enlightenment that the average person doesn't have. This is why sometimes psychics are known as "seers." They can "see" things others cannot.

The best approach to dealing with a child who has extrasensory gifts may be to take the middle road: don't ignore it, but don't feed into it too much, either. If you believe in psychic gifts, let your child know, but also let him know that for now, he needs to be a kid and discover life like everyone else.

It may be a mistake to make your child think that he's special and different from anyone else because of his intuitive gift. If you tell everyone you know that your child has psychic abilities, what do you think will happen? You'll be surrounded by people who want help from him—and what kind of life would that be for your child?

Also remember, not all those dead souls are situated in a better place yet. They may be dysfunctional souls who could drain your child. Therefore, if your child says "I see dead people," go ahead and talk about it with her—this is an interesting occurrence, after all, and part of her life—but don't encourage her to go out seeking as many connections to the afterlife as she can. She might just find some troublesome souls she's not equipped to handle.

All Grown Up

Here's the best advice I can give to parents of children who see spirits: give these kids time to be kids. Don't encourage or discourage their gifts. When they're adults, let them choose what they do with their abilities.

If your child is really drawn to communication with the dead, he may ignore it for many years before becoming involved with it again when he becomes a young adult. If he has the call, he can put it on hold until he's old enough to research, investigate, and experiment with things concerning the unknown and make his own decisions about how to use his gifts.

I equate this to a child who loves acting. The parents know the child has talent but are afraid she won't have a backup career or a normal life if she gets into it too soon. They let the child do regular things; once the child has developed other interests and areas of her life, the parents are more comfortable with her following an acting career. They're confident that there's more to her life than this one aspect.

Ethereal Potpourri

We all have a sixth sense, but it's very weak in most of us and only rears its mysterious head on occasion. For example, studies show that 90 percent of people all over the planet have had the sensation of someone staring at them behind their backs, causing them to turn around.

Parents of psychic children often feel the same way. They encourage their children to lead as normal a life as possible without forgetting about the mystical aspects of their life. I would also recommend you tell your child that not all people on this planet understand such things and it's best to keep it quiet until they're adults. The obvious ramifications that come with kids who see dead people can damage their natural growth.

Jean's Daughter

A lady I know—we'll call her Jean—told me a story about her daughter, who has the ability to communicate with dead people. I talked to Jean about how this started and when she realized that her daughter truly had a psychic gift.

Jean was sitting on her bed crying one night because she and her husband were having serious marital problems. Her daughter, who we'll call Debbie, was eight years old at the time. She came into the room and sat next to her mother and asked, "Mommy, what's wrong? Why are you crying?" Jean replied, "I don't know where your father is or when he's coming home."

Jean said that her daughter felt so sorry for her it seemed to physically jolt her. Then out of the blue Debbie said, "She just told me Daddy's with his friend and he'll be home soon."

There was no one else in the room. Jean asked, "Who told you that?"

Debbie said, "Can't you see her? She's right there." She pointed toward the "person" she was talking about. Jean saw no one, but her daughter's eyes were fixed on something. Jean asked, "Why can't I see her?"

Debbie said, "Because she died a long time ago, but she's here to help us."

Jean was quite concerned. She asked, "What's this lady's name who your father is with?"

Debbie looked at her invisible friend and said, "She said daddy's friend's name is Susie and they're having Chinese food."

At this point, Jean was convinced that Debbie was creating a story to try to calm her down. She felt terrible for crying in front of her daughter. Jean told Debbie to go to bed and assured her that everything would be fine.

The husband came in soon afterward and said nothing. A few weeks later, her husband announced he was leaving Jean for a lady named Susie.

Getting to the Bottom of the Story

You might be wondering if Debbie had heard her father on the phone with Susie or seen a letter with her name on it. Jean claims there's no way this could have happened. And what about the Chinese food? Jean asked her husband about that night—if he had gone out to dinner with Susie. He was amazed at such a strange question. He told her, "If you're implying that I've spent a lot of our money wining and dining this lady, I haven't. In fact, the last time I was with her we only had Chinese takeout."

Well, Jean divorced her husband and Susie married him.

Jean's daughter still stays connected with her spirit friends whom she sees from time to time, although Jean doesn't push Debbie in this regard. Jean commented recently, "My daughter receives messages or communication, but it seems to be getting less and less frequent as she finds other interests. She may investigate this further when she gets older."

The Message

When a child is frightened or stunned (or desperate to help a loved one, like Debbie was), she may be able to hook into a higher frequency and pull in an otherworldly source of help. In some cases it could be an angel; in Debbie's case it was a spirit.

However, we really don't know how children end up with extrasensory abilities. They may just be sensitive to the dead, though on occasion they can be shocked into it, like Debbie was. In these cases, the child knows she has to look to another level of consciousness for answers. This is exactly what Debbie did. She didn't know what a higher level of consciousness was, but she found it—with her heart and soul.

Dale and Grandpa

Grace thought it would be nice to include her story to show that these communications can be very real. I've changed the names here, and only use first names at that.

Dale was a five-year-old boy at the time he discovered he was a cosmic communicator. He had a close relationship with his grandfather. Grandpa Charlie taught him to fish, took him to ballgames, and even taught him how to make microwave popcorn. It doesn't get better than that.

Grandpa Charlie passed on at age 81 from heart failure, as Dale was turning six years old. The child was devastated, but with loving parents, he was able to adjust to his loss.

One night Dale's mother, Grace, heard him talking in his room and thought he was talking to their dog. She went into the bedroom and saw that there was no one there. "Who are you talking to, Dale?" she asked. Dale replied, "I'm talking to Grandpa Charlie." Grace assumed it was part of the grieving process, as Grandpa had passed away only a few months before. "Shhh!" Dale cried. "Now I lost him again!" His mother said, "Again! What do you mean, *again?*" Dale said he had been talking to his grandfather on and off for about a month. Grace asked what they talked about. Dale replied, "All kinds of things, like school and things I do." Grace asked where Grandpa was now. "Oh, he's fine and with all kinds of nice people who have also died."

Grace suspected Dale had picked up on this idea of talking to dead people from watching TV and disregarded the comments, thinking it would pass. Then Dale's father, Jim, came in and said Dale told him he was talking to his grandfather. Jim said, "The next time you talk to your grandfather, ask him where my new fishing pole is. I think I lost it." He chuckled and walked away, also thinking that his son had invented the situation to get him through the grieving process. The next day, Dale said to his father, "Grandpa says you left it at Ben's house," referring to Jim's friend. Jim replied, "Good try, but had I left it there, Ben would have called me two days ago. I think Grandpa needs to work on his answers."

A day later, Ben called Jim and told him his fishing pole was in his backyard and they both must have forgotten about it. Jim thought this was strange because his son would not have known that—Jim himself couldn't believe he had forgotten his fishing pole in Ben's backyard!

Dale's parents chalked this up to coincidence or a lucky guess and ignored it. Then, for fun, Dale's mother said, "Okay, I have one for Grandpa: ask him why my sister isn't calling me and I can't get in touch with her." Dale came back that evening and said, "Grandpa said there's a problem with her phone."

The next day, Dale's mother got a call from her sister, who said the phone company had had to rewire her entire phone system; she hadn't received Grace's messages until today. Grace asked, "Why didn't you call me on your cell phone or return the message I left on your cell phone? Your home phone isn't the only way you could have called." Grace's sister said, "I don't know. I kept thinking about dad [Dale's grandfather] and just felt like I didn't want to call for a while." Grace started wondering if this could have been her dad's way of proving a point that Dale had been telling the truth about communicating with him.

Just to check, Grace asked Dale to ask Grandpa another question. "Ask Grandpa Charlie if I'll get that new job tomorrow." Dale came back later and said, "No, they gave it to someone else already and she's working there now." Grace could not believe this, because she had basically been told she already had the job. (This assured her that her son was just a lucky guesser and she was glad she never encouraged his behavior!) The next day came and she didn't get a phone call from the company. She called and asked to speak to the person who was supposed to hire her. He told her they had already hired someone with more experience who had interviewed at the last minute. She asked him, "When did you hire her?" His response was, "A few days ago. I'm really sorry; I was meaning to call."

When asked if he ever talked to anyone else on the other side, Dale said, "Yes, but no one I like as much as Grandpa. So I tell them to please go away and they do."

Dale is now 10 years old and claims he still talks to Grandpa on occasion, but his parents do not encourage it and have asked him not to mention it to other people.

The Least You Need to Know

- Small children often have imaginary friends. Sometimes it means nothing; other times, it may mean these kids are intuitive.

- Treat psychically gifted children like anyone else; encourage them to be children!

- You can't really test children without them thinking they are special or different, but you might want to try one simple inquiry to see how intuitive they are.

- Sometimes when children are distressed, they tap into a higher frequency to find answers to help those they love.

21

Animal Intuition

In This Chapter

♦ The sixth sense in the animal kingdom

♦ How animals sense when spirits are near

♦ What do animals know about death?

♦ Can we share spiritual communication with animals?

Obviously, it's not easy to get a straight answer from an animal. Even though there are professional "animal communicators" who "talk" to dogs, cats, and other species, it's not the same as being able to ask, "Why are you barking at Grandma's picture? She's been dead for 10 years!"

It's been well documented that animals have a sixth sense, or a feeling of impending trouble that kicks in well before a natural disaster takes place. If they can sense what's coming through their finely tuned powers of perception, is it such a stretch to think that they may be able to sense the changes that come when a spirit is nearby? Can humans learn to tune in to this frequency?

In this chapter, we'll explore how animals react in the presence of everyday threats and how that relates to their interpretation of otherworldly events.

Follow the Animals!

Although the idea of animals having a sixth sense is not new, it's come to the forefront after the Asian tsunami of December 2004, when relatively few animal carcasses were found among the hundreds of thousands of human casualties. Before the tsunami hit land, most animals went to higher ground. In Sri Lanka, an island south of India, it was reported by wildlife officials that at Yala National Park, elephants, leopards, tigers, wild boar, water buffalo, monkeys, deer, and smaller mammals and reptiles somehow sensed the impending danger and survived.

What Skeptics Say

Regarding the tsunami and other natural disasters, many skeptics say that what was not mentioned is that the tsunami was preceded by a forceful earthquake—in which case, it was that earthquake that alarmed the animals.

Reports of animals' sixth sense in detecting hurricanes, earthquakes, volcanic eruptions, and tsunamis—hours or even days before the disasters take place—go back centuries. Animals' sensory physiology—being super-sensitive to temperature, touch, vibration, sound, electro-static, and chemical activity and magnetic fields—gives them a head start in fleeing natural calamities. It's a sensitivity humans don't appear to have.

According to an *ABC News* report on the tsunami on January 1, 2005, an entire village in Indonesia was saved when villagers were warned by birds squawking in a most unusual manner. An eyewitness stated, "We heard the birds screaming in a way we had never heard before. They were warning us. We followed them to safety in the mountains." Another giant quake struck off the Macquarie Island on December 23, 2004, yet the penguins on the island escaped prior to the event.

There may be a metaphysical explanation for this. The earliest possible recorded event involving the sixth sense of animals, in 373 B.C., indicated that animals such as rats, snakes, and weasels deserted the Greek city of Helice in droves just days before an earthquake devastated the area.

There are similar accounts of animal anticipation of earthquakes—for example:

- Catfish move violently
- Chickens stop laying eggs
- Bees leave their hive in a panic
- Dogs and cats act strangely, showing signs of nervousness and restlessness *before* a ground shock

Some animals become disoriented or frightened, and some run away.

Another event happened a few days before a 7.3-magnitude earthquake destroyed most of Haicheng, China, on February 4, 1975. Along with information from scientists that there were changes occurring regarding water levels and land elevations, there were many reports of witnesses seeing changes in animal behavior—this was the convincing attribution. Huge schools of fish and frogs killed themselves trying to break through ice-covered rivers and ponds, and horses, cows, and pigs ran off. Fortunately, even city officials noticed the strange animal behavior and evacuated the city prior to the event, saving numerous lives. Over 2,000 people died and there were more than 27,000 injuries. Had the evacuation not taken place, it's estimated the number of deaths and injuries would have surpassed 150,000.

> **Eternal Thoughts**
>
> If all the beasts were gone, men would die from a great loneliness of spirit, for whatever happens to the beasts also happens to the man. All things are connected.
>
> —Chief Seattle of the Suwamish tribe, letter to U.S. President Franklin Pierce (mid-1800s)

What Animals Can Sense

Animals may be able to detect very small changes in the earth's magnetic field due to magnetite in their bodies. For example, it's thought that this is the cause of homing pigeons' navigational abilities and of whales' and butterflies' migration patterns.

It's a fact that many animals have senses humans don't have, such as the ability of snakes to sense chemicals through their unique vomeronasal organ. Bats, whales, and dolphins have "echolocation" and sharks are able to sense electrical fields generated by other fish. Fish have the lateral line of tiny hair cells that respond to fluid flow around the fish and allow it to detect obstacles and sense the movement of water even if it is completely dark.

Animal Warnings

It is believed animals possess supersenses—including a sixth sense—that are beyond the scope of normal sensory perception. In general, the sixth sense is known for its ability to sense danger. And it appears to be *entirely* psychological. Now, the sixth sense isn't always reliable. Sometimes it turns out to be a false alarm. But that does not mean it doesn't exist.

How do animals exhibit their sixth sense? Well, it depends on the animal. Here are some typical behaviors of impending doom from the animal kingdom:

◆ Wild animals typically gather in groups or go into human-inhabited areas.

◆ Cats may hide or run around frantically, trying to escape outdoors. They may also meow in an unusual manner.

◆ Dogs usually hide. They may also howl, whine, bark, or become restless, aggressive, or very protective of their owners.

◆ Horses and livestock often refuse to enter barns or pens or to be tied up. They group together in open areas, acting nervous or pacing.

◆ Caged birds may hang on their wired enclosures, flap frantically, or become abnormally quiet.

◆ Elephants are extremely sensitive to ground vibrations and often scream and run for higher ground.

◆ Flamingos abandon low-lying breeding areas.

◆ Zoo animals go into shelters and will refuse to come out.

Ethereal Potpourri

The sixth sense is not fully understood, even by scientists. Interestingly, some experts believe that ancient humans may have had a highly developed sixth sense, but that it was lost as we evolved and needed it less and less.

What's really interesting is that animals seem to communicate the danger to one another without speaking. Whether one animal senses the danger and tells the others or they all simultaneously sense something's up, we just don't know.

Note that not all animals will do these things. (Maybe some animals are more intuitive than others, just like humans!)

What's Wrong with Fluffy?

Because animals have sensory abilities that we can't even imagine having—the ability to sense a change in the magnetic field of the earth, or the slightest change in the ground's vibration—it's not such a stretch to imagine that they can also sense other things we can't see, like spirits. Remember, it's been reported that when apparitions appear or spirits are nearby, the electromagnetic field changes, temperatures drop, and compasses start to spin. If animals are so sensitive, why *wouldn't* they notice these changes in the atmosphere?

In this section, we'll look at some stories of animals who've done some pretty extraordinary things. Pet owners love to talk about their furry little loved ones, so it was easy for me to find stories about pets with possible connections to the other side.

Grandpa's Here ... Woof!

A friend told me of a story about the strange behavior of her dog, Morty, a mixed breed. This woman, her son, and her daughter were sitting at home watching television. It was just a regular evening; nothing special was going on. The weather was calm; there were no storms, lightning, snow, etc. Things in the neighborhood were quiet. The family settled in for a peaceful night on the couch.

Morty was lying on the floor in his usual place. Suddenly, he sprang up and started barking at a photograph of a dead relative whose picture was hanging on the wall. The picture had hung in the same place for at least 15 years. The mother checked to see if a spider was hanging down from the frame or if there was an insect crawling on it. Why would the dog be barking at the picture, she wondered?

The dog kept on barking, looking from the picture to his masters and back again. Eventually, the family was able to calm him down, but for the rest of the night, they wondered what had caused his unusual behavior.

The mother was an atheist. She believed in living a good life, but she didn't encourage religious beliefs or a belief in the afterlife in the home. However, she claims this incident made her wonder if the dog was trying to send them a message: was the departed relative in the home, trying to make contact? The next day, the family received word that someone very close to them had died. The mother felt that perhaps the dog was trying to warn them about this death.

For a skeptic who didn't believe in life after death, this was quite a revelation. Since this happened, the mother thinks perhaps there *is* an afterlife—she also thinks it's a very real possibility that animals can sense things that we can't!

My Cat Plays with Ghosts

A lady I interviewed—we'll call her Sally—is a bookkeeper, of sound body, mind, and spirit. She relayed an ongoing story of her cat and her resident ghost. (Yes, I said *resident* ghost. And yes, she is *still* of sound body, mind, and spirit.)

Sally acquired a cat, Sara, when her elderly neighbor moved away. Sally knew the cat well, and the cat loved Sally, so this was an easy adjustment for both of them.

One day Sally was sewing in her bedroom and she thought she spotted the entity whoosh by. She didn't make any sudden movements; she just continued sewing. This was the resident ghost coming in. Because the entity never bothered her, Sally always just went about her business. She knew the spirit might hang around for 10 minutes and then leave again, as this was the ghost's usual habit.

Well, Sara the cat came into the room and suddenly started to bounce up and down. It looked as if the cat were playing with someone. Now, Sara wasn't a playful kitten—she was getting old and she was normally quite inactive. This display of athleticism was abnormal for her, to say the least.

Sally sat at her sewing machine watching the cat play. She thought the cat was trying to get her attention, so she got up and clapped her hands, calling the cat's name. The cat ignored her. Sally left the room and the cat continued to interact with … well, with what appeared to be nothing!

After a few minutes, Sally saw a whoosh leaving the room and the cat suddenly stopped its actions and lay back down on the rug like normal.

Pet Pig Pearl Perks Up

I laughed when I heard someone named her pet pig Pearl. (Say that 10 times quickly!) Pearl is the pet pig of a lady I met in Mexico a few years ago. Dorotea had a leash for Pearl and walked the pig everywhere. She also took her to the art gallery that she owned. Day after day, Pearl would just sit there in the gallery with Dorotea. The pig hardly made a peep, a grunt, or a movement.

Dorotea told me that one afternoon, Pearl suddenly stumbled up on her chubby little feet and started walking around about the gallery. She wandered into the main gallery where customers were viewing paintings. Pearl had never been restricted from the area because she never moved from the back room until she was given a little yank of the leash. Dorotea couldn't understand what Pearl was doing. She thought Pearl was sick. She walked the pig outside but Pearl wanted to go back into the gallery. This was a behavior Dorotea had never seen.

When they went back into the studio, Pearl sat herself down in front of an oil painting that was Dorotea's aunt's favorite work of art. Dorotea knew that her aunt was in the hospital in Mexico City; she had had a stroke. She wondered what the connection between Pearl, the painting, and the aunt might be. It was an unusual situation to analyze, to say the least.

About an hour later, Dorotea received a phone call that her elderly aunt had passed away that afternoon, just about the time Pearl had parked herself in front of the painting. To this day, Dorotea is convinced that Pearl was trying to send her a message that her aunt had passed and her spirit was in the studio to say her final farewell.

Pearl is still alive and still prefers to just sit and sit. No incident like this has happened again.

Where, Oh Where, Has My Little Dog Gone?

In Chapter 15, I mentioned that it's believed that animals who have been loved and cared for in this life most likely cross over into the next life when they die. Because they've been taken into a family and accepted as one of its members, they've more or less developed a humanlike soul.

Do animals mourn the passing of their animal friends? It's very likely that they do grieve the loss. In fact, we see this in animal depression or loneliness. The animal may mope around, hang its head, act lethargic, or look for the other animal. You can almost feel its sadness. But comfort is around the corner for these mourning creatures. Just as humans may see an apparition of a person whom we loved visit us in a flash and experience a feeling of happiness, animals can most likely experience the same thing—except they may be one up on us. Their sixth sense is more finely tuned, for starters, so they may see apparitions more easily than humans do. And when they *do* see their departed pals, their communication is most likely easy, since they "talk" to one another without speaking.

Ethereal Potpourri _____

Since animals cross over, it's also possible for them to pop in on us from time to time, just like our departed human loved ones do, in the form of an apparition or other ghostly form. Pet owners have reported seeing their departed furry friends, usually in a familiar setting, like the animal's favorite napping spot or in the room where the animal liked to spend a lot of time.

Dream Connections

We know that animals are very perceptive and that some of them appear to be able to tell us about the impending death of others, or let us know when spirits are near, or tell us when some catastrophe is about to strike. This is all very useful information for us humans, of course, and maybe that shouldn't come as any surprise—after all, domesticated animals, at least, are very devoted to their owners. But don't these animals ever try to tell us something about themselves that we might otherwise not know? And if they did, would we understand?

Ethereal Potpourri _____

It's believed that some level of sixth sense is available to humans if we try to understand and bond with nature and open our eyes and ears to what nature has to teach. When there is love for animals and a willingness to learn and accept them as they are, our ability to understand them grows. The mind and heart open and expand. With time and openness, a deeper understanding and communication with animals is possible.

Here's an interesting story about a human-animal spiritual connection. In her article "Einstein's Challenge; A Strange Affliction" (*PetFolio* magazine, February-March 2005), Juci Somogvi of Reno, Nevada, tells the story of her hale and hearty horse, Einstein, who was bitten by a spider, developed an infection, and nearly died as a result. She details his struggle to survive and his slow but amazing recovery.

So what's so special about this story? Somogvi was alerted to her horse's condition through a dream. She writes, "In July, on a typical Thursday night, I went to bed and when I woke up, I remembered my not so typical dream of my horse, Einstein. He was in his stall rolling bizarrely and couldn't get up, as if part of his leg was missing. The image came back immediately, and feeling uneasy, I hurried to feed him that morning.

"I was relieved to see he was on his feet, but realized something was wrong. His eyes were huge with pain and he could barely stand. I led him out of the stall to assess how bad it was but could barely coax him to walk. He almost fell down with every step. We barely made it to the pasture where he went down instantly. My dream flashed— it wasn't looking good. I thought this was the end."

Was this a case of the animal sending a message or the owner being unusually perceptive—or both? We may never know, but because Somogvi had a visualization—in her dream—of just how serious the situation was, she wasted no time getting treatment for her animal, which may very well have prevented him from crossing into the next life!

The Least You Need to Know

- ◆ Animals have a sixth sense, especially when it comes to natural disasters.

- ◆ Pets sometimes may be able to pick up on communications with spirits.

- ◆ It's likely that animals mourn the passing of their animal friends, and can see and communicate with those pals who have passed over.

- ◆ Animals may be able to communicate their suffering or pain through our dreams.

Chapter 22

Past Lives and Reincarnation

In This Chapter

♦ Reincarnation: recycling the soul

♦ Who decides when and how you come back to this life?

♦ Why you must mend your karma

♦ Fears and phobias related to the past

♦ Relating to people from another lifetime

Many people believe that after the physical body dies, the soul goes through a life review and recovery period and then returns to the planet to learn additional lessons. This process of soul recycling, called reincarnation, may also explain why people act in certain ways, have unexplained fears or talents, or are drawn to particular individuals.

In this chapter, we'll explore some of the beliefs about reincarnation, including whether animals come back around a second or third time (and/or whether *you* may be headed for a life as a dog).

The Soul of It All

Many religions and spiritual systems believe in reincarnation. As you'll recall from Chapter 2, that's the belief that only the physical body dies; the soul keeps returning to the planet to spiritually evolve and learn lessons that help its evolution to a more enlightened state.

Life Review

There are varied ideas about reincarnation, but one interesting theory is what happens to the soul *before* it comes back into another life form. Some say it travels to another dimension or plane in the afterlife and experiences a life review, which is sort of like watching a movie of your life on Earth. Once the show is over, a higher power decides whether you have to come back—and what form you'll take the next time around.

If you've lived a life on Earth that was filled with love and respect for the planet and for other human beings and animals, you may not have to return at all. You may be allowed to proceed to another level or plane, which goes by different names depending on the tradition or faith that you follow (heaven, paradise, Nirvana, and so forth).

Taking a Soul Nap

Once the soul goes through its life review, it goes through a period of rest if it must reincarnate. For this reason, the soul may not return right away. It could take years—even centuries—for it to make its way back to this life. There's a time and place for everything. The soul returns according to the needs and the knowledge it must gain in the next reincarnation. For example, if for spiritual growth and life's lessons, a soul needs to gain knowledge that wartime might provide, it will wait until such a time exists on the planet. If the soul must learn about true love, it may be held back until the one it is supposed to truly fall in love with is on the planet as well.

The evolved soul is given special consideration. If a soul has reached a heightened level of existence and doesn't need to come back but chooses to for whatever reason, it might wait for that perfect time. For example, if a soul wanted to contribute to the space program, it would have to wait for that era when it can be of the greatest help.

Where does the soul go for its much-needed R&R? Perhaps in a plane where other souls are waiting. Or maybe it waits in heaven or paradise itself, but unfortunately is only permitted a temporary visit until it can come back and settle in permanently.

Eternal Thoughts

> **Eternal Thoughts**
>
> The soul comes from without into the human body, as into a temporary abode, and it goes out of it anew it passes into other habitations, for the soul is immortal. It is the secret of the world that all things subsist and do not die, but only retire a little from sight and afterwards return again. Nothing is dead; men feign themselves dead, and endure mock funerals ... and there they stand looking out of the window, sound and well, in some strange new disguise.
>
> —Ralph Waldo Emerson, author, poet, and philosopher

Paying Off Your Karmic Debt

You may recall from Chapter 1 that karma is the theory your actions will come back to you. So if your life review doesn't go as well as you'd hoped, you may have to go around the cosmic block again in order to fix your errors, learn your lessons, and mend your karma.

Even if you were fair in your dealings in life, you might still have to pay the price for some negative things you did. In that case, you'll return to a life that will teach you that lesson. The kind of life you led before determines what type of individual you will return as.

For example, let's say you were a wealthy man who made your money dishonestly, and treated women horribly, to boot. You lived by the mantra, "All's fair in love and business." You may come back as a woman with five children who's struggling to find work but who would never cheat anyone. Your mantra during *this* life might be, "Why is this happening to me?" This is the *what goes around, comes around* theory, or the cycle of cause and effect we refer to as karma.

Sometimes a soul has evolved and doesn't have to incarnate but chooses to come back anyway. These souls are "volunteers" of sorts that return for a specific purpose: to help those here who need to develop and follow a more balanced and enlightened path.

People often want to know if they can pay off their karma in this lifetime. The answer is yes. If you start to lead a life where you become aware of the mistakes you've made and try to fix them, you may be able to succeed. The trick is to recognize where you went wrong in a past life—or even in this life—and correct it. This can lead to the beautiful afterlife that awaits you.

Past-Life Regressions

When we die and return to the planet, we have no recollection of previous lives—they're removed from our consciousness. However, by conducting a *past-life regression* via hypnosis or meditation, you may be able to recall other lifetimes. You may uncover when, where, and who you were in different lives. This is a fascinating process and it can often allow us to understand why we act the way we do in the present lifetime.

def•i•ni•tion

A **past-life regression** involves entering into a trancelike state for the purpose of recalling your former incarnations.

I have provided a simple method here to help you tap into your own past lives. Before you begin, schedule a time when you can devote your full attention to the process. Locate a quiet and private space away from diversions. Turn off phones, radios, and anything else that would make a sound.

Then follow these steps:

1. Lie down with your eyes closed. Concentrate on breathing through your nostrils and become aware of the sensation of your breath as it enters and leaves the nostrils.

2. Once you're relaxed, visualize a protective white light or cloud around you. Ask your higher power to protect you. Say or think that you don't want to experience any negative lifetimes.

3. Visualize entering an old-fashioned locomotive. Try to imagine as many details as you can. Are the seats red velvet or are they gold? Do you see tables, chairs, wall decorations, and so on? (You can also visualize a bus, boat, spaceship, or any mode of transportation.)

4. As you journey, you're going back in time. The train goes through a tunnel. When it comes out on the other side, you'll see the first stop, which will be your most recent past life.

5. Visualize standing up. Go to the door when the train stops. The door opens. What do you see? Stores and cars from days long ago? The lost city of Atlantis? Are you in a Native American village?

6. Get off the train and then look at the clothes you are suddenly wearing. This will give you a sense of the time period.

7. A spirit guide dressed in attire from the era will meet you at the depot. He or she will guide you and serve as your protector.

8. As you walk through this setting, you won't be seen by anyone. You'll see yourself as you were in that time. In other words, there will be two of you, the one who's observing and the person you used to be. You'll be watching yourself. You'll hear voices and conversations—you should even hear your (former) name. You can go to your home, your workplace, or anywhere else you want to visit, and you can meet anyone you're interested in (such as a lover). There are no rules or guidelines.

9. When you're through, you'll be escorted back to the train. If you want to go on to another stop you can, or you can travel home. Take care not to tire yourself out by going to too many stops. More than three stops at a time might get confusing. However, if you think you can continue on, do so for as long as you like.

Slowly come out of your altered state of consciousness and focus before you stand up. You may be groggy, but take the time to write down what you've experienced so that you can analyze it when you're fully awake. If you're unsuccessful the first time around, try again another time.

Keep in mind that there are professionals who can help you in this quest. To find a past-life regressionist, look in New Age bookstores or on the Internet.

A regressionist may charge you anywhere from only $65 on up. But don't let the price fool you. I have seen many regressionists who are excellent charge a fee that's almost too good to be true ... even $20!

Some people feel it's best to work with professional hypnotherapists who deal in this type of consultation. Others feel that if the person is intuitive or a professional psychic reader, they can do the same job.

Spotting fake regressionists is like being on the lookout for any other scam. Ask questions without being insulting, and ask for references. Inquire how long they have been doing this and how they got started. Unfortunately, not all regressionists will feel the need to sell themselves to you. But remember, as a consumer you have the right to ask questions. As always, use your intuition.

If you just don't have a good feeling from the individual when booking the appointment, give this person a pass and find someone who you are comfortable with. (Or maybe even knew in a past life!)

? What Skeptics Say _____

The Skeptic's Dictionary (www.skepdic.com) tells us "past-life regression (PLR) is the alleged journeying into one's past lives while hypnotized. While it's true that many patients *recall* past lives, it's highly probable that their memories are false memories. The memories are from experiences in this life, pure products of the imagination, intentional or unintentional suggestions from the hypnotist, or confabulations."

All About Genders

People who believe in reincarnation typically think that when you make the transition back to Earth you can return as either male or female, no matter which sex you were when you died or which gender you may have been in your other lives. It may take you becoming female to have an understanding of what you did wrong as a male a lifetime ago, and vice versa.

Gender Confusion

Frequently, people will wonder why some people are born gay or bisexual. Those who study reincarnation have an explanation that sounds reasonable to others who believe in past lives. Let's say that you were a woman in your past 10 lifetimes. On your 11th time around, you come back as a male. You may be confused without knowing why. Well, here's one possible explanation: your soul was so used to being feminine that the soul fights being born into a male body.

Believers in reincarnation also speculate that bisexuals have come back primarily as one sex for several incarnations but are able to adjust more to the new body than someone who's homosexual; they just can't adjust 100 percent.

In Touch with Your Other Side

We always laugh about big brawny guys who love to knit, clean, or participate in an activity that's considered feminine. We also raise eyebrows when we see the very lady-like gal sitting on a tractor bringing in a crop or building an addition to her house.

Although we thankfully live in a society that doesn't limit or judge our activities by gender anymore, past-life researchers feel that these characteristics may also be due to past life experiences.

Having these leftover gender characteristics from your former lives doesn't mean you're gay or bisexual. It simply means that perhaps you're still feeling residuals from having lived as the opposite sex. You subconsciously remember certain activities you once enjoyed and carry them into this lifetime. Nothing wrong with that!

I Always *Thought* You Were a Dog ...

During past-life regressions, some people remember being an animal. These accounts can be very confusing—but are they *real?*

Some feel that if you did something really horrific in another lifetime, such as murder or cheating someone to the point of their demise, you're reduced to an animal form, after which you may learn your lessons and then incarnate into a human form again. This is highly debated by those who say we incarnate to learn about other people, relationships, and daily living. To return as an animal as a form of punishment probably doesn't help the evolution of the soul.

However, some cultures believe that reincarnating into an animal is just one form of spirituality. They believe their ancestors' souls reside in sacred animals while the soul prepares for reincarnation. The animal is a holding place for the soul, more or less, which is why certain animals are not eaten and are treated with the utmost respect. The Egyptians, some Buddhist traditions, and some Native American tribes believe that people come back as animals. The aborigines thought that their warriors were incarnated as dolphins. Obviously, the beliefs also state it is wrong to kill these animals.

Ethereal Potpourri

The question always arises as to whether animals reincarnate. The majority of pet owners look at their faithful friends as family members, so the idea that their souls pass on and come back can be very comforting during a time of grief. It's not believed an animal will incarnate within the same lifetime. In other words, if your cat died five years ago, it's unlikely it will appear as a kitten at the Humane Society two years later. Animal souls need a resting period, just like human souls.

Some theories believe there is a collective consciousness where the souls of animals end up. When an animal is to be born, a new soul is born from that consciousness and passed into the animal. Another thought, which is more controversial, is that animals are considered a lower level of existence, and at that level the soul simply "is" and doesn't learn spiritual lessons. The animal may learn to obey, to help people, and so forth, but, the theory argues, that's not really the evolution of the soul; it's programming.

Why Does That Scare Me?

People who have phobias (unreasonable fears of places, other people, heights, or animals, for example) might be able to reconcile these fears by confronting events that happened in a past life. The reason for fears that can't be accounted for in a present lifetime may make perfect sense if you use the "this happened to me in a past life" attitude.

For example, people who have a fear of fire but can't recall a negative experience including flames either as a child or adult may have been burned in a past life. The same goes for bridges. Some people would rather drive 50 miles out of their way than cross a bridge. Perhaps a hundred years ago they fell off a bridge and that memory exists in their subconscious.

This theory can be used to explain any fear. Fear of snakes? Perhaps you were bitten by a snake. Fear of crowds? It could be that you were killed or hurt in a crowd. This concept can explain quite a number of things. Therefore, these fears may not be premonitions of something that's *going* to happen in this lifetime, but leftover fears of something that's *already* happened.

A regressionist may not be able to help you actually get over your fear, but can help you understand why it exists in this lifetime. With that knowledge, sometimes the fear will start to subside.

Leftovers from Other Lives

We've all seen people catch on to things so quickly we can't believe our eyes: Youngsters who play piano as if they've studied for years and years. People who have a natural talent for drawing without ever having been instructed in art.

How many times have you seen someone show an inordinate amount of talent with very little training in a certain skill? Are these people geniuses, or have they lived before and developed talents and exceptional skills in another lifetime? Their gifts may well have been carried over to the present life span. Although consciously we don't remember what and who we were in the days of yore, we often still tap into the capabilities we had before.

Picking Up Where You Left Off

Edgar Cayce (1877–1945), an American psychic, was called the "sleeping clairvoyant" or "sleeping prophet." He also was referred to as the "other Nostradamus" (Nostradamus was a renowned prophet in the 1500s). Some refer to him as the greatest psychic of our time.

In a 1934 lecture on the *continuity of life* included in *The Edgar Cayce Reader #2*, Cayce explained that he was not a scientist, so he was not able to speak in a scientific way; he was also not an educated man, so he could not speak like a scholar. Therefore, Cayce's views on life after death came from experience, observation, and what he had read.

Cayce felt the question, "What does the term 'continuity of life' really mean?" was one people had asked throughout the ages. "What happens when a man dies? Does he live again? What is death and what happens next?"

def•i•ni•tion

According to Cayce, **continuity of life** refers to the consciousness of being one with God that continues after death.

Cayce believed these questions were individualized; people have to form their own opinions and concepts concerning life after death. Cayce personally believed that "when God breathed into man the breath of life he became a *LIVING SOUL*—individual soul, if you please. The Spirit of God is life, whether in a blade of grass or in man! The soul of man is individual and lives on!"

Although Cayce was a Christian and professed love for Jesus Christ, his ideas were unconventional at the time and many Christians did not understand his process of receiving information. He would lie down with his eyes closed in an altered state of consciousness and answer questions and pick up impressions of future events. He once told a story about a child he had never met who walked up to him and handed him a part of his candy bar for no reason. When Cayce asked the boy, "Why are you giving me part of your candy?" the boy said, "I remember when we were hungry on that raft."

Did the boy have a dream of a man who looked like Cayce—or was he somehow recalling a past-life experience and connected to Cayce's soul? It seems as though children are more open to these experiences, perhaps because they're free of the pressures of society and haven't been educated enough to discount how they feel and intuitively "see."

An excellent website for more information on Edgar Cayce is www.sleepingprophet.org.

Been Dead, Done That

As adults we may have always had a desire to do something special, but with busy schedules we can't always achieve those goals. Perhaps you've been aching to take a pottery class, or you've dreamed of visiting China. Are these just human desires, or are we trying to connect to something or someplace that was familiar to us in another lifetime?

I've spoken with people who've traveled abroad, having never been to a particular country and never seen a certain area or building in books or on television—yet they knew what they were going to see. Once they arrived at their destination, they felt as though they'd been there before. This feeling of recollection before is known as *déjà vu.*

def•i•ni•tion

Déjà vu, French for "already seen," is the feeling that you have experienced something—a place, a situation—before, even though the experience is new to you.

Déjà vu can catch us off guard at the least expected moments. It might strike you as you're driving your kids to school—which is not as startling, since this is something you probably do with some regularity—or it might come upon you in a new situation. You may feel right at home, for example, as you're walking down the street in an unfamiliar area, sensing that you've done this before. You instinctively find your way around a strange town, certain that you know which direction is correct. Do you have a built-in compass ... or are you just recalling the roads you used to wander?

Déjà vu doesn't only exist because of reincarnation. We can also experience déjà vu in this lifetime. Some believe that at night our souls can travel while we sleep—so your soul may have traveled into the future, seeing this exact event. (See Chapter 16 for more on soul travel.)

People Who Keep Coming Back for More

"I know I have no reason for this, but I just don't like that person!" Have you ever said or thought things like this? A perfectly nice individual may be introduced to you and before they even say hello, you've already judged that person and don't care for him or her.

On the flip side, you may see someone in a crowd and think, "There's something about him or her that I feel drawn to." I'm not talking about physical attraction, but soul attraction. This type of thing is actually quite common. If it's never happened to you, then surely you have a friend or two who instantly *knew* upon meeting their life mate that this person was The One.

Sometimes there are logical reasons for this. A person may remind you of someone with whom you had a bad experience—or they could remind you of someone you used to love. But those who don't remind you of that mean third-grade teacher or your old boyfriend may have been your enemy or lover in one of your former lives. That is, you just sense something about a person that you don't care for, even though you cannot relate him or her to anyone you have ever met in this lifetime.

Relative Discord

We know we're "supposed" to like our children, parents, grandparents, aunts and uncles, and anyone else who's connected to us by blood. But the reality is, sometimes we just don't. Try as we might, it's sometimes difficult to find redeeming qualities in the people we're supposed to hold nearest and dearest to our hearts.

People tend to feel very guilty when they don't care for a relative's personality or character—but some of this familial discord may also be attributable to past lives. I know it seems extraordinary, but the soul gets around and we don't know where or when it's going to pop in.

Your awful Uncle Joe, for example, could have been your mean boss in the kitchens of Japan when you were a cook for a royal household. Your mother could have been your cousin who stole from you in ancient Greece. Your brother could have been an executioner in Revolutionary France. (You've always suspected as much, right?) You just don't know what kind of baggage someone else may be carrying around from their past lives; if you can learn to look at them as the compilation of everyone they may have been, you might learn to like them—or at least understand them—better.

The same thing goes for people who we don't really know but who we feel instant affection for. The lady you're drawn to at the fabric store may have been your father in another lifetime. In these cases, it's best to just go with your gut instinct—you just never know who's who!

Soul Mates?

Oh, that overused term, "soul mate." A soul mate is supposed to be "it" for us—the one, the only, the love of our lives. In actuality, we all have more than one soul mate. They're usually love interests from different lifetimes.

Now, we've all had friends who've had lovers who treated them badly—mates who weren't good for their growth and well-being. So why would anyone stay with someone who limits them in the most important ways? It may be because they're connecting to something in that person's soul—something that they loved in a past life.

Apply this to your own life: if someone is clearly not helping you become the best person you can be (and, in fact, is actually working *against* your best efforts) but you just can't release him or her, think about the possibility that you could be experiencing residual feelings from the past—the *distant* past! Move on and just be happy you were able to meet one more time in this time and place.

In other words, this is probably just "a past-life thing," and not meant to be a relationship in *this* lifetime.

The Least You Need to Know

- ◆ The soul can be reborn again into another human body so it will learn lessons before it reaches its final resting place.

- ◆ You can do your own past-life regression.

- ◆ When selecting a past-life regressionist, use your intuition to judge if that person is right for you—and don't be afraid to ask questions about the person's experience.

- ◆ Phobias may be attributed to something that happened to you in another lifetime.

- ◆ Talents and interests may stem from jobs or gifts we developed in another place and time.

- ◆ Negative relationships sometimes occur because we're drawn to the soul of someone from the past.

Appendix

Glossary

afterlife   The existence or continuance of the soul after death. A life in a different dimension or different plane where we continue to grow spiritually without the pain and stress of the physical body.

agnostic   Someone who claims no knowledge of the existence of gods, God, or any deities. He withholds judgment on the subject until solid evidence is brought forth.

apparitions   What we typically think of when we hear the word "ghost." They appear suddenly and in a recognizable form, whether it's a human or an animal.

Ascended Masters   Religious figures who have fully united with God; for example, Jesus and Buddha.

astral body   The body that's sent out during soul travel or astral travel.

astral travel   Putting oneself into a trance and visiting other dimensions of the universe and planes of the afterlife. This is also called soul travel.

atheist   Someone with an absence of a belief in a single creator, God, or any deities.

aura   An energy field that surrounds each living thing.

automatic writing   Writing while in an altered state of consciousness or trancelike state.

Barzakh   In Islam, the place where the soul goes after death. It waits here until the final judgment day.

Buddhism   An ancient religion founded in India more than 2,500 years ago. Followers believe in karma, reincarnation, and Nirvana.

channeling   Receiving information from a spirit, higher power, or other supernatural source that is not of the mind of the channeler or the person who is receiving the information.

Christianity   A religion centered on the belief that Jesus Christ is the son of God. Followers believe that the soul is judged at the moment of death and is sent to heaven or hell. Catholics also believe the soul can be sent to *purgatory*.

consciousness   Refers to a spirit being alert and aware of its surroundings. It's able to do certain things with intent.

cosmic law   A universal law that gives people on Earth the insight of the basic principle of self-preservation against harming themselves or others. It is a principle that defines right from wrong regarding the moral value of life.

debunker   A person who is considered a scientific skeptic. He actively attempts to discredit claims of the paranormal, the afterlife, and any other ideas of things beyond the physical that can't be proven scientifically.

déjà vu   The feeling that you've been somewhere or done something before. This feeling may be due to *reincarnation* or *astral travel*.

Divine Records   A library of sorts, containing all the knowledge of the universe since the beginning of time.

double-blind   A standard scientific method used to prevent the outcome of research from being influenced by prejudice or opinion.

The Dreamtime (or **dreaming**)   The aboriginal cycle of time. It includes past, present, and future, existing all at once. There is no beginning and no end to life according to this theory.

Electronic Voice Phenomena (EVP)   Sounds such as voices that are caught on electronic media. EVP devices are used to try to pick up messages from those on the other side, who attempt to rearrange sounds to send messages because they no longer have voice boxes. You can hear the voices only when the recording is played back.

grave goods   Objects that the ancient Egyptians buried with their dead. These are items the dead person would need in their next life, like eating utensils and/or luxury items such as jewelry.

guided meditation   Involves a facilitator leading one person or an entire group into a trancelike state.

Hindu   An ancient religion founded in India. Followers believe in karma and reincarnation.

Islam   "Surrender" or "commit to God." Islam is a religion based on the teachings contained in the Qu'ran. Followers believe that the departed soul enters into an intermediate state called the Barzakh, where it stays until the final judgment day.

Judaism   A religion based on the teaching of the Old Testament and the Torah, or "law." Jews believe that upon death, the soul may ultimately judge itself.

kami   Shinto gods, which may include natural elements and/or ancestral spirits.

karma   The Buddhist belief that our actions in this lifetime determine the shape of our next life.

life review   The review of your life by the Supreme Being, which takes place after this life ends but before you incarnate into a new life.

lucid dreaming   The conscious understanding while dreaming that you're in a dream state. You can control the process and the makeup of the dream. This gives you the ability to talk to people or entities in your dream, such as spirit guides.

mind's eye   See *third eye*.

Muslim   A follower of the teachings of Islam.

near-death experience (NDE)   An experience of crossing over to the afterlife that occurs when a person is either declared dead or is close to death. The person eventually returns to this life.

New Age   A set of beliefs that don't gel with traditional religion. New Age followers are spiritual, open-minded individuals searching for their own path to the afterlife.

Nirvana   According to some beliefs, the highest state of being the soul can reach. Once the soul reaches Nirvana, it doesn't have to incarnate anymore.

orbs   Small balls of energy that may indicate an apparition is about to make itself known. Orbs are not visible to the naked eye.

orthodox   Conforming to an established conventional or conservative religious group or doctrine.

out-of-body experience   The feeling that you're leaving your physical body and a second body—exactly like your physical body—is floating outside of it.

past-life regression   Entering into a trancelike state for the purpose of recalling your former incarnations.

place haunting   See *place memory*.

place memory   A voice or image that has burned itself into the atmosphere of a home or area. Also called a *place haunting*.

poltergeist   Literally "noisy ghost," refers to energy that creates havoc in a certain location. Experts believe that poltergeists are actually the manifestation of negative energy (such as stress) and not a true haunting.

possession   When an entity takes over a person's body. Also called *spirit possession*.

psychokinesis   A mind-over-matter situation. This theory tells us that our own thoughts can sometimes unconsciously be used to move objects and or to misshape them, usually when an individual is experiencing great anxiety and tension. Also called *telekinesis*.

purgatory   The state between heaven and hell where a soul purges itself of its sins. This is a belief exclusive to Catholicism.

reincarnation   The belief that after the physical body dies, the soul returns to this life in another human form.

séance   A gathering of three to twelve people, typically assembled in a circle, attempting to receive messages or communicate with the spirit of a person who has died.

second body   The body that's sent out during soul travel or astral travel. Also called the *astral body*.

self-realization   The act of achieving the highest spiritual level, a level where the soul doesn't have to incarnate again.

shadow people   Figures seen out of the corner of our eye for a few seconds or less that look like a fleeting shadow of a person but aren't recognizable. Also called *shadow figures* or *shadow beings*.

Shinto   "Way of the *kami*" (or "divine"). This is a religion practiced almost exclusively in Japan. Followers worship natural elements of ancestral spirits, also called *kami*.

sixth sense   The ability to receive information by means other than the five senses.

skeptic   From Greek, meaning "one who doubts."

soul travel   See *astral travel*.

spirit guides   Deceased individuals who offer advice to the living. Everyone has one main spirit guide, but more are available to guide us.

spirit possession   See *possession*.

Spiritualism   A type of religion characterized by a belief that we can speak to the dead by using a medium.

Tao   The final resting place for the Taoist's soul; it's perfection and immortality. It's akin to the Buddhist's interpretation of Nirvana.

Taoism   A fundamental Chinese concept that implies or translates as a method, principle, or doctrine; the "way" or "path" one should follow.

telekinesis   See *psychokinesis*.

telepathy   The ability of a person to communicate with others, alive or dead, from one mind to another. No tools or equipment are needed. Telepathics simply "hear" in their mind.

third eye   The idea that between our eyes, on our forehead, we have an invisible eye from which our intuitive impressions stem. Those who have their third eye "open" have psychic abilities. Some people refer to it as the mind's eye.

tools of divination   Items such as tarot cards, pendulums, and crystal balls that are used to predict the future, look into the past, or examine the present.

transmigration   Similar to reincarnation, but includes the belief that a soul can return in animal or even plant form.

triads (of angels)   The hierarchical order of angels, which consists of three levels. Each level, in turn, contains three levels of angels. Each level is tasked with specific duties.

Underworld   The name for the land of the dead in ancient Egypt. A recently deceased person had to pass through a labyrinth in the Underworld in order to reach the afterlife.

Vedas The main scriptural texts of the Hindu religion. These teachings have been passed by word of mouth through the generations.

zombie A dead person who has been brought back to life by sorcery or black magic. They have no free will or soul but can wander amongst us.

Resources

Books

The afterlife is such a broad topic, you could read about it till ... well, till kingdom come! As this publication covers just the tip of the afterlife iceberg, further reading is highly encouraged. No matter how many concepts you believe in or question, chances are someone has asked the same questions and written about it.

Ahlquist, Diane. *The Complete Idiot's Guide to Fortune Telling*. Indianapolis: Alpha Books, 2006.

———. *White Light: The Complete Guide to Spells and Rituals for Psychic Protection*. New York, NY: Citadel Press Kensington, 2002.

———. *Moon Spells: How to Get What You Want from the Phases of the Moon*. Avon, MA: Adams Media, 2002.

Arcangel, Dianne, and Gary E. Schwartz. *Afterlife Encounters: Ordinary People, Extraordinary Experiences*. Charlottesville, VA: Hampton Roads Publishing, 2005.

Atwater, P.M.H., and David H. Morgan. *The Complete Idiot's Guide to Near-Death Experiences*. Indianapolis: Alpha Books, 2000.

Browne, Sylvia, and Lindsay Harrison. *Life on the Other Side: A Psychic's Tour of the Afterlife*. New York, NY: NAL Trade, 2002.

Cayce, Hugh Lynn. *Venture Inward*. New York, NY: Paperback Library, 1964.

Dalzell, George E., and Gary E. Schwartz. *Messages: Evidence for Life after Death*. Charlottesville, VA: Hampton Roads Publishing, 2002.

Denning, Melita, and Osborne Phillips. *Creative Visualization*. St. Paul, MN: Llewellyn Publishing, 1992.

Dubois, Allison. *Don't Kiss Them Good-Bye*. New York, NY: Fireside, 2005.

Eadie, Betty J. *Embraced by the Light*. New York, NY: Bantam Books, 1994.

Goldberg, Dr. Bruce. *Astral Voyages: Mastering the Art of Soul Travel*. St. Paul, MN: Llewellyn Publishing, 1999.

Hammerman, David, Lisa Lenard, and Carol Bowman. *The Complete Idiot's Guide to Reincarnation*. Indianapolis: Alpha Books, 2000.

Lundahl, Craig R., Ph.D., and Harlod A. Widdison, Ph.D. *The Eternal Journey ... How Near-Death Experiences Illuminate in Earthly Lives*. New York, NY: Warner Books, Inc., 1997.

Miller, Jamie C., Laura Lewis, and Jennifer Basye Sander. *Heavenly Miracles: Magical True Stories of Guardian Angels and Answered Prayers*. New York, NY: William Morrow, 2000.

Morse, Melvin. *Parting Visions*. New York, NY: Random House, 1997.

Ogden, Tom. *The Complete Idiot's Guide to Ghosts and Hauntings*, 2nd ed. Indianapolis: Alpha Books, 2004.

Schwartz, Gary E., William Simon, and Deepak Chopra. *The Afterlife Experiments: Breakthrough Scientific Evidence of Life After Death*. New York, NY: Atria, 2003.

Sheridan, Kim. *Animals and the Afterlife: True Stories of Our Best Friends' Journey Beyond Death*. Carlsbad, CA: Hay House, 2006.

Shermer, Michael. *How We Believe: Science, Skepticism, and the Search for God*. New York, NY: Owl Books, 2003.

Time-Life Books, ed. *Mystic Places*. Mysteries of the Unknown Series. Alexandria, VA: Time-Life Books, 1987.

———. *Phantom Encounters*. Mysteries of the Unknown Series. Alexandria, VA: Time-Life Books, 1988.

———. *Psychic Voyages*. Mysteries of the Unknown Series. Alexandria, VA: Time-Life Books, 1987.

———. *Search for the Soul.* Mysteries of the Unknown Series. Alexandria, VA: Time-Life Books, 1989.

———. *Time and Space.* Mysteries of the Unknown Series. Alexandria, VA: Time-Life Books, 1990.

Turlington, Shannon R. *The Complete Idiot's Guide to Voodoo.* Indianapolis: Alpha Books, 2001.

Wills-Brandon, Carla. *One Last Hug Before I Go: The Mystery and Meaning of Deathbed Visions.* Deerfield Beach, FL: HSI, 2000.

Zammit, Victor. *A Lawyer Presents the Case for the Afterlife—Irrefutable Objective Evidence.* Australia: Ganmell Pty. Ltd., 2006.

Zimmermann, Denise, and Katherine A. Gleason. *The Complete Idiot's Guide to Wicca and Witchcraft*, 3rd ed. Indianapolis: Alpha Books, 2006.

Websites

Websites are abundant, but unfortunately the information one finds in them may not always be accurate. The following are sites I feel have not only correct information but provide a more detailed look at some of the ideas mentioned in this book.

- **http://veritas.arizona.edu/** is the site of the VERITAS Research Program in the Department of Psychology at the University of Arizona, "created primarily to test the hypothesis that the consciousness of a person survives physical death."

- **www.aaevp.com** offers information about the American Association of Electronic Voice Phenomena, or EVP.

- **www.csicop.org** is the home page of The Committee for the Scientific Investigation of Claims of the Paranormal.

- **www.davidthompson.com.au** is the official website of David Thompson, who is said by many to be the "World's Foremost Direct Voice and Materialization Medium."

- **www.hauntednewjersey.com** furnishes knowledge on EVP recordings and other information on hauntings.

- ◆ **www.iands.org** is the home page for the International Association for Near-Death Studies (IANDS).

- ◆ **www.ibrt.org** is the website for the International Board of Regression Therapy. It provides a list of regressionists with bios and information on contacting these individuals.

- ◆ **www.randi.org** is the website for the James Randi Educational Foundation. It promotes critical thinking about paranormal and supernatural ideas.

- ◆ **www.skeptic.com** is the website for the Skeptics Society, a scientific and educational organization that promotes the scientific method.

- ◆ **www.sleepingprophet.org** provides information about the biography of psychic Edgar Cayce, his experiences, and predictions.

- ◆ **www.victorzammit.com** provides a wealth of information from Dr. Victor Zammit, an attorney of the Supreme Court and High Court of Australia. He is considered by many to be the foremost defender of the afterlife.

Life After Death Journal

Throughout this book, I've talked about different ways of contacting the dead. Now, I know that not everyone is interested in this sort of thing, but for those of you who are, it helps to keep track of your attempts and note which methods have worked and which haven't. Use this journal to write down all the details. The goal is to develop a successful method by trial and error.

Be honest in your reporting and recognize that even a "failure" can be a springboard to another method that will work. There are no mistakes when it comes to what the Universe is trying to teach us.

Dreams

The departed often appear to us in our dreams. If you dream of a dead loved one or acquaintance, you'll want to write the account of what happened:

◆ What kind of mood were you in earlier in the day, before your loved one came to you in a dream?

_____

_____

_____

_____

◆ Did anyone talk to you about the deceased person during the day? Could this have triggered you to dream about them?

_____

_____

_____

_____

◆ Were you looking at memorabilia of the deceased that day?

_____

_____

_____

◆ Did you watch any television shows, movies, or hear radio shows that reminded you of the departed individual?

_____

_____

_____

◆ Did you make some sort of request that day for the loved one to come to you in a dream, or did they just appear?

_____

_____

_____

◆ What did the dead individual look like in your dream? Were they happy, sad, peaceful?

_____

_____

_____

◆ Did the person speak to you (or did you speak to him or her)?

_____

_____

_____

_____

◆ Did you see other people in the dream? Did they speak?

_____

_____

_____

_____

◆ Who were the other people and what expressions did they have?

_____

_____

_____

_____

_____

◆ Describe your dream as best you can with as many details as possible.

_____

_____

_____

_____

_____

_____

_____

_____

_____

_____

_____

_____

_____

_____

_____

_____

_____

_____

_____

_____

_____

_____

_____

_____

_____

_____

Tarot Cards

You don't have to be a professional Tarot reader to attempt to contact the dead. Shuffling and turning the cards on your own is fine; just keep track of the events surrounding your readings:

◆ What time of day did you conduct your reading?

_____

_____

◆ Who was present? Were you alone?

_____

_____

_____

◆ Where did you do your reading?

_____

_____

◆ Have you ever used Tarot cards before?

_____

_____

◆ What type of deck did you use? (There are different types; jot down the name of your deck.)

_____

_____

◆ Did you shuffle the cards?

_____

◆ Did you do a Tarot layout according to the directions that came with the cards or did you invent your own?

_____

_____

_____

_____

◆ Did any face cards become apparent in the layout that would describe the appearance of the departed? (The Queen of Swords might depict a woman with dark hair and dark eyes, for example.)

_____

_____

_____

_____

_____

_____

_____

_____

◆ What were the meanings or definitions of the cards you pulled?

_____

_____

_____

_____

_____

_____

_____

_____

_____

_____

_____

_____

_____

_____

_____

_____

_____

◆ Did the information the cards revealed to you make any sense in regard to the departed person you were attempting to contact?

_____

_____

_____

◆ How many times have you attempted this method?

_____

_____

◆ Would you try this method again? Why or why not?

_____

_____

_____

_____

_____

◆ If you went to a professional Tarot reader, write the results of the reading.

_____

_____

_____

_____

_____

_____

_____

_____

_____

_____

_____

_____

_____

_____

_____

_____

_____

_____

_____

_____

_____

_____

_____

_____

Pendulum

Using a pendulum to communicate with those on the other side is an interesting option. It offers yes or no answers. Information you may want to note about your sessions with a pendulum include:

♦ What type of pendulum did you use?

_____

_____

♦ Was the pendulum store-bought or did you make it?

_____

_____

◆ Where did you conduct this session?

_____

_____

_____

◆ Who was present? Were you alone?

_____

_____

_____

_____

_____

◆ Which direction was "yes" for the pendulum? Which direction was "no"? (For information on how to determine which direction is which, see Chapter 12.)

_____

_____

_____

◆ Did you feel as though you were receiving answers from someone on the other side, or did you think that you were moving the pendulum yourself?

_____

_____

_____

_____

◆ Did you change the type of pendulum you were using in the middle of the session?

_____

_____

_____

◆ How many questions did you ask? Write down all the questions and the answers you received.

_____

_____

_____

_____

_____

_____

_____

_____

_____

_____

_____

_____

_____

_____

_____

_____

_____

_____

_____

_____

_____

Crystal Balls or Spheres

Crystal gazing, or scrying into a reflective object, takes a lot of concentration and practice, but if you can develop the knack, it's very rewarding. What might you want to take note of during these sessions?

◆ When, where, and what time did you do your crystal gazing?

_____

_____

_____

_____

◆ Who was present? Were you alone?

_____

_____

_____

_____

_____

_____

◆ What type of crystal did you use?

_____

_____

_____

_____

◆ If you did not use a crystal, what type of object did you use?

_____

_____

_____

◆ How long did it take before you saw a haze or image? Describe the images you saw.

_____

_____

_____

_____

_____

_____

_____

_____

_____

_____

_____

_____

_____

_____

◆ Do you feel you received a message from someone in the afterlife?

_____

_____

_____

_____

◆ If you weren't successful in receiving a message or image, are you going to continue to try? (Remember, this method takes lots of practice and patience.)

_____

_____

◆ The next time you attempt scrying, what will you do differently?

_____

_____

_____

_____

◆ Record anything else about the gazing you think is important.

_____

_____

_____

_____

Séances

Some people think séances are scary, some think they are silly, and yet others think of them as a way to focus energy to those on a different plane or dimension. Perhaps it's worth a try. If you do give it a shot, take note of these issues:

◆ Did you hire someone to hold a séance or did you do it yourself?

_____

◆ If you hired someone, who was it and what are his or her credentials?

_____

_____

_____

_____

◆ How many people were at your séance, including yourself?

_____

_____

_____

If you made contact, write down an account of what happened.

_____

_____

_____

◆ Where and when was the séance performed?

_____

_____

_____

_____

◆ Did you hear noises or sounds?

_____

_____

_____

_____

_____

_____

◆ Did you feel a presence of any kind, other than the people in attendance?

_____

_____

_____

_____

_____

◆ If you made contact, write down an account of what happened.

_____

_____

_____

_____

_____

_____

_____

_____

_____

_____

_____

_____

_____

_____

_____

_____

_____

_____

◆ If you used a professional, would you use her or him again and/or give the medium a high recommendation?

_____

_____

_____

◆ Would you attempt a séance again? If so, what kinds of changes would you make next time?

_____

_____

_____

_____

_____

_____

Professional Mediums

A professional medium may be someone who does séances, or he or she might be a survival evidence medium—someone who connects with the other side through telepathy. If you hire a professional, jot down the following information:

◆ Record his or her name.

_____

◆ Where did you find this medium?

_____

_____

_____

◆ When and where did this communication take place?

_____

_____

_____

_____

◆ How much did you pay?

_____

◆ Was the cost worth the results? Why or why not?

_____

_____

◆ What are the details of the medium's communication with the deceased? (Was contact made? Did the information make sense to you?)

_____

_____

_____

_____

_____

_____

_____

_____

_____

_____

_____

_____

_____

_____

_____

◆ Did the medium record the session or did you?

_____

_____

◆ If the session was not recorded, why not?

_____

_____

◆ Would you do this again? Why or why not?

_____

_____

_____

_____

Recording All the Details

Don't forget to add the little details when making entries in this journal. As you look back on this information, something that doesn't make sense right now may make sense in the future.

If you choose to use this journal and try some of these methods, remember practice makes perfect. Don't get discouraged.

Also, as I mentioned in the book, there are those who feel it's not for us to try to pull the dead back into our realm. Don't feel as though you have to employ these methods; make a decision that you're comfortable with. And stay open-minded. You may not be interested in contacting the dead with any of these methods at this time, but perhaps you'll be interested later.

Most of the methods listed in this appendix are fine for contacting the dead in the most general sense. If you're interested in contacting a specific deceased person, read Appendix D. It contains a detailed method for contacting the deceased in 10 days!

Ten Days to Making Contact with the Departed

Throughout this book, I've discussed many different methods of contacting the departed. In this appendix, I'm going to give you an alternative approach to speaking with a departed loved one. This is a detailed step-by-step plan that we haven't yet discussed.

Contacting the dead brings closure to grief-stricken individuals who are having a difficult time moving on. The grieving process is sometimes made easier if people know they can do something to bring themselves happiness and peace of mind again.

If you're trying to pull someone back to this dimension in order to argue with them or try to extract information from them that would drain their soul, I advise against it. This method is all about finalization. It's a way of saying, "I love you and I'm glad to know you're safe and sound on the other side," not, "Where did you leave the key to the cabin in Wisconsin?"

I've written this section as a 10-day approach, but it's really an individual thing. (In other words, it might take more time or even less time than 10 days.) I set a goal of making contact in 10 days but you can set your own goals. It won't affect your outcome. Do as much as you're comfortable doing on any given day and then take a powder until your next session.

You might want to space things out and try a step every other day or every third day. The important thing is to be *consistent*.

As in Appendix C, I've included plenty of space for you to record the results of your attempts.

Day One

Contact starts with intent. Therefore, the very decision to get in touch with your departed loved one brought you that much closer to making contact.

Before you get started, pick a time of day when you'll be available to try to make contact for at least 10 days. If you think that you can't do this in 10 consecutive days, then decide in advance if you will do this process every other day, once a week, or so forth. Having a plan helps you maintain the rhythm of the energy you'll develop.

Consistency helps you open up a channel; the soul on the other side might need some time to realize you're "online," so to speak, at the same time every day (or every other day, etc.). Souls don't keep track of time the same way we do, but they may have a sense of when your energy is calling out to them. They tend to listen for the call.

Think about it this way: if you receive a phone call from your sister every Monday morning, then you'll probably hear the phone ring even if there's a lot of noise in the house. This is because you're listening and waiting for the call.

1. Choose a time you can attempt to make contact and keep in mind that you'll only need about five minutes. There isn't one time of the day that's better than another: nights, afternoons, or mornings all work fine for contacting the departed.

2. Eliminate sources of interruption. Other people can be in the house, but make sure *you* are alone in a room. For example, a woman I know tells her family she is going to take a shower when she attempts to communicate with the dead; this is the only way she can have some time to herself.

3. Choose a location you can use over and over again to establish consistency. And you should narrow it down to a rather specific spot. Using the same house all the time, for example, is too general. Try to stay within a smaller radius, like a single room or specific location within a larger space within the same house.

4. If you want to play instrumental music or include other enhancements such as candles, that's up to you. But it must always be the same music and the same aroma or same type of candle.

Once you've made these decisions, stop. Don't continue any further until day two. You need to work yourself into this mode of contact slowly.

Journal Notes for Day One

♦ Which room did you choose as your contact spot?

_____

♦ What other enhancements, if any, will you use?

_____

_____

_____

♦ What time of day have you chosen?

_____

♦ How often are you going to spread out this method? Will your goal be to make contact in 10 days? Twenty days? Thirty days?

_____

_____

_____

_____

Day Two

On the second day, go to the same room at the same time of day and create the same mood as the day before. (Not *everything* must be exactly the same. You can change your clothing!)

1. On day two, you must have an area in which you can be seated. It doesn't matter if it's a floor, chair, bed, or sofa.

2. If you have music, turn it on. Candles or incense can be lit now.

3. You *don't* need to try to focus or concentrate. No deep breathing or meditation is required here.

4. Now, try to relax a bit and simply say in your own words that you're trying to get in touch with your loved one.

   Example: "Mary, it's me, Cynthia. I am trying to make contact with you. I will be back here at the same time tomorrow. Are you out there?" Wait for approximately 60 seconds, then leave the room and go back to your regular activities. Don't linger and don't say things such as, "Mary, please, please hear me."

5. If you do get a response, keep your own reply short. You might say something like, "I'm glad you came through. Thanks."

That's the end of day two. Seems too simple, but sometimes simplicity is the charm.

Journal Notes for Day Two

♦ Where did you sit?

_____

_____

_____

♦ What exactly did you say when trying to get your communication out into the ethereal plane?

_____

_____

_____

_____

◆ Did you pick up any message or sign right away?

_____

_____

_____

_____

◆ Did you feel any sense of anyone near you?

_____

_____

_____

_____

Day Three

Same place, same time as day two.

1. Have a seat and relax.

2. Again, using the person's name, say something like, "I am back again, Mary, trying to make contact with you. It's me, Cynthia." Then use the person's last name and your last name: "Mary Doe, it's Cynthia Jones, your daughter here on Earth." This is a way to ensure you're sending out energy to that specific person.

   On day two, you used only your first name along with your natural energy. You cracked the door open a bit, and now you're opening it just a little bit more. This is like when you're at the mall and hear someone call your first name. You're not sure if someone was calling you or someone else with the same name. You might not even bother to look around. If someone called your name again— and added your last name this time—first of all, you wouldn't be surprised since you already heard your name called; and you'd know that it is indeed you the other person is looking for.

3. Wait for 60 seconds, saying nothing more. If you get a response via a telepathic message or some type of sign, don't do anything. Simply say, "I will be back again. Maybe you can build up your energy to communicate more clearly." Remember, the dead are trying to get the hang of this whole communication thing, too. It's not common to make contact on the third day, but it's also not out of the question. It depends on the two parties involved.

4. If you don't receive a response, leave the room.

So ends day three. As you can see, this shouldn't be taking up too much of your time.

Journal Notes for Day Three

◆ Were you more relaxed today than yesterday? Why?

_____

_____

_____

_____

◆ Did you feel you sent out a message that maybe broke through to another dimension? Or did you feel you just sat on your chair, nothing happened, and you might be wasting your time?

_____

_____

_____

Day Four

You know the routine. Relax and give the departed individual a call. This can be done either telepathically or out loud.

1. This attempt can be more casual. Talk to the person as you would if they were still alive: "Hey Mary Doe, it's me Cynthia Jones again. Remember me, your daughter? Hope so. You out there anywhere?" Humor is welcome. Those on the other side maintain their earthly personalities for some time—until they are so far evolved that they have moved beyond being interested in what's happening on Earth. However, that could take decades or even centuries, so go ahead and crack some jokes if you feel like it.

2. Don't ask questions or scold them for not answering. Remain lighthearted and positive. Try not to cry or otherwise bring negative energy into the conversation right now. For example, *don't* say something like, "Mary, how can you do this to me? I am so sad and need to move on. Can't you just let me know you're okay? Please!" Nope, that's not the right direction for this form of communication.

3. If you do make some sort of contact or something moves or you receive a message in your head, don't ask for anything. Just thank the person for communicating with you. Remember: this soul is coming back to an environment that's not even close to the peacefulness it's surrounded by now. The person doesn't need to be pressured or made to feel sad. Keep it "short and sweet."

   You're going through a system of communication. This is like looking for a phone number in the phone book. One number doesn't work so you call directory assistance. Now you call the number and there's no answer. You just keep trying and the process moves forward.

That call is over for day four.

Journal Notes for Day Four

♦ How did you feel today in general about this session?

_____

_____

_____

_____

_____

◆ Did you feel you made any kind of contact?

_____

_____

_____

_____

◆ If so, what happened?

_____

_____

_____

_____

_____

_____

_____

_____

Day Five

Hurrah! You're at the halfway mark!

You might be wondering if there's a guarantee you're going to receive confirmation that your loved one is listening—maybe in the form of a wink and a nudge to let you know that there is life on the other side and they are okay? Such guarantees don't exist, of course. But your chances of reaching out and touching the dead are getting better as you move through the process. You've set up a channel of communication that is present even if the deceased isn't coming through immediately.

Day five begins with the same process: sit down, relax for a few seconds, and start talking. Continue to stay positive, casual, and keep your words brief. Example: "Mary Doe, it's your daughter again, Cynthia Jones. Mom, how ya doin'?"

This time you can add a little chitchat, but don't go overboard.

1. Wait for approximately two minutes this time because they may be starting to move closer.

2. If there's no contact, move out of the room.

3. If you do get a message or feel as though you have a presence with you, thank them for answering your call and let them know you will be back tomorrow (or whenever you have decided according to your original plan).

4. Remember, the dead don't really have a sense of time like we do. So you might want to say, "I'll try to contact you about four more times and then I will let it go, so I hope you will be around." Let them know there is a deadline (sorry—no pun intended) so they have a sense of going back to their life on the other side.

Journal Notes for Day Five

♦ Was anything you did different today than any other day thus far?

_____

_____

_____

♦ If you feel you made contact, write down the details.

_____

_____

_____

_____

_____

♦ How do you feel about this process so far? Is it a waste of time; are you making progress; are you withholding judgment until the end?

Day Six

Back in your location and back in the same environment ...

1. Let your loved one on the other side know that you are there solely with the intention of trying to communicate, with no other agenda. Example: "Mother, it's me. I just want to attempt to communicate with you so I know you are all right." At this point you don't have to mention names, as the lines of communication have been established.

2. Don't put them under the pressure of sending you a sign or making the lights flicker or the winds blow your curtains. Let them do what they want. And keep in mind their communication might just be a thought that comes into your head.

3. If you have a sense that the person you are trying to touch base with is coming through, thank them and tell them you love them or whatever you want to say. This is all about communicating without expecting or wanting anything except to know that they're at peace.

Journal Notes for Day Six

◆ What's the weather like today? Why do I want to know, you ask? Because from here on out, I want you to get very detailed in your description of how your day went and the environment around you. I want to see you start to pay attention to everything around you. It will help you become more aware of a presence that comes to you in your communication project.

_____

_____

_____

_____

_____

_____

_____

◆ Did you feel you made contact today, and if so, what happened?

_____

_____

_____

_____

_____

_____

_____

_____

◆ You have four more days to go. Is this getting tiring, boring, or are you looking forward to it each day?

_____

_____

_____

◆ If you are making contact every day, do you feel you want to say more to the person? If yes, what do you want to say? Is this message in keeping with the message of peace and closure?

_____

_____

_____

_____

_____

Day Seven

Same place, same time—the setup's not going to change!

1. Send out the call, but this time you can be stronger and a little more detailed! Example: "Mary? I am here once again trying to communicate. I don't want to rush or pressure you, but if you could communicate with me now instead of waiting it would really be nice. I don't know where you are or what may prevent you from communicating or what has allowed you to already let me know you are well, but I would like to know in my heart and soul that you exist on another dimension. If you can, let me know by whatever method is easiest for you."

2. When you give the departed that kind of permission, watch out the next day. you might get a reply sooner than you think, but not just in that room you have been secluded to for the last seven days. The dead can come to you anywhere—even in your dreams! So just be extra aware of all things around you that might be a sign or communication from your loved one.

Journal Notes for Day Seven

♦ Did you make contact? If so, what happened?

_____

_____

_____

_____

_____

_____

_____

♦ In the last seven days, at what time were you most confident that you may have felt a presence?

_____

_____

_____

♦ How did you feel after thinking that you may have made contact?

_____

_____

_____

_____

_____

Day Eight

At this point, you're either loving this or you can't wait till it's over (or you've closed the pages of this book). Please keep going. Try to think of this as an adventure.

Shoulders back, face up, and proceed to your place of contact.

1. This time, just talk to the departed person as if he or she were there—but remember: no complaining.

    Example: "Hey Mary, I really miss you and would just like to know that you are okay. I have been trying to reach you now for seven sessions. You can choose any way you want to make contact with me."

2. If you already feel you've made contact, continue on. Let the person know you are only going to continue this for three more sessions (*don't* say "days") and you cherish every contact. If you haven't heard or felt a peep yet, simply say, "I hope you will come through. It would mean so much to me. But if you can't, I understand." Remember, no pressure.

3. Be patient. I know time is running short, but don't say things like, "Mary, I don't know what in the heck is going on but I have been at this for eight days now. Give me a break. Are you okay or what?" This kind of thing will really make the departed retract from you. (Geez, won't they be glad they're out of your realm?!)

4. This time wait for up to five minutes. In that time, try to "see" them on the other side, however you imagine it. Think about good times and try to put emotion behind your thoughts. It's okay to cry as long as it's coming from real emotion, and not a plea for them to come to you.

5. If you make contact, tell them that you know it hasn't been easy for them to come back to let you know they are fine. Tell them that's all you wanted to know and thank them.

6. If you don't make contact, tell them that the next attempted meeting may be the one.

Journal Notes for Day Eight

◆ Did you make contact? If so, what happened?

_____

_____

_____

_____

_____

_____

_____

_____

◆ Are you still looking forward to these sessions or will you be glad when you reach day ten? Why?

_____

_____

_____

◆ During the day, when not conducting the communication, have you sensed that someone is trying to contact you even if you are not in your standard place? How does it make you feel?

_____

_____

_____

_____

Day Nine

Okay, it's day nine. You only have two more steps to go. If you haven't made any kind of contact or felt any type of presence even for an instant over the course of all these days, don't give up hope!

Take your normal place.

1. If you have made contact, continue on and just make the most of the love you're feeling and the knowledge that your loved one is in a wonderful state of existence.

2. Let your loved one know that you are going to try to communicate with them only right now and one more time. Let them know that because all of the frequencies are in place for the two of you to make contact, now is the perfect time for them to come to you.

3. At this time, you can finally be a little selfish and tell them that it would mean a lot for *you* to have some form of communication—if only for a few seconds—so you can put closure to their death. Also mention that you don't want to know anything at all except they are in a good place so you don't have to feel such a loss.

4. Cry if you want. Go ahead, bawl your eyes out. You are releasing emotion and it can be powerful and may make those dead ones who are not totally ready to come across for a last goodbye a little more apt to make the journey. Why couldn't you have just sat and cried from day one? Well, in my opinion and experience, you have to break into the deceased's presence slowly. Crying may overwhelm recently deceased souls, at least until they're comfortable with the communication process.

Journal Notes for Day Nine

◆ Did you make contact? (Yes or no? Your answer can't be "I think I did." You know if you did or didn't. Be honest with yourself.) If so, what happened?

_____

_____

_____

_____

◆ Did you cry at this session or any of the other days? What happened afterward?

_____

_____

_____

◆ Do you feel that you want to ask questions to your departed loved one? If yes, write them down.

_____

_____

_____

_____

_____

_____

Day Ten

This is your last day, and by now you know where to go and how to set up ... so go ahead and do it. And then begin:

1. Let the deceased know that this is the last time you will attempt communication. If possible, you'd like them to please come into your presence as soon as they understand this message. (Meaning *right now*.)

2. If you have not yet felt that they were there with you, let them know that they should make their essence stronger, if possible. Example: "Mary, I think you are trying to come across but the feeling is still weak. Can you do something to give me reassurance? A sign or a sound or a thought?" (The reason you can now ask for signs is because the departed is getting used to the open channel; giving some sort of sign won't be as much of a drain on them at this point.)

3. Stay in your area of interchange for up to 10 minutes, and try not to feel desperate. Don't get frustrated or sad. Even if you think you didn't make contact, you were most likely heard.

Even if you're disappointed, keep in mind that the dead don't have a sense of time, so you might get a message when you least expect it. Also remember that some souls are more advanced than others. If you know someone who's been in contact with her deceased mother and you weren't able to make contact with yours, it could be that her mom simply has a knack for this kind of thing—or that she's been on the other side longer and has learned a thing or two about crossing back over—things that *your* mother doesn't know … yet.

Maybe this didn't work well for you this time, but you're intrigued enough to give it another try. Wait for a few months or a year and try again. Maybe this soul just needs some time to learn how to make contact with this world.

Journal Notes for Day Ten

♦ Was there any time that you believed you made contact or felt a presence? What day was it? Why do you think it happened at that time?

_____

_____

_____

_____

_____

◆ What was communicated to you? Or was it more of a sense that the soul was with you?

_____

_____

_____

_____

_____

_____

_____

◆ Would you try this again at a later date? Why or why not?

_____

_____

_____

◆ Do you think you were heard? (Oh, let me answer that one for you. Yes, you were.)

_____

_____

_____

◆ Use the following space to jot down any other details about the experience.

_____

_____

_____

_____

_____

_____

_____

_____

_____

_____

Above all, never lose faith or give up hope. There _is_ life after death and we are only pioneers at making contact.

But when there's love involved, nothing is impossible. It just takes patience and understanding that the soul goes on. We know that we'll all unite when the time is right, so love, be happy, and know all things are possible.

Index

Create a Powerful and Positive Life!

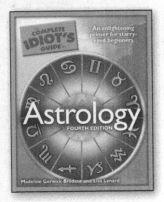

ISBN: 978-1-59257-581-7

ISBN: 978-1-59257-575-6

ISBN: 978-1-59257-539-8

ISBN: 978-1-59257-418-6

ISBN: 978-1-59257-614-2

ISBN: 978-1-59257-651-7

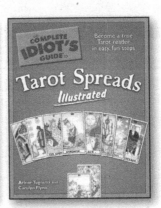

ISBN: 978-1-59257-550-3

ISBN: 978-1-59257-637-1

ALPHA

idiotsguides.com